FIRE W

The Story of Wu Yung

First Published in 2000 by OM Publishing

06 05 04 03 02 01 00 7 6 5 4 3 2 1

OM Publishing is an imprint of Paternoster Publishing,
PO Box 300, Carlisle, Cumbria, CA3 0QS, UK
and Paternoster Publishing USA
Box 1047, Waynesboro, GA 30830-2047
www.paternoster-publishing.com

British Library Cataloguing in Publication Data

A catalogue record for this book is available from
the British Library

ISBN 1-85078-355-1

Cover design by Diane Bainbridge
Typeset by Textype, Cambridge
Printed in Great Britain by
Omnia Books Limited, Glasgow

Contents

A Word from the Author

First of all, I want to thank Brother Peter Lin Chih-ping, who for a long time incessantly encouraged me to record the way God has worked in my life. Each time he saw me he would ask when I would start.

'It'll be soon,' I promised. 'It'll be soon.'

Undaunted by my delay, he regularly phoned me to ask, 'Haven't you started yet?'

Eventually I decided I could not put off the task any longer. I am getting older, and if I should suddenly pass away or have an accident, I would miss the opportunity of sharing what God has done for me, in me, through me, and in spite of me. I have therefore made use of a rather long stay in America to put aside my heavy workload and quietly put my experiences of a few decades in order and then record them.

I need also to thank Brother Ho Hsiao-tung, who put my recordings onto paper. His enthusiasm was touching. He completed this heavy and exhausting work in an amazingly short period of time, quickly giving the finished work to the Cosmic Light Publication Company so that it would soon reach readers. I appreciate as well the work of Liang Shang-yuan, to whom I gave the job of deleting passages that were repetitive and of correcting my lack of eloquence.

Here, however, I must ask my readers' forbearance. As I do not have the habit of keeping a diary, I have had to depend on my memory. I cannot always speak with great detail. Though I have tried my best to be accurate, the dates and years may not be very exact, nor the sequence of events altogether in order.

The testimonies I record are all God's doing. Though we may see ourselves, it is more important that we see God manifested through us.

When Jesus took his disciples up onto the mountain, and Moses and Elijah appeared to them, Peter exclaimed, 'Let us make three tabernacles: one for Moses, one for Elijah, and one for Jesus.' In so saying, he was ranking Moses and Elijah with Jesus. Immediately a cloud formed and completely enveloped the two Old Testament men so that the disciples saw no one but Jesus. Today the purpose of our witness must also be this – not to exalt ourselves, but to lift up Jesus, so that he alone is seen. Why? Because without God's working inside us to reveal his own deeds, all our behaviour is empty. Although God's manifestation of his own glory contains an element of humanity, its chief purpose is to exalt Christ. And this is the purpose of my testimony.

Wu Yung

PUBLISHING

OMF International works in most East Asian countries, and among East Asian peoples around the world. It was founded by James Hudson Taylor in 1865 as the China Inland Mission. Our overall purpose is to glorify God through the urgent evangelisation of East Asia's billions, and this is reflected in our publishing.

Through our books, booklets, website and quarterly magazine, *East Asia's Billions*, OMF Publishing aims to motivate Christians for world mission, and to equip them for playing a part in it. Publications include:

- contemporary mission issues
- the biblical basis of mission
- the life of faith
- stories and biographies related to God's work in East Asia
- accounts of the growth and development of the Church in Asia
- studies of Asian culture and religion relating to the spiritual needs of her peoples

Visit our website at *www.omf.org*

Addresses for OMF English-speaking centres can be found at the back of this book.

Preface

I had just believed in the Lord when I first met Wu Yung in Taiwan more than forty years ago. Wearing a reddish blazer, the gentle and affable young man was distributing programme sheets at the door of Taipei's Hsuchang Street YMCA, where the Mandarin Church met. Later, when I occasionally attended the Sunday School meetings of the Youth Fellowship, he usually took me to a small room on the second floor to pray with a few brothers before the Sunday worship.

Once at a special outreach of the Youth Fellowship I asked Elder Wu who the invited speaker was. When he pointed a finger at himself, I said incredulously, 'Oh! Do you also preach?' I had thought he served only as chairman and usher.

Afterward I didn't see him for a time. Because I had contracted a lung disease, I stopped attending school to rest at home and was feeling rather downcast. One day, meeting Pastor Andrew Loo on the street, I asked him to pray for me. He encouraged me, saying, 'Don't be afraid. Brother Wu Yung got cancer, and though, after operating on him, the doctors confirmed that his recovery was impossible, he still lives today.'

I had seen Elder Wu Yung, then, in his first public appearance after having cancer. He preached with vigour and vitality, nothing like a sick man. And later that year I heard him preach at a three-day spiritual revival meeting and he also lead the singing in his sonorous voice when others preached.

Eventually I went to America and worked for eight years as a photographer in Washington, DC. Twice, during spiritual evangelistic meetings, Elder Wu was invited to preach at the church I attended, the Washington Chinese Church.

Because my aged and still unbelieving father lived near the Nanking East Road Church in Taipei, where Elder Wu ministered, I wrote asking Elder Wu to visit him. Though very busy, this man of God took the time to go, sharing with my father, among other things, how God had healed him of cancer. My father was greatly moved, eventually coming to love the Lord and to appreciate his new friend's preaching very much. After my father went to be with the Lord, Elder Wu took charge of his memorial service.

Every time I returned to Taiwan from America, I visited Elder Wu. In fact, I met him in meetings in many places outside Taiwan. During this period, many organisations and individuals, including myself, expressed the desire to record Elder Wu's life story, but Elder Wu turned us all down.

But when I returned to Taiwan in 1987, I heard that Elder Wu had promised to record his testimony on tape. Excited, I went to his house and spent a long time discussing with him about making tapes. After his Thailand trip, he said, he would have more time to make the recordings. But when the phone rang before we were more than a few minutes into our conversation, I began to doubt that he could ever finish recording a lifetime of stories.

My doubts were legitimate. There was no news about progress for a long time. The idea was like a stone sunk in a big sea, without a trace. Every time I saw him and inquired about the status of the recordings, he simply smiled and said nothing. What a surprise, then, to receive in August 1990 a small parcel of ten tapes from Elder Wu! In an accompanying letter from Cosmic Light, Inc. I learned that Elder Wu had taken time while in America to record a total of thirty-six tapes. I was ecstatic and started recording the content of the tapes immediately.

Feeling greatly honoured to take over this job and thrilled at what the tapes revealed, I worked from morning till night to finish the task. The original tapes contained over three hundred thousand words altogether. May God bless the story of Elder Wu's life to bring help to many people and glory to God!

Ho Hsiao-tung

Foreword by James Hudson Taylor III

In old Singapore's Chinatown he could mobilise a demonstration twenty thousand strong against the British colonial government in less than three hours. They deported him for it and said he could not return for ninety-nine years.

Wu Yung was a Chinese patriot who loved his people with a passion. Back in his home province of Fujian they discovered a maestro quality in his singing. There Wu taught music until the tide of civil war engulfed his homeland and, reluctantly, he moved again with his new bride to Taiwan.

His conversion and call to Christian service was also accompanied by almost predestined-like pressure. His mother-in-law to be would not hear of her daughter marrying this charismatic young leader until Wu Yung had personally confessed faith in Jesus Christ. He accepted. Then cancer struck. The surgeon operated but sewed him up again with the prognosis that the malignancy had spread beyond any hope of recovery. Committed Christian friends gathered around his hospital bed as Wu dedicated his life to God and his service. And serve he has! I know of no Chinese Christian leader who has travelled any more widely, preaching in Chinese churches around the world.

What is the secret of Wu Yung's spiritual leadership and power?

It is to be found in his total commitment to Christ and his call. One sad incident, recorded here in *Fire Within*, illustrates the point. Again and again Wu's father had tried to inveigle him into returning to Singapore after the government had lifted its ninety-nine-year ban. But Wu felt God had placed him in Taiwan for a strategic spiritual purpose. The father's final effort ended in tragedy. He and the family church joined in 'a conspiracy' to invite Wu Yung back as pastor. With careful steps their 'plot' unfolded. First they invited him back to hold an evangelistic mission. He would stay at home, where, on the last evening the father would spread a sumptuous feast with all the dishes he knew his son liked best. Before that fateful meal began, Wu's father asked him to grant him a request. Wu replied that he would love to do it, but didn't know what it was. The father then asked him to return to Singapore to pastor the church. What was Wu to say? Quietly he told his father of God's call to the church in Taiwan and of expanding work there among students and intellectuals. He did not feel free, therefore, to accept the Singapore church's gracious invitation. Pounding the table in anger, the father left the room, the meal untouched. Within a week he was dead. The rest of the family accused Wu Yung of killing their father. If this was not enough, just at that moment a letter came from a group of disgruntled members in the church in Taiwan encouraging him to accept any invitation that might be forthcoming from churches in Singapore. The Wus were devastated. What was God saying? Had they missed something? Returning to Taiwan, they quietly made their way to Sun Moon Lake for a time to prayerfully sort things out. Leaders of the congregation discovered their whereabouts and sent a delegation to apologise for the actions of the small minority and to invite Wu Yung to continue his pastoral ministry among them. And so he has for more than four decades.

Wu Yung is a leader of vision and bold faith. He has engaged in a wide-ranging itinerant evangelistic and Bible teaching ministry among Chinese communities around the world in which thousands have come to Christ and tens of thousands more have been nourished and built up in their faith. This global ministry opened Elder Wu's eyes to the strategic role the Chinese church could have in the fulfilment of the Great Commission. In 1965 he established CMO – Christian (formerly Chinese)

Mission Overseas – which has sent out cross-cultural mission-aries to Okinawa, France, Indonesia, Thailand and Myanmar. Over the past ten years Elder Wu has encouraged the association of churches which he leads in Taiwan to work with the burgeoning churches in China in training urgently needed new leaders.

In the late 1960s, as more and more Christian graduates began to flow out from the universities in Taiwan, Elder Wu recognised the need for those called to Christian service to be given sound theological training.

Even though he himself had not had formal seminary training, like D.L. Moody a century earlier in the US, he joined with other leaders in establishing China Evangelical Seminary in Taipei. As CES Board Chairman, his challenge to the charter faculty was to train Christian apologists for the Chinese church as well as pastors and missionaries.

Since 1970 nearly one thousand graduates have gone out to serve. The Theological Education by Extension programme in Taiwan and North America has seen more than ten thousand lay Christians enrolled in extension courses.

Like Pastor Hsi, the nineteenth-century Confucian scholar and Christian leader of Shanxi province; Dr John Sung, China's great evangelist of the 1920s and '30s who earned a PhD in chemistry from Ohio State University; and Pastor Wang Mingdao, whose preaching kindled the fires of China's Christian student movement in the turbulent decades before 1950 and whose Christian faith was tested by fire during twenty-three years of imprisonment thereafter – Elder Wu Yung is a compelling illustration of the fact that it is not, as some have claimed: 'One more Christian, one less Chinese' but rather 'One more Christian, one more beautiful Chinese'. In response to this, Wu Yung would echo the words of the Apostle Paul when he said, 'But we have this treasure in jars of clay to show that this all-surpassing power is from God and not from us.'

James Hudson Taylor III
Hong Kong, SAR, China

1

Babyhood to Exile

No one would ever have predicted that I would become a preacher, least of all I myself.

The journey into exile from Singapore to Shanghai was very long. As the ship made its way in a wide swing around the jungled Indo-Chinese peninsula and the convoluted bulge of China's coastline, I stood on the deck almost every day staring at the billowing ocean. A teenager heartlessly torn from family and friends, I felt encompassed by a grey mist, totally unable to see ahead. *What future will I have?* I asked myself. Whatever are my prospects?

In the past I had a home, but now I was homeless. In the past I had someone to depend on, but now I was a wanderer, alone. Having not yet reached legal age, I didn't know how I would survive without my parents in an unfamiliar land. Without relatives to help me out, I could become a beggar and starve on the street, and no one would care. The more I thought about my predicament, the more my dread of the future increased and the more I grieved over my past actions.

A family with gender discrimination

I came by the bull-headedness that led to my deportation from Singapore honestly! In many ways I was like my grandfather. In fact, the circumstances that led up to my birth conspired only to make me even more headstrong than my genes dictated.

My grandfather and my father after him were farmers in Xiamen, a city in China's Fujian province. After my father married, my grandfather looked forward to having grandchildren. According to my hometown custom, a man had to have a grandchild before he could grow his beard. But when his daughter-in-law's first baby was a girl, my grandfather refused to grow his beard, in protest.

'Uncle Wai, you are already a granddaddy. Why haven't you grown your beard?' somebody on the street challenged him one day.

'Why should I grow a beard?' my grandfather replied angrily. 'I don't want to be as shame-faced as Mr Wang, who grew a beard even though he had only a grand*daughter*!'

My poor mother! What disgrace she felt! When she became pregnant a second time, she desperately hoped to have a boy so that her father-in-law would be satisfied.

When the second baby was born, my grandfather was eating lunch in the next room, eagerly awaiting news of the birth of a grandson so that he could grow his beard. But when the midwife came out from Mother's room with news of the birth of a second girl, my grandfather was furious. Without thinking, he hurled his bowl of rice at the door of the room where my disappointed mother cradled her new daughter.

Of course, as my mother approached the birth of her third child, she became very anxious. What would she say to her father-in-law if the baby were another girl?

This time, when the baby was born, my grandfather was working in the field. At word that he had a third granddaughter, he marched home with his spade and broke all the dishes in the kitchen. Afraid to stay in her room to rest after the birth because of my grandfather's temper, my mother forced herself to get up and to do household chores. Within hours she was fetching water from the well, washing clothes, and cooking meals. Soon after this she began suffering from rheumatism.

When my mother was about to have her fourth baby in 1920, the entire family hoped not to have another girl for fear that my grandfather would turn the whole house upside down.

Fortunately the fourth birth granted everybody's wish, for the baby was a boy, and that boy was me. Our whole family was filled with happiness, and the honour of my mother was restored. And in celebration, my grandfather began to grow his beard.

The whole atmosphere of our home brightened. I was spoiled, of course. Whatever I wanted people had to give to me, and whomever I called had to come. As a result, I became an exceedingly stubborn and wilful child.

Scrounging vegetables and rice to live

But during my babyhood China churned with unrest. Man-made calamities combined with incessant natural disasters to make existence miserable. With bandits and warlords both acting without scruples, people found it difficult even to survive. My family was no exception. Eventually following the lead of others emigrating to other Southeast Asian countries, we moved to Singapore.

At the time of my family's uprooting, I was just a toddler. As Chinese in general were not highly educated at that time, a man who could write a general letter or do bookkeeping could work as a secretary in a shop. Because my father received little education and, in fact, could hardly write his name, he could do nothing of the kind. To feed his family of six when we reached Singapore, he worked as a docker at the pier.

When I was six or seven, my father was injured seriously enough to require his staying home to recuperate. Immediately the family faced a financial crisis, desperate to know how to keep food on the table.

In my family only the boys went to school; none of my elder sisters received any education, nor were they allowed to go out in public. If for some reason they had to go out, my parents would accompany them. For this reason the burden of feeding the family fell heavily on my young shoulders. Often after school I had to take a basket to the market to scrounge leftover

vegetables or go to the pier with peck and broom to collect
grains of rice that fell from bags when coolies unloaded cargo.
What I brought home was sorted, washed and cooked for our
family's food. Collecting the rice especially was agonizingly
tedious, and I felt the shame of it keenly. But it was the only way
to keep our family alive.

Disastrous speech competition

When I was in grade four, my teacher entered some of us in a
speech competition. Though we were not given our topics before
the event, our teacher taught us how to present a prologue and
how to conduct ourselves on stage, hoping to give us an edge
towards winning awards. Just before the competition we drew
lots to pick our topics and again to determine the order in which
we were to speak. The topic I picked was 'To love buying national
products', a patriotic theme as at the time the Japanese were
invading China. But the worst of it was that I picked number one,
and being the first one to speak, I had no chance to listen to how
other people handled their topics or to think what to say.

After I heard the judge call, 'Number one', it took all the
bravery I could muster to walk up onto the stage.

'Judges and teachers,' I said, nervously trying to clear my
voice, 'today I represent the fourth-grade students participating
in this competition . . .'

So far so good, as my teacher had given us some training in
the prologue.

But I could go no further. Unable to explicate the hows and
whys of loving to buy national products, I could only stand
there, with my hands clutching miserably at my clothes. The
more nervous I became, the more I was unable to say anything.
In front of me were more than a hundred schoolmates staring at
me. With my tension about to burst, I finally cried out, 'Wow!'
and then sobbed, causing the audience to laugh. At that point
my teacher, feeling very disgraced, came up onto the stage to
escort me down.

That whole week, as I walked around campus, I dared not lift my eyes to look at my schoolmates.

Who would ever guess after that debacle that someday God would give me grace to speak many, many times from the pulpit?

The harm of superstition

For many years I put religious faith in the same category as superstition. This bias, in fact, made me unable to accept the Gospel, even though I had heard it. I tenaciously held to the view that as only the uneducated were superstitious, only the uneducated believed in the existence of God.

The part of superstition in my mother's actions in my early life, in fact, helped shape my bias against both superstition and faith. Two events particularly stand out.

I loved swimming and swam every Saturday, Sunday, and holiday I could. One day while enjoying a swim in the sea, I noticed the water nearby vigorously swirling and gushing upwards. Not understanding why it was so turbulent, I felt a little frightened. I quickly dried off, put on my clothes, and ran home to tell my mother about the strange phenomenon.

Upon hearing my tale, my mother was obviously pleased. Smiling, she said, 'Oh, child, you are blessed because a dragon was sucking the water! A man who sees a dragon,' she assured me, 'will receive a blessing. In the future, if that man does not make big money, he'll become a great government official.'

Well, I became disillusioned with such beliefs as in the years to follow I neither made a lot of money nor became a great government official. I came to realise as I grew up that what unsophisticated, uneducated people did not understand they ascribed to a god. The wind god caused the wind. The thunder god caused the thunder. In my mind, belief in a supreme God fell into that same category.

The second event that prejudiced me against belief in the supernatural was the premature death of my eldest sister. Superstition's role in this tragedy greatly reinforced my mindset against what I saw as the beliefs of the ignorant. This sister was the dearest person to me. Of a kind disposition, she took great pains to look after me and the rest of her younger brothers and sisters.

In giving birth to her own child, my sister developed a condition which today is not a serious problem since it responds to antibiotic drugs. But in those early years, especially in an uneducated family like ours, it was life-threatening.

My mother believed that my sister's problem was the result of someone's having offended the gods. Fearing that going to a doctor might offend the gods further, Mother went first to the temple to draw lots to seek a cure from Buddha. When she returned home, she mixed incense ash with water to make medicine for my sister to drink. Unchecked, however, the disease raged on.

Desperate, my mother went from temple to temple seeking written spells from various monks. These she burned, again mixing the ashes with water for my sister to drink. Instead of getting better, my sister's condition continued to worsen.

Finally there was no choice but to fetch a doctor. The doctor, however, seeing that my sister was on the verge of dying, was angry. 'You . . .' he said to my mother, 'you have caused your daughter's death!'

My mother was so dumbfounded that she was speechless. She had acted on what she believed. How could her efforts have ended like this?

Deprived in a few days of a dear sister, I was deeply hurt. Superstition had taken from me a sister I loved. I vowed not to be a part of such foolishness.

My anti-British bent builds

Because most of the Chinese immigrants in Singapore came with a very low educational background, they developed an inferiority complex. Not I. Though some people bought products made in Britain and called them 'old family products', even as a young boy I could not accept this. Were such people not inferring that the British were our ancestors? In rejecting their own roots, they were making the British into first-class people and relegating the Chinese to second-class. If a British person was walking toward a Chinese, the Chinese person would walk in a roundabout way, acting as if he was not worthy to meet the British face to face. I resented this.

With no need of passports or entry permits during the years of my youth, Chinese poured into Singapore, swelling its population until it was more Chinese than British (today nearly 80 per cent). When immigrants came, all they had to do was to line up, be counted, and go ashore. At the gate sat a British person with a whip, striking each incoming person with his whip as he counted. When I saw the British treating the Chinese like cattle or horses as I played at the pier, I burned at the racial disgrace.

I began to despise foreigners, disgusted at the fact that they were always sitting at the top, with Chinese little more than slaves. With these anti-British feelings smouldering inside me, when I was a little older I began to participate in anti-British activities.

The head-shaving incident

One day a British officer of the Singapore Education Department came to our school and demanded that we students shave our heads. 'Many of you are growing long hair. Some comb it to the left, some to the right. You look unkempt.' Even those who used haircream to look sophisticated and neat, he accused of wasting time and money. 'At this young age you should acquire good habits and save money for your parents,' he said. 'That would be very beneficial for your future.' His eyes scanning our faces to make sure we were paying attention, he continued, 'Today is Saturday, tomorrow is Sunday. You go to have your heads shaved tomorrow, and then you will look orderly. On Monday I shall return to inspect.'

The anti-British sentiment within me began to boil. Disturbed over this unreasonable demand, I stood up as soon as the man had left and asked my classmates, 'Do you think it is all right for him to ask us to shave our heads?'

No one responded.

'Classmates,' I persisted, 'how can we be so very thoughtless? Leaving the hair on our heads can protect our brains. The weather in Singapore is very hot, and our hair can be a shade for our heads so that our brains won't be dried up by the hot sun.' It seemed like a good point to me. 'In the past the British sold opium to us Chinese to make us use it,' I went on. 'As a consequence the Chinese became known as the sick men of the East. Now if we let our brains get dried up by the sun, would it not mean that we have made ourselves stupid fellows? To be sick is serious, but to be stupid is worse. Adding stupid Chinese to sick Chinese, what hope is there for our race?'

After these words I asked my classmates, 'So should our hair be shaved or not? Those who are opposed to shaving their heads, raise your hands!'

.   All my classmates raised their hands.

'Well, then, tomorrow we won't shave our heads. When the officer comes on Monday, he won't see all bald heads.'

The British officer came on Monday fully expecting to see a room full of shaved heads. But when he entered the classroom, he could not find even one. Fuming, he asked, 'I ordered you to shave your heads. Why haven't you done so?'

Nobody said anything.

The man asked again, 'Who is the person who stirred you up and made you decide not to shave your heads?'

Again, no one spoke.

But being a public matter, the incident called for an investigation. Once investigated, the truth was like stones peeping out from receding water. Eventually, the authorities found out that I was the instigator. They wrote a letter to my father.

As my father was illiterate and unsuspecting, he asked another person to read that letter to him. Angered and shamed that his son had led a revolt at school, he put the letter on the table to await my return.

I run away

'You really have too much nerve! You even dare to stir up trouble for a monarch,' my father yelled at me.

'What are you talking about?' I asked.

'What am I taking about? You stirred up the students in your school to rebel against the Education Department; you told them not to shave their heads.'

'Dad! This is not the same age as when you were growing up,' I yelled back.

'What do you mean, "not the same age"?'

I said, 'You are a citizen of the early Qing Dynasty. I live in the age of the Republic.'

'And what do you mean by "citizens of the Qing Dynasty" and "people of the Republic"?'

'People of the Qing Dynasty are used to being slaves, but people of the Republic are free from slavery.'

My father bristled with anger. 'How absurd!' he said. 'A brat trying to teach his elder!' With that, he slapped me on the cheek.

But I kept on. 'Dad, there was a female reformer in France who had a motto: "Give me liberty or give me death!"' My father knew less than I that I was mixing Joan of Arc and Patrick Henry. But it didn't matter.

'What do you mean, "Give me liberty or give me death"?' my father asked.

'That means liberty is more important than life,' I retorted bravely.

'Well, you say, "Give me liberty or give me death",' my father said measuredly, 'then you should die and get out of here!'

At these words I wanted all the more to give vent to my anger. That very night I rolled up my bedding and left home.

I spent the night at a friend's house. But I was unable to sleep. At home, being spoiled as the eldest son, I was used to my mother fanning me to sleep, and if I had heat rash, she always rubbed prickly heat powder on it. This night no one did either of these things for me. I tossed and turned, awake and miserable. Only then did I realise the rashness of leaving home.

But now that I had left, how could I go back?

When I woke up the next morning, I went out on the street to buy something to eat with the little money I had in my pocket. Fearful of being seen, I arranged with a hawker to prepare some satay (barbecued meat on a stick) for me and to deliver it to the door of a house near the park. I inferred that it was my house, though, of course, it was not.

Unfortunately, while the hawker was barbecuing satay for me, the owner of the designated house came out. When he seemed to be waving at me, I wondered what he meant. Actually he was waving to his dog to come to his side. But as he pointed at me again, the dog ran toward me, smelled me, and bit me.

Now, with the pain of a dog bite adding to my loneliness, I thought much of home. But I would not return.

Still, a subtle idea began to form in my head. Although my father was a coolie, he was honest and straightforward. All his fellow workers respected him, making him chief. Since he had position with them, I knew that he could ask them to go out and search for his lost son. I wondered if it just might be worth wandering out on the crowded street where I would surely be found by one of my father's workers, who would then take me back home.

The plan worked. Soon one of the dock workers sent to look for me spotted me and made sure I got home. Though I was a bit afraid of a beating from my father, I was glad to be home. Not only did my mother embrace me as though she had found her lost treasure, my father seemed to be very happy too, though he kept his face stern. My father, in fact, did not beat me, but rather loved me all the more.

Leaving home the second time

When I returned to school the next day, my head was shaved as was everyone else's.

But that didn't mean that my heart wasn't churning with

feelings of injustice. And when the school held a sports day not long afterward, I wrote an impertinent poem about our shaved heads. Then I put music to it, mimeographed it, and distributed copies to all my classmates. The song had many stanzas. I remember only one. It went:

> Shining heads reflect the playground,
> The scorching sun is right above,
> Bald heads' sweat is steamed away,
> Bald-headed guys – too ugly to love –
> Like old monks you meet,
> Like lepers on the street.

The song was meant to mock all of us who had shaved our heads, and we all sang it as loudly as we could while we were marching in the sports day procession.

The school authorities were not amused. They judged that the singing was not only inappropriate, but represented a revolt, an intentional uprising. And eventually they found out who the instigator was: Wu Yung – again!

Again the school officials contacted my parents and threatened to expel me. Very angry, my father came down hard on me for continuing to stir up trouble at the school. He forbade me from venting my feelings at school and from leaving the house. Again I rolled up my bedding and stealthily left home.

My leaving devastated my mother. She became so ill as not to be able to leave her bed. The doctor who was called to see her said that hers was not a physical ailment, but simply a psychological one. When my father didn't grasp the difference, the doctor explained, 'You bring her son back, and her ailment will be cured.'

But this time I did not show myself on the streets. No one knew where I had gone. I had disappeared without a trace.

Eventually, however, Malaysian relatives reported seeing me in Penang, in the northern part of Malaysia. 'Since I have to work,' my father said to my mother, 'let me buy you a boat ticket so that you can go to Penang to stay with relatives. They can help you find our son.'

After arriving in Penang, relatives told my mother that they had seen me going and coming from a certain school. So early the next morning she planted herself outside the gate of that school to wait. No son. One, two, three days passed without any sign of me. Undiscouraged, she continued to go every day.

Finally one day I rode past on my bicycle. Though I saw her standing at the entrance of the school, I didn't recognise her. She looked too old and haggard to be only about forty. When I rode closer to her, our eyes met, and she recognised me. Surprise and gladness brightened her face – until I quickened my pace and rode past her, withering her smile like a dry leaf in the flame. How could this son of hers have become so cruel? She had carried me for nine months and nurtured me. Now I had just sped by without even extending her a greeting. How could her son do such a thing? The blow was just too much, and she fell to the ground with a loud cry.

When I heard the cry, I immediately turned my head and saw my mother on the ground, unable even to pull herself up. I got off my bike and looked back. My mother was struggling to get up, with one hand holding onto the electricity pole and the other hand waving to me. 'Oh, Child! Come back!' she cried. 'Child! You come back!'

I dropped my bicycle and ran to embrace her. She hugged me while tears streamed down her cheeks. Even cold-blooded hearts cannot help being moved by the touch of a loving mother, and at that point I decided to go home with her.

On the way home I could not help wondering if my father would be able to forgive me. I shouldn't have worried. Even before I went inside our house, I heard the sound of exploding firecrackers celebrating the return of the family's prodigal son. That night my father invited friends to a big feast because his son had been found. The whole family was filled with happiness.

Later I would know how much this scene paralleled the welcoming home of the prodigal son in the Bible. It would help me grasp how God's heart is gladdened when sinners repent and turn to him for forgiveness.

Dealing with Rev John Sung's evangelistic team

I was still studying in English school when Dr John Sung came to Singapore. As had happened all over China, the famous evangelist stirred revival in Singaporean churches. As the fire of the Gospel kindled zeal, Christian believers formed an evangelistic band and took to the streets and lanes to spread the Good News. They seemed to be everywhere.

I was not pleased. I still believed that religious faith was nothing but the opium of the mind, that as material opium could cause bodily injury, so opium of the mind could also cause terrible damage to the mind. Since opium was so terrible, it followed that those foreigners who initiated the preaching of the Christian message were disgusting and the Chinese who spread it were even more disgusting.

I remembered that in the past, when Christianity first came to China, rebels repudiated foreigners, calling them the 'number one moustache' and those Chinese who spread these foreigners' religion 'number two moustache'. Back in those days having these titles tacked onto a person was cause enough for execution.

Deciding that I should oppose the Chinese who were spreading Christianity for the foreigners, I stirred up some students at my school to stop Dr Sung's evangelistic band when they came to our neighbourhood. We emptied some duck eggs, filled them with malodorous goo, and then sealed them again. When members of the Christian band came to our streets and lanes, we would follow them, and as they sang their hymns, we would throw those goo-filled eggs at them, darkening their faces and stinking up their clothes.

Now as I recall these shameful acts, I again marvel at God's marvellous love and forgiveness. To think that I, who once threw stinking eggs at an evangelistic band, would later be changed by God to become a minister, to spend my whole life spreading the Gospel, of which I am now not ashamed! How matchless is the grace of God!

I act out my anti-British feelings

Because Singapore was a British colony, the Chinese were expected to take part in celebrating the British Memorial Day. But after the Japanese made a surprise attack on the Mukden garrison and conquered the whole of Manchuria in 1931, Chinese national and racial feelings strengthened, even in Singapore. So, despite Memorial Day being a big British holiday, the Chinese chose to incorporate their own ceremonies into the observation of the day, singing their own national anthem, bowing three times to the portrait of their National Father, Sun Yat-Sen, and finally meditating on his will for three minutes.

One Memorial Day I decided to teach the pro-British Chinese a lesson. I positioned some children, each with a chain of firecrackers, several children per row, and when everybody closed their eyes to meditate for three minutes, the children were to ignite their firecrackers and throw them into the crowd. The exploding firecrackers not only made a lot of noise, but also physically hurt the people who came into contact with them. The result was a great pandemonium, with many people screaming and running.

I did not stop there. When the mayor of Shanghai, Mr Wu Tie-cheng, came to visit the overseas Chinese in Singapore, over ten thousand people came to the pier to welcome him and to express their love for their mother country. As it was a time when patriotic feelings were gaining momentum among the Chinese, the crowd formed a surging throng, intent on parading to demonstrate Chinese co-operative strength before the British government.

The British, of course, felt their authority threatened. Besides, the parade was blocking traffic. When the authorities ordered the parade to disperse immediately, the huge crowd balked. The government once again gave the order to disperse, and the people once again refused, intent on demonstrating the power of the people. In the end the British decided that they had no alternative but to use harsh tactics. So they arrested some of the ringleaders of the protest and took them to the police station. As the resistance was spontaneous, it was not prepared to stand up to attack, and soon the people dispersed.

Parade initiators, however, felt that they were being persecuted for showing support to their own country and sent deputies, I being one of them, to seek help from the Chinese embassy. We hoped the ambassador would negotiate the release of the detainees.

But as we faced the ambassador, Mr Kao Ling-bo, he said to us, 'Because you are living on other people's colonial land, you should respect the authority of other people's government and obey its regulations. You are to live in peace with the British government. So don't make this into a big incident.'

I was upset. Already the bitterness within was just waiting to be vented. Years of observing the prejudices of imperialism had been building pressure inside me. It irked me, for instance, that only British people were allowed to be customs inspectors or captains of ships. Were Chinese minds not as capable as Western minds? Were we Chinese to live forever under such shameful prejudice? When I saw the ambassador's unwillingness to intercede for those who were arrested, I felt all the more intolerant. I decided, therefore, that since our own officials would not help us, we would have to help ourselves.

Taking advantage of the foment and enthusiasm for action, I urged fellow Chinese to stop all marketing interactions in the city as a protest against the British government. Because overseas Chinese particularly were all worked up, within hours most shops in Singapore were closed. The action was a heavy blow to the British government.

Strong nevertheless, the British refused to release those arrested.

So we mobilised people to surround the central police station. Some ten thousand people turned up to demand the release of the prisoners. The British, though, remained stern to the end, knowing that if they consented to the release, they would be submitting to the demands of the overseas Chinese and thus recognise their authority. This they could not do. The crowds for their part lingered long and would not disperse. Gridlock set in.

The British eventually won out, however, for the people that gathered were still basically just a mob with no strategy for continued resistance. Thus after repeated assaults, they gave up and dispersed.

Imprisoned but uncowed

In the investigation that followed, I was found to be among the instigators of the recent protest. Not long afterwards I was arrested. Though I was too young to be convicted under British law, the government used emergency powers to arrest and imprison me.

Because, although poor, my family spoiled me from early childhood with good, tasty meals three times a day, I could not tolerate the coarse food ('big-wok rice') that inmates ate. Every morning, even when it rained or when she didn't feel well, my mother came to bring me food. She was afraid that I would not eat the unpalatable prison fare and end up in bad health. Even now, when I recall her love, I still feel deeply my unworthiness.

Taking into consideration the fact that I was so young, the British government tried to use a reformatory to change me. They hoped that the prison chaplain could make me into a Christian. When I asked the chaplain how Jesus came about, he believed he had a good opportunity before him, so told me in great detail about Jesus. When he told me that Jesus was born of a virgin, conceived by the Holy Spirit, I said to him, 'You are an educated man. How can you say a virgin gave birth to a child? Isn't such a story just a fairy-tale?' To this I added many unrepeatable words of blasphemy.

Seeing how headstrong I was, the chaplain said, 'Since you don't believe what I say, why don't you read what this pamphlet has to say? Perhaps it will help you with your questions.'

When the pastor handed me that pamphlet, I squeezed it into a ball and threw it right at his face, saying, 'Since you can't persuade me, how can you ask me to read this pamphlet? Take it and get out!'

Exile and agony

As British people have always been respectful to pastors, the authorities regarded my insults to the prison chaplain as traitorous. Soon after, they ordered me out of my cell and said to me, 'Since you are so very stubborn, if you want to cause an uprising, you can go back to your own country to do it. This is British soil, not Chinese soil.' With that they sentenced me to exile from Singapore.

'We have already informed your parents of the day of your departure. They will be at the pier with your luggage,' the spokesman said. 'You may say farewell to your parents and then return to your own country.'

When I heard what was in store for me, I was horrified. Just eighteen years old, I had not even reached legal age. Suddenly love for my parents welled in my heart. Ever since I was young, they had toiled hard to look after me. My mother fanning me on hot nights, the good food they struggled to provide for me – so much they did for me. The memories had left deep imprints in my heart. When I realised that I was to be separated from my parents with no foreseeable date of reunion, grief engulfed me.

The separation from my parents at the pier turned out to be the saddest event I have ever experienced.

Guessing that the British would expect me to break down, I made up my mind that I would not show sorrow before them. I couldn't bear the thought of their moralising over me. By staying calm no matter what happened, I would show the British how courageous I was.

As I got out of the prison van that day, I saw my parents waiting there with my luggage. It is still almost impossible for me to describe their mournful expressions – so broken, so hopeless. As I left the vehicle, I dared not look at either my mother or my father straight in the eye for fear of crying. I clenched my teeth and went directly towards the pier without even a glance at them.

My parents understandably mistook my refusing even to say

goodbye to them as deliberate cruelty. As I walked resolutely toward the ship, my father ran after me, crying out in a voice that reflected his agony, 'Do you see what you've given us in the short years of your life? It's the white hair on our heads!'

It was true. My behaviour wasn't just a case of a young man's mischief. My violent hatred of the British had brought such grief, trouble and agony to this old couple that they had aged prematurely and their hair had turned grey. But with things having come to such a point, what else could I say? I felt I had no choice but to harden my heart and walk silently forward.

My father paused a moment, then continued, 'You turn around and look at us. What have you given us for your eighteen years? Just streams of unending tears!'

These words pierced my heart like a knife. I felt unable to move another step forward. Yet, despite my shaking hands and feet, I clenched my teeth and with all my being fought the tears which threatened to disgrace me before the British.

Then my mother ran to me and said in a sad, trembling voice, 'Oh repent! My child! Repent! What you gave us for more than ten years are just two broken hearts.'

When I heard that, my tears were like torrents spilling from a broken dike; I could no longer control them. To myself I said, *My selfishness and impulsiveness has brought all this to pass – their grief and grey hairs. I've brought this disaster on them and broken their hearts.* I also thought that if I could see them again one day, I would let them know that I was not the same faithless person of the past. *I must change myself,* I thought, *so that these two old persons' hearts might be comforted.*

My pride still unable to let go, I hardened my heart and boarded the ship alone. When from the ship's railing I saw my mother sobbing and my father holding her tightly to himself, I almost fainted away. The trouble I had stirred up for my family pierced my heart. As the eldest son I had not only brought them no happiness, but I had caused them agony of the severest kind. My sin was heavy.

As the ship set sail, I knew, like it or not, I had to live with the consequences of my actions and face my future all on my own.

The tears that washed my face every day on the way to Shanghai could wash away neither the reality of the hurt I had left behind nor the uncertainties of what lay ahead.

2

On My Own

Light and shadow in Shanghai

When the ship finally docked at the outer pier of the Huangpu River at Shanghai, I was left to find some kind of shelter for myself. With my luggage on my back I stepped off the pier, very much alone.

Without family, I would have to depend on friends – but would friends receive a person with my reputation? I didn't know, but I had to try.

Though I had with me the address of a classmate, I didn't know which direction to go to look for him. I could think of nothing to do but to ask help from passers-by. Unfortunately, the larger the city, the colder people are toward others. I could find no one who would take an interest in a scared eighteen-year-old. Because I didn't know the Shanghai dialect, people just turned their heads and walked away.

Finally, I asked a Westerner for help. He was unexpectedly kind, offering to take me to the address I was looking for.

After following the stranger about an hour I asked him whether we had arrived at our destination. 'Please don't ask,' he said. 'Just follow me!'

It was then that I noticed that this man walked unsteadily, and his speech was unclear. He was drunk!

I decided to give up tagging after the drunken Westerner, instead to think out a way for myself. But where should I go? I went up one street and down another all over Shanghai making inquiries. Wherever people pointed me, I would go. As one dead-end followed another, finding my friend among the five million people of Shanghai seemed more and more hopeless.

Suddenly there my friend was – on the street in front of me! I recognised him, for when we were young, we were best friends. Both of us at that time were top students. Here he was in Shanghai, living in one of his cousins' houses, and, as I found out, open for me to move in with him. Now, thinking back on this almost impossible 'coincidental encounter'. I believe deeply that this was not a coincidence, but rather a working out of God's care for me, despite the fact that I didn't yet know him.

Now with a return address, I wrote immediately to my parents. Mercifully in the months ahead they sent me money for my board and keep.

But having a place to stay and help from my parents was just the beginning of blessings in my new circumstances. During my spare time I was able to attend classes at the Jian Nan University, a school specially designed for overseas Chinese. Thus I was not forced to stop my education.

Not only so, but my classmate's uncle and aunt were musicians – one a soprano vocalist and the other a violinist – who held concerts in their home. In fact, the famous violinist Ma Si Cong was a close friend of theirs. So, naturally, I came under this aunt and uncle's musical influence. Judging my voice to be very good, they encouraged me to learn to sing, which I did, as it was an interest of mine. Thinking back upon this, I believe that my music lessons were the good will of God as the ability to sing would give me great assistance in ministry in the days ahead.

Life in Shanghai was very happy for me. Although exiled from Singapore I was not reduced to being a beggar on the street (as I well might have), but I was able to continue my education and learn to sing.

Shanghai in the late 1930s was a mixed world, for some 'heaven' and for many 'hell'. The wealthy lived extravagantly in Western houses and drove private automobiles. At the same time streets were full of beggars. The poor included both refugees from the interior of China as the result of the ongoing Sino-Japanese War and uprooted people from the northern bay area, where there was little employment. Without warm clothing against the winter's cold, many street people wrapped themselves in newspapers to survive. So tragic was the scene of shivering humanity in mid-winter that I could not bear to look. I knew too well that I could have been among them.

One day, as I was buying groceries on Jingan Temple Road, I saw a beggar snatch a loaf of bread from a lady just leaving a shop. When the lady chased after the beggar, he hurriedly took a big bite of the bread, then, with a nervous giggle, held the loaf out to her. The lady recoiled from taking the contaminated bread, and the beggar gleefully disappeared down the street with it.

At that time Shanghai was divided into international settlements; i.e. a British Concession, a French Concession, etc., each with its own laws. The police from one could not go beyond their own sector's boundary to make arrests. One day I saw a beggar yank a basket of fish, meat, and eggs from the hands of a lady shopper and run for the French sector. The policeman from the British sector who chased the thief had to stop at the boundary. From there he could only watch the beggar laughing in broad daylight on the other side.

The dividedness of the city worked against the refugees and other people living on the streets as well. As each sector had its own Bureau of Public Works and as these were usually staffed by foreigners, the desperate found little care or help. One day when a cold wave swept down from Siberia, temperatures dropped to below zero. By the next morning a hundred and forty corpses were found closely packed together, all frozen to death. For a youngster it was truly a bitter tragedy to watch. My reaction was a growing resentment against the Japanese army, whose invasion caused so much of the misery.

Having come close to being among the homeless in those desperate times, I was constantly reminded of others' extremity. One of the most graphic reminders came one day when my friend invited me to eat at Jin Jiang Restaurant, famous for its

Sichuan-style food. When we came outside after our meal, I noticed a customer vomiting outside the door, the result perhaps of having had too much to eat or drink. His vomit covered the pavement. Suddenly a beggar dashed in, scooped up the vomit and ate it. I was horrified. Here was hunger forcing a human to do what normally only dogs would do.

When the heart is not right, nothing is right

I blamed politics for the death and despair in Shanghai. If its politics were good, I reasoned, then life for the people would be reasonably good. Leadership must make reforms. Yet there seemed to be no end to bad politics. In history, when one dynasty became corrupt, another arose to replace it. In the course of a few thousand years, dynasty followed dynasty, with new dynasties no better in the end than preceding ones. Satisfactory rule so easily deteriorated with the passing of time. Commendable ideologies in their working out proved to be little more than pipe-dreams. No dynasty or political system, I decided, could rise higher than the moral quality of the people involved.

A parable I once heard fits this reality. One morning, the story goes, a son and his mother were having breakfast together. After trying his coffee, the son complained that the coffee wasn't sweet.

'Stir it a few times,' the mother replied, thinking the sugar hadn't dissolved yet.

'It still isn't sweet,' he told her after stirring and tasting it again.

'Stir it some more!' she said – then suddenly realised that she had forgotten to add the sugar!

Coffee without sugar cannot be sweet no matter how many times your stir it. It is only after I accepted Jesus and believed in God that I discovered that this world will never be truly good. Without God any kind of reform is useless, for without him this world cannot govern itself. Confucius once said, 'Ruling a country depends on national policies. National policies depend on harmonious homes. Harmonious homes depend on self-control, and self-control depends on rightness of heart.'

But how can a heart be right? This is not an issue of education, because education has no means to make a heart right. Law can govern only our outward actions, not our inner condition. While education, a trained conscience, and moral understanding can sometimes constrain the human self, a person will still do things in the dark that they wouldn't dare do in the light. Even before I believed in God I understood this very clearly. But at this stage in my life I did not think further about what can make a person right.

Actually, how unreliable the human conscience can be was illustrated one day when several policemen arrived at the door of the family with whom I lived. They came to take us all to the police station, charging us with stealing our first landlord's furniture. Totally baffled, we protested our innocence. Nevertheless they locked us up for two days. It came out later that our second landlord had stolen the furniture, which the first landlord had deposited with him. When the thief was caught without an explanation, he passed the blame on to us. At that time I didn't know that the Bible said: 'The heart is more deceitful than all else, and is desperately wicked; who can understand it?' But I had begun to see the truth of it.

Learning the habit of thriftiness

During my time in Shanghai my parents regularly sent me money to live on. Each time it came in the mail I could not help thinking about them. I knew that money came as a result of their hard labour and sacrifice. How much sweat my father, working as a dock-hand, must have shed to earn that sum!

Weighing my parents' sacrifice, I would consider long and hard whether any purchase were necessary. I kept up this practice the whole time I was in Shanghai.

Though many people visited West Lake when travelling through Hangzhou and visited many ancient sites when touring

Nanjing, the wartime capital, I never went to any of these places. Spending money for something this unnecessary, I knew, would make me feel guilty. Living a thrifty life became such a habit that I continue to live frugally to this day.

Missing an opportunity to find Christ

One of the friends I made in Shanghai was a Christian. As Christians have a personal obligation to spread the Gospel to others and lead others to Christ, my friend was no exception. But I continued to hold a very deep prejudice against religion. At the same time, I felt I could not fly in the face of my friend's kindness, so to please him, I began attending worship with him at the Fujian Church on Jing An Temple Road.

The experience, however, was lost on me. I did not understand nor remember what the pastor said. Though I sang the hymns, I thought they were dull. When the congregation prayed, I waited impatiently for them to finish. Knowing my discomfort and knowing that religion was not something to be forced on people, my friend eventually stopped inviting me to his church, judging that any further insistence would have ruined our friendship.

Facing starvation

As the Japanese expanded the war in the Pacific, they took over Shanghai's foreign sectors. What had been under British and French control was now under Japanese control, and they soon made their presence felt. When Japanese soldiers made a search of a friend's house nearby, the master of the house used English to negotiate with them.

'Why do you not speak Japanese to us?' they demanded.

'I have never learned it,' he replied.

'Then why do you learn English? It's not an English world any more, but a Japanese world,' they shouted. As punishment, the soldiers made our friend balance a table on his head from morning until evening. The incident warned us of Japan's frenzied ambition to conquer the whole world.

The Japanese army began to move south. As bamboo falling before its mowers, everything swiftly gave way before Japanese might. Within a short period the aggressors occupied Indo-China, the Philippines, Malaysia, Indonesia, and Singapore. Soon all of Southeast Asia was forced to fly the flag of the rising sun.

With Japan's occupation of Singapore, my money from overseas ended. As I and the family of friends with whom I lived all depended on foreign exchange for our living, we faced serious problems. Everybody had to think about their own survival. I decided to return to my ancestors' village in Xiamen, thinking that I might well still find relatives there and could live in the old house left by my parents and grandparents. So I bought a boat ticket from Shanghai to Xiamen.

But Xiamen then was also occupied by the Japanese army. When the boat arrived, they allowed only those who had applied for travel permits to go ashore. The rest of us had to stay behind until relatives came to verify our status.

When a Japanese went to inquire of my kinsmen for me, they told him that they didn't know me. Having learned of my past history in Singapore, they were afraid that I would create problems for them. Besides, with the hardships of wartime, one more person meant one more burden.

When the Japanese messenger came back, he was angry. 'Your audacity is bigger than the sky itself,' he scolded, 'for you dare to cheat the Great Japanese Emperor.'

I found it hard to see how I had cheated the Emperor. I was the one who had been cheated, by my relatives no less. Not only was their rejection like bitter herbs in my mouth, but the Japanese detained me as a result. Having heard about Japanese brutality long before, I was terrified.

The Japanese left me unharmed, however, but transported me to a small island between Quemoy and Matsu. As the place was used by fishermen as a rest stop and by low-class smugglers as a transfer station, I wondered how I would survive. As my money was all used up, I began selling my possessions. Yet what I got from selling even an imported fountain pen provided food for only two days. My Chinese suit which my mother had made was so obviously country-style that it was practically worthless. Eventually with nothing left to sell, I faced starvation.

Escape to Quanzhou

'There are boats here that go to Quanzhou,' a smuggler told me. 'You had better escape there, because if you don't, the Japanese might kill you.'

I took the man's advice, and soon after left on a midnight boat.

I was soon seasick. Tired and weak with fear and anxiety, my body could not cope with the rolling motion of the boat.

Yet on board was a family who, despite the rough water, ate and drank as usual, all the time laughing and talking together. They were Christians on their way to the mainland of China. They didn't seem a bit afraid of the raging sea. For the first time I discovered something of the difference between Christians and non-Christians. I could see clearly the reality of God in these people's lives.

As obvious as the contrast between them and me was, however, I was unwilling to think deeper on this issue nor to come to grips with my own prejudice. In thinking of myself at this stage, I am reminded of a parable of a child and his father walking down an unfamiliar road. As the sun gradually went down in the west, the father asked his little son, 'Are you afraid?'

The child said, 'I am not afraid.'

But as the sun disappeared below the horizon and the sky turned dark, the child moved close to his father and gripped his hand tightly. After a while the two approached a wild, uninhabited place, and the boy's heart began to pound. As he moved even closer to his father, his father asked him again if he were afraid.

Determined to be strong, the boy once again replied, 'I am not afraid,' though in his heart he was extremely frightened.

Likewise our hearts and our mouths often do not line up with each other. That was true of me as I sat in clammy misery facing an unknown and fearful future.

Sometime past midnight the boat approached a port called Xiangzhi, outside Quanzhou. We didn't dare get too close to shore for fear that the boat might run aground or that we would be discovered by the army. Going in as far as he dared, the captain dropped anchor and ordered his passengers to swim ashore.

One after another the people jumped into the briny water, me included. Having learned to swim in Singapore, I had no problem following the others.

My luggage, however, did not fare so well as the boatmen threw our baggage into the sea after us. While the experienced among us had wrapped their luggage securely in plastic sheets, my stuff got soaked.

Arriving on the beach, all the passengers decided to rest there for the night and start their journeys at daybreak. When I asked people around me to wake me early, they all assured me they would. Having been quite ill, I was afraid that I would oversleep if left to myself. More than anything else, I did not want to be left behind.

I slept soundly. When I awoke, the sun was already directly overhead, and I was alone. I began to panic. Unfamiliar with the place, I had planned to follow the other passengers. Now as it was, I had no idea where to go or what to do.

For half a day I hesitated, not knowing what to decide. I noticed that to one side was the sea, while on the other was the mountain. Believing that people in general lived close to the base of mountains, I eventually decided to walk toward the mountain.

But soaked with seawater, my luggage was very heavy. Because of the weight, I could carry only one piece at a time. So I would walk with one suitcase, set it down, and then go back for another. I made progress at a snail's pace.

The sun was low in the sky when a local security man

discovered me and asked where I had come from. When I told him that I had come from a small island near Xiamen, he became immediately suspicious of me as that was enemy territory. Treating me as if I were a criminal, he took me to the village police station. I felt very alone.

In response to interrogation I told the authorities in trembling voice how I had gone from Shanghai to Xiamen, where the rejection of my relatives had aroused the suspicion of the Japanese, who sent me to that island. I told them that my immediate family was in Singapore. They did not believe me until I showed them letters from my parents and the foreign exchange receipts I had received in Shanghai.

Although the village authorities did not imprison me, they kept me in the police station. Until someone could be found to bail me out, I could not leave. Incredibly a local primary school teacher took pity on me and put up bail for my release.

But now where was I to go? Remembering friends I knew in Shanghai who were now teaching at the Double Ten Secondary School in Zhangzhou, I wondered if they would help me. As the idea seemed worth a try, I set out to walk to Zhangzhou.

I had gone no further than a half a day's walk, however, when the security man found me again. He wanted to know where I was going.

'I want to go to Zhangzhou,' I told him.

'What for?'

'To seek help from friends there,' I answered honestly.

'You still have not even clarified your identity here,' he said. 'So if somebody else suspects you, you'll really be in trouble. Since you are already in Quanzhou, you'd better go have a look at the downtown area.'

It seemed that I had no choice but to follow his advice. So I started back to Quanzhou. But along the way I remembered something that changed my mind.

Change of fortune in Yongchun

I remembered that I had received a letter saying that money I had
left in Shanghai with the family with whom I was living was
waiting for me with their relatives in Yongchun. So I quickly
headed north. I desperately needed that money.

It was the right decision. Not only did I find my friends'
relatives and retrieve the money they had been holding for me,
but I met a group of overseas Chinese who knew some of my
Shanghai friends. After some conversation they welcomed me to
live with them and invited me to teach in their school. So I had
both a home and a job.

Because it was wartime, accommodations were simple. I had
to share not only the same room, but the same bed with a
colleague. Finding other people's breath offensive, I requested
that we sleep with our heads at opposite ends of the bed. But the
smell of my roommate's feet was worse than the smell of his
breath! During the war, people, not able to afford leather shoes,
wore plastic ones that trapped the sweat inside. With my companion's sweaty feet at my face, I spent the night tossing about,
sleepless. So the next morning I asked him if he could please
wash his feet before he went to bed.

'Why do I need to wash my feet before going to sleep?' he
wanted to know.

'Because your feet smell worse than the toilet,' I told him.

'Oh, so my feet smell, do they? And what about yours? Your
feet smell worse than cat dung!'

Fortunately we were still young and were also friends in need.
Our quarrel was soon forgotten. But the incident did show me
how quickly we see others' weaknesses and faults and how slow
we are to see our own.

After I had been in Yongchun for some time, the provincial
government asked our school what we could contribute to the
celebration of the Double Ten National Festival. We said that we
wanted to perform a drama.

Reviewing famous dramas we might want to try, the

headmaster asked the staff who would be the director. I said I would like to try.

As no one challenged me, the job was mine.

Deciding to tackle two dramas, 'Peking Man' and 'The Black Characters Twenty-Eight', I immediately began recruiting actors and holding rehearsals.

The performances actually turned out to be quite successful, not because I was a drama expert, but because the place was small and those who came to watch did not have high expectations. Thus I became a great king among little men and was thought to be a famous director. Thinking about it now, it seems a little funny. How great my naivety! I did not know how high the sky was nor how thick the earth!

Downfall of a gentleman

At Yongchun was a gentleman with everyone's respect, appreciated for his morality and his writings. The man was humble, noble, and easy-going. As he had proved himself a man to be trusted with money, many overseas Chinese sent money back to their families through him. Everyone looked up to the man, including me.

Suddenly the tables turned, and Yongchun exploded in rage. Like water spilling out of a boiling cauldron, people poured out of their homes to join in the commotion. The gentleman whom everyone respected was now tied to a big tree and left to bear the public's scorn. Women spat on his face; other people put dirt onto brooms and dumped it over his head. For several hours the man bore the town's insults. When I saw what was happening, I was shocked.

Later I found out that in delivering funds for overseas Chinese he had fallen in love with one of their wives and was secretly carrying on an affair with her. Suspicions arose, and eventually relatives laid wait for him, catching the adulterous couple in their treachery.

Seeing this man's downfall had a profound effect on me. I realized that reputation could not restrain a man from committing a crime, that law could not control a man's behaviour, nor was education a panacea. I saw that once lust finds opportunity it pushes man to shameful action.

I have never been able to forget the trauma of that man's downfall. Later in life I would often use it to show how social mores, law, or education cannot restrain a person from following their sinful nature. Even we Christians, if we are not careful at all times and live daily in close contact with God, are open to temptation and failure and must depend on God to overcome selfish desire.

Another chance to believe

Since taking voice lessons in Shanghai, I continued to practice singing as often as I could. Nearly every morning at daybreak, before going off to teach at the village school, I would go up onto a small hill to sing. One day the dean of Pei Yuan Secondary School in Quanzhou heard me singing and came looking for me. 'You've got a very good voice,' he said when he found me. 'Would you be willing to be a music teacher at Pei Yuan Secondary School?'

'Yes, I would,' I said with little hesitation.

But Pei Yuan was a Christian school. With my prejudice against Christianity, I chaffed at the school's worship times. When students and staff closed their eyes to pray, I thought they were like lunatics. When I saw them holding their Bibles with obvious respect, I thought, *What can be accomplished with such an education? It's the twentieth century, and they still study that Western book of divination!*

When people at the school found out that I was anti-Christian, they tried to win me to faith in Christ, arranging for various people to share the Gospel with me. One man they sent to tackle my stubborn unbelief was quite eloquent and knew his Bible well. Whenever I was free after school, he would visit me and ask if we could chat together.

Day after day the man came. He talked about Jesus, about

what was meant by heaven and hell, about the importance of faith. All were things I had rejected from childhood. My mind did not change. To me religion remained the opium of the mind. Only an uneducated man would ascribe credence to such absurd teachings. I could not bring myself to entertain such nonsense as truth.

The man was quite persistent, however. One day he prattled on until I could take it no longer. 'Let's talk honestly for a minute,' I said sternly. 'A person like me cannot be persuaded with a few of your words. You are dreaming if you think you can persuade me to believe in Jesus. I would sooner let you chop off my head and use it as a football!'

At that point, considering me hell-bound and completely reprobate, he stopped coming.

The Lord God almighty could well have done the same.

3

Marriage and Miracles

Courtship ends in refusal and rashness

I met Lai Bao Lian in Yongchun. But to finish her education, she returned to her hometown of Quanzhou. After I moved to Quanzhou as well, we saw each other frequently. Deciding that her proximity was an opportunity made in heaven, I soon began courting her seriously. Soon we were secretly talking about marriage.

But in the still-conservative ways of village life in China, young people could not marry without the consent of parents. So I recruited a colleague of mine, who knew my intended wife's parents, to be matchmaker for me.

By the time my colleague arrived at my girlfriend's home with my marriage proposal, her mother had already learned about our relationship and had already begun investigating my family background. But though she knew I was from Singapore, she could learn no more because she ran into a communication blockage, the result of the Japanese occupation of Singapore. To give a daughter to a man with an unknown background risked too much, she decided, and she sent me a straightforward refusal.

My friend was mortified. He returned to school with a downcast face. One look told me that the situation was not favourable for me.

When my friend confirmed my fears of rejection, I became completely pessimistic. I saw no reason to continue living since I had lost the person most dear to me. Yet because I considered suicide behaviour of a weak person, I did not want to kill myself.

In wondering what to do, I thought suddenly, *I'll join the army*! At that time the whole country was recruiting young soldiers, using the slogan, 'Ten thousand youths for an army of ten thousand.' I would die on the battlefield, I decided, for that would be a death with honour.

But not wanting to join the army alone, I came up with the idea of rallying a group of young men to go with me. Immediately I began planning my opportunity to recruit students and staff at school. Thus one morning I stood at chapel and gave a speech entitled, 'All men share a common responsibility for the events of their nation.' My delivery was systematic, and my audience easily moved: young and enthusiastic, strong in their patriotism and bitterly opposed to the aggression of the Japanese.

'Now is the time for us to pay back our country,' I challenged. 'I am willing to give myself to be a member of the resistance force. If you also have this determination, please raise your hands.'

To my surprise, many young men raised their hands to signify their willingness to follow my example. In the enthusiasm of stirred patriotism, I urged the would-be volunteers to march with me from the auditorium to the Village Governmental Soldiers Recruitment Department to be registered. As a result I appeared in the local news reports as a hero.

A change of mind leaves me in a dilemma

But I was in for a surprise. Returning home from signing up, I found a letter waiting for me from Bao Lian. 'Please try once again!' she wrote. 'My mother has already changed her mind towards our marriage. Please ask that young gentleman to come to my house once more, because we now have hope!'

What a turn of events! Suddenly I did not know whether to proceed or to retreat, whether to laugh or to cry. On one hand I was very happy, but on the other, very embarrassed. Though hope was rekindled for marriage, I was publicly committed to fighting the Japanese. Surely, I thought after much deliberation, getting married is more important than joining the army. At least I wanted marriage more than becoming a hero on the battlefield. So I asked the colleague who had served as matchmaker earlier to make the proposal one more time.

'I don't want to go,' he said with lowered face, his voice pleading. 'Isn't one failure enough? How can you ask me to go a second time?'

'Here, look!' I said, showing him the letter from my girl-friend.

'All right,' he agreed reluctantly. 'I'll try one more time.'

This time my matchmaker friend was successful. My future mother-in-law gave her consent. But she did so, not so much because she was convinced of my worthiness, but because she couldn't stand her daughter's constant crying and pleading. Besides, Mrs Lai knew that in a few more years, when her daughter was of age, she would not be able to stop the girl anyway.

As excited as I was at the good news, I was also nervous. How was I to settle the matter about my promise to join the army? Joy and jitters intermingled in my heart most disconcertingly. In the end I went ahead and set the date for the wedding, planning to deal with the possible consequences of reneging on my commit-ment to the military later.

Bolts of cloth save my wedding day

A friend who had spent much time with me in Shanghai had just arrived in Quanzhou when he read the news of my engagement to Bao Lian in the newspaper. Immediately he hurried over to our school to congratulate me.

Discovering that a little more than a month remained before the wedding, my friend was concerned. 'Since marriage is a big event in life, your preparations should be first-rate,' he urged. Then he asked, 'Have you prepared for it?'

'What should I prepare?' I asked naively.

'What should you prepare? Don't you know? Where is the new house? How about a wedding suit? Have you sent out invitation cards yet? Do you have enough money for the feast? What are you planning to do about the dowry?'

I had been feeling fine before he came. Now my head was swimming.

'How much money have you saved?' he wanted to know.

'I have nothing! I teach school and use up what I earn. I can't even save a cent!'

'Goodnight! Are you crazy?' he blurted. 'You can't save anything, and yet you're planning on getting married next month? What are you trying to do, disgrace yourself?' He paused a moment and asked me again, 'What are you going to do?'

'I don't know what to do,' I said helplessly.

'Let me solve your problem,' my friend said. 'Your problem is money; if you have money, you can do anything. There is still a load of imported cloth left at my house. I'll write a letter for you to take to my home so that my mother will give you the goods. After you sell them, you'll have enough financial resources for your wedding.'

I was deeply moved that I had a friend who would generously give me so much help in a time of desperate need. I thanked him with tears.

But the road was not smooth yet. After I had travelled to Penghu and fetched the fabric from my friend's mother, I was on my way back to Quanzhou with visions of selling it when I met an overseas Chinese from Vietnam whom I had known in an earlier time. He was in Penghu helping to look after his father-in-law's shop. He asked me about the cloth. 'Are you in business?' he asked.

'No, I'm not in business. I am a schoolteacher,' I told him.

'Then why do you carry so much cloth with you?'

I told the man about needing to exchange the cloth for cash for my wedding.

'How are you going to sell it all?' he wanted to know.

I told him I planned to take it to Quanzhou and look for someone to sell it for me.

'Quanzhou is a long way. Let me sell it for you here!' he offered.

I felt happy with the arrangement. After all, having him sell the cloth for me rather than hauling it all the way back to Quanzhou seemed sensible. So I gave him the fabric.

Since the cloth was imported, it all sold within a short time. Yet, unbelievably, my acquaintance took the money earned and lost it all gambling. When I heard the news, I felt as if I had been hit by lightning. On the one hand I felt sorry for the friend who had given me the cloth, and on the other hand, the loss left me without financial resources for my wedding. I was so indignant that I could not even speak.

When I went to the scoundrel's house to confront him with my dilemma, his father-in-law unexpectedly took over the responsibility of this worthless son-in-law and gave me all the money due me. So, though the incident gave me a bad scare, it did me no real harm. I stayed there for another two or three days, then returned to Quanzhou.

With the money in hand I managed the preparations for the wedding quite easily, though hurriedly. I owe ten thousand thanks to the friend who helped me in such a great and timely fashion.

Bao Lian and I were married in Quanzhou on 2 February 1945. At that time, as inland China did not have modern transportation such as cars, I had to go to my mother-in-law's house to receive my bride perched on an open sedan chair. I was quite an attraction along the way, as groups of friends and students from Pei Yuan Secondary School were standing on either side of the street to cheer me on. After arriving at the door of my bride's home, I received her out of her house and helped her into a second sedan chair, this one with a cover. Then together the two conveyances delivered us to the big chapel of Pei Yuan Secondary School for the ceremony. Finally, though hindered by obstacles and frustrations in the making, the big event of my marriage proceeded successfully, and Bao Lian and I became man and wife.

Trouble catches up with me

Not more than a day or two after the wedding, the trouble I felt nervous about caught up with me, and I had to deal with the situation head on. I had not registered for the army out of patriotism at all, but as a reaction to the failure of my marriage proposal. Backing out of my own commitment was bad enough. But having led the large group of young men to register with me and then having backed out myself left me with many enemies. The parents of the young men particularly attacked me fiercely. 'You yourself dare not to die,' they complained, 'but you ask our children to go to die!' So indignant were some who worked at the Quanzhou newspaper company that they published a news item under the heading, 'The *Yung* (which means courage in Chinese) of Wu Yung. Where did this *Yung* go? It went to the marriage bed!'

The headline and news item screamed from the front page. Quickly I became a despicable news figure and an object of gossip on everybody's lips in Quanzhou. People would come after me on the street, and children would point, saying, 'It's him! It's him!'

The loss of reputation and the public's scorn weighed heavily on my shoulders. Eventually under the pressure of this infamy, my bride and I decided to make our future some place else. Because of friends and connections in the area, I wrote to the branch of the Central Police School in Meilie, Fujian, and received a wholehearted invitation to come to teach. We decided we would leave Quanzhou as quickly as possible.

The power of love

Though I did not like leaving my wife so shortly after our marriage, I felt I had to go first alone to Meilie, a two-day walk to the interior of Fujian. I was about to arrive at the town when I heard someone behind me say, 'You in front, are you Mr Wu?' It was a security man coming out of the woods. Because he startled me, I did not answer him right away. Only when he asked me the second time did I answer him that I was.

Immediately the man handed me a telegram from my mother-in-law. The telegram said that my wife was seriously ill and that I should hurry back. Once I had grasped its message, I started shaking all over. I had no choice but to go back.

I would have given almost anything for a pair of wings. Instead I hired a sedan chair to carry my belongings. After piling my luggage onto the chair, I told the lead carrier that I would not ride myself, but that I wanted to set the pace on foot. If I walked, he and his fellow carrier would walk; if I ran, they would run; and if I crossed over obstacles, they also would cross those obstacles. When the man found that my luggage was no heavier than eight or nine kilograms, much lighter than a person, he agreed to my conditions.

'What's your hurry?' he asked.

'My wife is seriously ill,' I told him. 'I need to get to her quickly.'

Almost miraculously the return trip took us only one long day. When I arrived home at almost midnight and knocked, my mother-in-law answered the door. 'How did you get here so soon?' she asked, hardly believing her eyes. 'Hurry! Come inside!'

By that time my feet were stiff with pain, however, and I could not make it in by myself and had to ask one of the sedan chair carriers to help me inside.

In the living room I sat down to take off my shoes and found that my feet were swollen, blistered, and bleeding. Why hadn't I felt this pain on the road? The great power of love for my wife!

How glad Bao Lian was to see me! With my return, she felt more secure and was comforted, and she was soon on the mend. I decided not to leave her alone again. We would go to Meilie together.

My wife believes in Jesus

During her recuperation, my wife attended an evangelistic revival meeting in Quanzhou and believed. The speaker was the young Rev Hsu Sung-kuang, later to serve for many years as pastor of the Jubilee Year Church in Singapore.

Bao Lian had invited me to go with her. But still convinced Christianity was a tool of imperialism, I at first refused. Unable, however, to hold out against my wife's persistence, I eventually went, reluctantly.

I was miserable. Sitting there, I felt as if I were being punished. No matter how eloquently Rev Hsu spoke, my heart remained fully closed to what he said. I was extremely bored. I was a perfect example of the biblical teaching that says that when a person is still in his flesh and unregenerate, he cannot understand spiritual things, but rather thinks they are foolishness. I left that meeting totally unmoved and unrepentant.

But God was not finished with his work in my heart.

Miracles on the way to Meilie

When Bao Lian's health was restored to the point that she could stand the long trip, we headed for Meilie together by bus.

Our first stop was Datian. We got off and checked in at a hotel. While there someone told us that we needed a road pass to proceed, something that I did not know. 'A police school is hiring me to be their teacher,' I explained. 'As I am a teacher of policemen, they wouldn't dare detain me.'

Feeling sure I was right, I made no move to obtain the required permit. But on that very night a Datian policeman knocked at our door and asked for our road pass. I told him we didn't have one.

'Where are you going?' he asked.

'Meilie,' I said.

'What are you going there for?'

'To teach in a police school,' I answered, expecting a change of attitude when he heard what I said. I even showed him my letter of invitation.

But, to my surprise, this policemen was not convinced by my story. 'Who is this woman?' he asked suspiciously.

'This is my wife,' I said.

'Do you have anything to prove that she is your wife?' he persisted. At the time prostitution was quite common inside the hotel. And since I could show no documentary evidence to verify Bao Lian as my wife, he insisted that we get dressed and accompany him to the police station. It was half past two in the morning.

At the police station my wife sat down in a corner and lowered her head to pray. But I was like an ant on a hot skillet. I was up and down and pacing constantly. Finally, unable to endure my frustration any longer, I said to the policeman, 'Excuse me, sir, but tomorrow I must be on my way. Our tickets are already bought.'

'There is only one way for you to leave,' he said. 'You must post bail.'

Suddenly remembering that a friend's brother worked in Datian, I asked if I could look for a friend to post bail for us. The policeman agreed, but I had to admit that I didn't know where this man lived. 'I never expected to be caught in a situation like this,' I explained. 'That's why it didn't occur to me to ask for that friend's address beforehand.'

'Since you don't know the address,' he said, 'where would you look for him?'

'This little village has only one big street,' I ventured. 'If we knock and inquire from house to house, we should be able to find where he lives.'

Giving in to my fervent request, the policeman armed himself with a gun and escorted us out onto the street. Going from house to house, I asked many people if they knew my friend's brother. All I managed to do was to make everybody angry at us, having caused the whole street to be searched.

By the time we gave up looking, the roosters were crowing, and the sun was almost up. The policeman had just decided that we should return to the police station, and I was feeling very discouraged and lost, when someone from behind us with a lantern suddenly cried out, 'Mr Wu, is that you?'

I turned around immediately. 'Oh, yes,' I said, 'I am Mr Wu.'

He ran to me and lifted his lantern to look at me. When I discovered that I didn't know him, I asked him how he knew me, since we'd never met before.

'Last week did you not eat at Mr Wang's house?' the stranger asked with a smile. 'Mr Wang is my colleague, and he was giving us a farewell meal before we went off on a distant trip. You were among those who were invited, and I overheard you talking with other people. When I heard you talking with the policeman, I remembered your voice and so recognised you.'

When the man saw that I was being detained by the policeman, he asked what had happened. I told him about not having a road pass.

'Don't worry,' he encouraged. 'My brother is an official of the village government. I can call him right away to release you on bail.'

For our miraculous release from custody, my wife kept thanking the Lord Jesus, believing that our release was his answer to her prayer. I believed that our meeting the man was just a wonderful coincidence.

The next day my wife and I took a bus to Yong'an, planning to transfer there to a vehicle bound for Meilie. When we were about to arrive in Yong'an, the bus inspector announced, 'Please take out your road pass. The military police must see your road pass before allowing you to enter the city.'

I cried bitterly in my heart, for we had just been detained for a whole night because we did not have that road pass, and now the authorities were asking for it again!

I began asking around in the bus for an extra road pass. I was desperate for a way out of our dilemma.

'Our house is outside Yong'an,' said a kind young man, 'so we don't need to enter the city. I can let you use my road pass.'

I was filled with thanks. It was incredible that I had such great fortune to find so many helpers wherever I went.

However, when I looked at his road pass, I was unsure of what to do, for he was traveling with a wife and child. Being newly married, we had no children. 'What about the fact that we have no child?' I asked the young man.

'Don't be so stupid!' he said. 'You just say that your child got sick and died on the way. Then they will not question you further, but will sympathise with you instead.'

To me the plan sounded good. But not to my wife. As a believer in Jesus, she could not go along with the lie. The issue was clear to her – we had no child and couldn't pretend that we did, much less that it had died. She took the road pass from my hand and returned it to the man. 'Mister,' she said, 'we thank you for your kindness very much. However, I am a Christian, and I cannot do this.'

I was very angry. We had gone through this mess before! Christians or non-Christians – what was the point? Women! Foolish prejudice! Inwardly I said, *Well, I'd like to see how we are going to enter the city! You Christians should be a little more concerned with the practical.*

My wife did not say a word but lowered her head to pray. The action made me all the angrier. It wouldn't have been so bad, except that there were other people on the bus, and I was embarrassed. Wouldn't they think she had a mental problem?

While my wife continued to pray, I craned my neck to see whether we were approaching the city gate yet and whether there were military police and other law officers waiting there or not. Then, all of a sudden, sirens wailed, and we were told to disperse immediately in order to escape possible bombing from Japanese planes. As we took cover, many people spilled out of the city gates. After we had waited ten minutes or more without spotting any Japanese planes, the people who had fled the city began filing back in. We just followed the throng through the gates. We were in Yong'an without road passes! My wife was elated. 'See!' she said, 'my Lord heard my prayer.'

I couldn't help remember the miracle of finding someone in Datian willing to bail us out of prison. My wife had said then that it was her Lord who had heard her prayer. Now it was the sounding of the air-raid siren and our being able to enter Yong'an without a road pass that she was linking to having prayed. This time even I didn't dare say that it was a mere coincidence.

Arriving in Yong'an, we discovered that because there was no bus going to Meilie that day, we would have to stay the night in a hotel. But the money I had brought with us was already nearly all used up. If I bought meals, we would not have enough for the hotel. After discussion we decided to go to the hotel and see what would happen. When the clerk came to ask us if we wanted a big room or a small room, I said to him, 'I want to leave my luggage here. We want to have a walk outside before we make our decision about a room.'

In reality I was planning to pawn some possession such as my fountain pen for some money, for during wartime a Parker could be pawned for quite a few dollars. At every pawn shop, however, all we got was, 'You leave your pen here. If there are people who want to buy it, then you can come to collect your money.' But we needed the money right away. Having visited every pawn shop on that street without success, we lingered on the street, not knowing what to do.

All I really wanted to do was to cry. So when my wife ran under a bridge, I thought she must be going there to cry in private. Instead she went there to pray. 'Oh Lord,' she pleaded, 'it's as if we are getting near the Red Sea, and we need your help.' She was still praying when a girl spotted her there from on top of the bridge and ran down to embrace her. She was a former student of my wife. 'What are you doing in Yong'an?' the girl wanted to know.

'We're on the way to Meilie.'

'Where are you going to stay?'

'Our luggage is inside the hotel,' we answered.

'Don't stay in the hotel,' she begged. 'Stay in my house!'

Our problems were solved on the spot.

Three times I witnessed God's mercy in answering my wife's prayers. Three times he had seen us safely through difficulty, even danger. Though we felt desperate, we were alive and well and taken care of. For the first time in my life I began to wonder if this Jesus in whom my wife believed could be real. If he were not, how could something so coincidental happen three times? My view of God had begun to soften, and I began to accept some things about him – with reservations, of course.

Japanese surrender changes our lot

We had been in Meilie for some time, with me teaching at the Central Police School, when suddenly one night we were awakened by the noise of exploding firecrackers and people shouting for joy. The Japanese had surrendered unconditionally! We were so excited that we could not sleep. And for a few days all the people in the school jubilantly celebrated the victory.

The end of the war with Japan was to change our lot. Not too many months after Japan's defeat we were given orders to move to Taiwan.

Our otherwise unremarkable time in Meilie was to end with a small, unhappy surprise. One day after we had begun packing to go, we came home to discover our seventy-something-year-old landlady scrambling down the ladder from our attic room. As her limbs were rather stiff, she almost fell off in her panic at seeing us. Naturally we hurried forward to help her, though a bit puzzled why she needed to go to our room

Not until I climbed up to our small abode did I know exactly what the intruder had been doing. I found suitcases unzipped, drawers opened, and things in general disarray. It seemed that she was taking this last opportunity before our leaving to steal things from us. It really made us feel terrible.

In any case, the incident with the landlady was a sad ending to this chapter in our lives. We could only wonder what was in store for us on the island of Taiwan. Though God had begun to invade my life in these early days of our marriage, I could never have guessed what he had 'up his sleeve' for Bao Lian and me.

4

A Policeman in Post-War Taiwan

Welcome and pitfalls

When the American warship that took our group of police academy transfers to Taiwan dropped us off, we found a society that bore the imprint of fifty years of Japanese rule. Not only did almost all the inhabitants speak Japanese, but the Japanese government had made every effort to encourage the Taiwanese to live a Japanese lifestyle.

Still, the people were not Japanese, and no amount of education could remove racial prejudice. Upon our arrival in Taiwan the native population gave us an ecstatic welcome. Every corner of the beautiful island was decorated with lanterns and coloured hangings. It was an overwhelmingly joyous occasion. The Taiwanese were celebrating the end of their island's status as a Japanese colony and its return to China. And we were celebrating our own liberation from Japan.

In his struggle against the Japanese, General Zeng Guofan attributed his successes in the field to his training methods, particularly those employed to safeguard his troops against carelessness after a victory. He understood that victory all too often leads to a weakened defence, leaving an army vulnerable to attack by its enemies.

Unfortunately in entering Taiwan, we mainlanders did not heed General Zeng's wisdom. As victors, many of the transplants worked during the day but drank heavily, consorted with prostitutes, and engaged in whatever enjoyment they could find during the night. These were men with families, but families left on the mainland.

Only twenty-four years old, I was impetuous and rather hot-blooded. But I was also newly married and aware of my obligations. How could I keep myself pure in this incredibly tempting environment? Love for my wife. Love is a very strong force. That I kept my matrimonial faithfulness even though I was not yet following the Lord God was surely evidence of His continued hand on my life.

In fact, God was about to draw me to himself.

Facing the reality of God

Shortly after we arrived in Taiwan, Bao Lian suffered complications following our first daughter's birth. Medicine in the 1940s was not as developed as it is now, and her fever rose to a point where it threatened her life. The doctor could do nothing.

At the end of my tether, I remembered what had happened on our way to Meilie. My wife's prayers had made the difference then. Now out of options, I decided to ask God for help. At that point all my arguments about religion being the opiate of the mind and the tool of imperialistic cultures fled before my concern for my wife. Even though I did not believe in Jesus, in love for dear Bao Lian I went to a quiet place to pray alone.

I prayed for nothing for myself. I prayed to the Jesus in whom my wife believed to give her mercy and salvation from her sickness. Just as the Scriptures promise, 'Those who seek will find', the Lord let me find him. Not long after I cried out to Jesus the hospital administrator informed me that a ship carrying medicines, including penicillin, had just arrived. With penicillin the doctor was confident my wife would recover.

My wife did indeed begin a rapid recovery and was soon out of danger. I was overjoyed. God really did exist! His loving kindness and mighty power acted like battering rams against the strong defences within my heart. With my concept of him and faith changed, past prejudices vanished without a trace. At last he had placed me firmly on the path leading to my eventual conversion.

I quit the police force in protest

More and more I found myself disgusted with the behaviour of fellow workers. Colleagues went in and out of hotels every day. Their lives were so befuddled as to seem perpetually drunk. I had little in common with any of them.

Public brutishness of fellow officers quickly tarnished our image and standing among the Taiwanese. One day, for instance, people were lining up for tickets for a movie as they had been taught by the Japanese, when our police force manager pushed his way to the ticket-seller's window. 'We are Chinese from the great Republic of China,' he muttered. 'Since when do we line up to buy tickets?' I was mortified. *How could we mainlanders conduct ourselves like that before the Taiwanese?* I thought. *This is going to be awful for us, for this man totally ruins our image as policemen.* Indeed, eventually this corrupted image did breed very serious roots of evil in Taiwan.

How little I as a person of principle fitted into the increasing corruption of the transition police force came to a head over illegal drugs. During this period the city government of Keelung, for lack of suitable workers, hired people from the police department to participate in the transition from Japanese to Chinese authority in the city. I was among the ones sent by our school. My job was to oversee the hygiene department.

One day, with clearance book in hand, I went to look for a departmental director in a certain hospital, a man who was Japanese. When he saw me in uniform, his face turned pale. Although his terror was obvious, why he was terrified was beyond me. I soon realised, however, that the man was expecting a worker from the city hygienic department, not a policeman, and he was convinced that he was in trouble. The truth was that he had hidden a load of illegal medicine and was sure that I had come to arrest him.

Asking a person who could speak Chinese to interpret for him, the man began at once to bargain with me. He was willing to give up all his illegal stash of medicine, he said, in exchange for leniency. To avoid arrest, he took me to a cave and showed me the hidden medicines. I inventoried them, entering each medicine and the amount in a ledger. At the report session on Monday, when I was reporting from a list I had compiled of the discovered drugs, I noticed that many people were staring at me incredulously.

That night after I returned to my dormitory, my superior accosted me. 'How can a person like you maintain your standing in society?' he asked sarcastically.

'What are you talking about?'

'What am I talking about?' He was obviously impatient. 'The cake was right next to your mouth, but you would not even take one bite!'

'What cake are you referring to, and what do you mean, I wouldn't take one bite?' I still did not understand.

'The medicine was not in the ledger. When you found it, you could easily have taken it all for yourself.'

I was amazed at what I was hearing. Although the medicine was not recorded in the ledger, it still belonged to the government. How could I secretly take it for myself? My superior, however, seemingly had no problem with my doing so.

Feeling strongly that only if a country's officials are upright will the citizens have a sense of security and respect authority and in disgust at what my superior was suggesting, I threw down that ledger before him and said, 'I'm sorry, Chief, I can't eat this bowl of rice. I quit!'

That ended my career as a policeman.

5

I Believe in Jesus

From saint to sinner to saved

After I left the police force I did not know where I could find a job. One day as I was walking down the road, I thought: *If society had more people who were upright like me, would not our politics be clean and just? Would not this society be pure white? Would not interpersonal relationships be greatly improved? Would not government workers be better respected . . . and their public authority be better accepted by the people?* Thinking these thoughts that day, I drifted more and more into believing how remarkable a person I was. In my own sight I was a saint!

But the Lord did not allow me that luxury very long. Reminded of a particular aspect of my behaviour, I found my opinion of myself lowered rather drastically.

For many years since leaving Singapore I had not kept in contact with my parents. Except for the early period in which I regularly received money from them, I had not written them a single letter, in spite of the fact that we Chinese place a high value on being filial to our parents. My mother and father did not even know where I now lived. The more I thought about my failing in this area, about the way I had kept my parents worrying about my welfare, the more my opinion of myself plummeted. Not only was I not a saint, I was worse than an animal. Even as I walked along, my conviction led me to tears.

At that moment I was passing the YMCA and heard people singing hymns. Hardly thinking, I went inside and sat down among the Christians. These were mainlanders who, because they did not know Taiwanese, rented the YMCA chapel to hold Mandarin worship services. That day among them the Spirit of God deeply touched my heart.

When a man knows that he has sinned, his heart softens, and once the soil is softened, the seed of the Gospel can be sown. Consequently on that very day I opened my heart to receive Jesus Christ to be my Saviour and began living a life of faith. I developed a great thirst toward spiritual matters and diligently pursued them. I was a changed man.

Forced to grow

Hungry as a baby bird, I attended every meeting at the YMCA possible. Soon the people of that church began to know me very well. One day, when the worship was about to end, the chairman of the meeting, Brother Lin Ping-yuan, announced from the pulpit, 'Now would Brother Wu Yung lead us in prayer?' I had never prayed in public before and was nervous about praying before so many people. I spotted my wife over on the women's side and quickly ran over to her and, grabbing her hand, asked her to do the prayer for me.

'They asked you to pray, not me!' she said, giving me back my hand.

Brother Lin must have known that I was nervous but was not willing to let me go, so he asked me again, 'Would Brother Wu Yung lead us in prayer, please?'

Having no alternative, I opened my mouth and started praying, and from that day onward, I was strong enough to pray aloud in front of others. Like Simon, who reluctantly carried Jesus' cross when compelled to do so, I prayed with reluctance. Did Simon's reluctance nullify what God was doing in his life? No. Paul refers to 'Rufus' mother and mine' in Romans 16. He had great respect toward Rufus' mother, who was the wife of Simon, by then a spiritual cornerstone of the church. Surely spiritual life and blessing can blossom from the roots of reluctance.

In fact, in the years since, in my ministry for the Lord in the church, I have learned that pressuring people to pursue the Lord's way pays off. If we wait for people to volunteer to serve, I don't know how long we might have to wait. If we push people into serving, the Gospel will be pushed forward too.

This principle worked in my own personal devotions as well. I was not used to waking up early in the morning. But forcing myself to get up one day at a time, I formed habits that boosted my spiritual life tremendously. In fact, having time alone with God each morning in my early Christian walk spurred a breakthrough which I myself could not have imagined.

Kept in Taiwan for a purpose

For some time I had intentions of returning to Xiamen. Friends who had taught with me at Pei Yuan Secondary School in Quanzhou had taken over the famous Hua Ying College on Gulang Island, opposite Xiamen. These folk were bosom friends of mine from the past. We got along with each other splendidly. There was almost nothing that we could not discuss or learn from each other. So when they found out that I was in Taiwan, they invited me to join them on Gulang Island to help them administer the school.

My wife and I were more than happy with the invitation and looked forward to going very much. We were from Fujian, and Hua Ying College had the added attraction of being Christian. Now that I was a Christian myself, I was sure that my relationship with this school would be better than my relationship to the Christian school at which I taught earlier. Imagining the joy of having so many spiritual companions, I was sure the path would be easier and smoother than the one I was treading.

The whole focus of our lives became going to Xiamen. More than a month passed without our finding a buyer for our house. Without the money from the house we didn't have enough for travel expenses. We felt impatient.

In the meantime, however, the communist army was marching southward, forcing us to waive our plan and wait. Not long after, when we finally did sell our house, Xiamen was occupied, and soon the whole of mainland China was under communist control. We would have to remain in Taiwan.

God knew the future. We did not. As I recall this forced change of plans, I remember the verse in Proverbs that says, 'The mind of man plans his way, but the Lord directs his steps.' If we had gone back to Xiamen slightly before the takeover, I wonder what kind of person I would have become. Already I had tasted the bitter fruits of mainland China and would have, I'm sure, eaten much more bitterness there as a Christian under an anti-God regime. In the free environment of Taiwan I have learned many things and have had the opportunity to serve with many fine people. I thank God for showing me this great mercy in intervening in our plans.

Racing with the sun

Four years before the communist takeover of the mainland I had begun participating in the services of the Hsuchang Street Mandarin Church, later to be known as Friendship Presbyterian Church. Since believing in the Lord, I had great enthusiasm to pursue any avenue of getting to know him better. So when one day shortly after my conversion the leader announced the beginning of a young people's Sunday School class and asked for a show of hands of people who wanted to join the small group already committed, I raised my hand.

From that point on, the young adults met for Sunday School from 9 am to 9.50 am every Sunday. The Mandarin worship service followed at ten. At the beginning our class had only seven members, and all were over twenty years old.

At first the church sent Brother Wu Hsing-pao to teach our class. Older and with more spiritual experience than the rest of us, he had the maturity to expound the Bible to us. But before long the government sent him back to the mainland.

The week following Wu Hsing-pao's departure we did not have a Sunday School teacher. Since we were all sitting there not knowing what to do, one of the fellows suggested that we choose a teacher from among us for that week. The first person chosen turned down the request since he had believed in the Lord for only three years. While he had just finished reading the New Testament, he said, he had not yet read the Old Testament. The second one said, 'I'm even worse! I have been a believer only two years, and I have not even finished reading the New Testament, much less the Old. I'm not even clear about the New Testament. So if he's not qualified, I'm even less so!'

In this way we went from one person to another, with everybody refusing, until it finally came to me. What about me? I had believed in the Lord for only a few weeks. If everyone else couldn't teach, how could I? Unexpectedly, however, I consented to teach for one reason: if nobody would teach, there would be no Sunday School. To me it seemed better for us to run the spiritual path together than each of us to run alone.

But what was I to teach? Far from being finished reading the two testaments, I had not read even to the last chapter of the Gospel of Matthew! Still I stood up and shared with everybody the passage that I had studied that day, trying my best to express what I understood from the verses.

Afterwards the last thing I expected to hear was that I had done well.

'Really?' I queried.

'Yes! Yes!' the group said, declaring that I should teach again the next week.

Just like that I consented.

After returning home, I told my wife about what had happened.

'You are really overstepping yourself,' she scolded. 'You have just believed in Jesus for a few weeks and have not even finished reading the New Testament and have never read the Old Testament. Yet you dare to become a Sunday School teacher!'

'I don't want to be a Sunday School teacher,' I protested. 'I only want to fill a vacuum in the Sunday School. That's why I reluctantly accepted the task when they asked me to speak again next week. What do you think I should do?'

My wife thought a moment and then said, 'One must receive before he can give. No receiving means no giving, because giving comes from receiving.'

'But how can I receive?'

'Starting tomorrow, you must race with the sun,' she told me.

'Who in the world can race with the sun?'

'I don't mean it literally,' she explained. 'But in the Old Testament it says that once the sun came out, the manna dissolved. Once the manna dissolved, the people had to return home empty-handed. If you want to find manna, you must make haste to do so before the sun rises.'

Then I understood. My wife meant that I must wake up every day before the sun comes up, for at that time the day's work has not yet begun. Without the day's duties to distract the heart, one can give himself fully to the Lord and to the study of his word.

So the next day I woke up before the sun rose, praying first and then reading the Bible. I have kept this habit until this very day. Much of what I have learned from the Bible is the result of this practice. I always encourage people to build their spiritual life on the foundation of morning devotions. If they are faithful in their study of the Bible and their communion with the Lord in prayer, they will have strength for each day, and their spiritual life will develop and mature. For me racing with the sun has made the difference between strength and weakness. But when I started, I had no idea of how God would use it in my life.

6

Railway Station Interlude

Testimony of honesty

Leaving the world of law enforcement, I became temporarily jobless. Though much older than I, a brother in the Mandarin Church, Li Pai-jen, took an interest in me. Concerned that I was out of work, he went to a friend with a high-ranking position in administration at the railway station to ask if he had a job opportunity for me.

'We have no vacancy in the railway station right now,' he said. 'But we need someone to manage the food department. If this man would be willing to take this position, we could hire him as manager.'

'You can start right away,' Brother Li told me, 'if you would be willing to take this job.' Not one to categorise a job as either dignified or lowly, I accepted the offer without hesitation. The way I see it, as long as a man works hard to earn his keep, any kind of job has value.

Within a couple of days I was at work as manager in the food department of the railway station, serving a huge dining hall accommodating over three hundred employees. My task was to plan the daily menu and to calculate how much rice to allot for each day. Once I got the feel of it, the planning was not hard, as one day was pretty much like the next.

After some time I noticed that quite a bit of rice was left over at the end of each day. The previous supervisor had allotted 24 ounces of rice per person per day, and at first we kept to that.

Actually, though, even before I came, the cook, noticing that a lot was wasted, had been cooking less than that. Theoretically the excess rice should have been accumulating. None could be found. No one knew where all this rice went.

I began experimenting with the amount of rice we needed. I decreased the amount allotted per person to 22 ounces a day. With three hundred people, that would translate into a saving of six hundred ounces of rice a day. But still the leftover rice was too much. I reduced the allotment another ounce. Still too much. Dropping the amount an ounce at a time, eventually I discovered that 19 ounces was enough to satisfy people's appetites. The total saving was over two thousand ounces a day, more than 20 times that in a month.

Higher management noticed, of course, and came to the railway station one day filled with praise for my honesty and prudence. I was grateful for the good testimony.

Quarrel over bamboo shoots

But all did not go smoothly all the time. At least the down times kept me from becoming full of pride!

Considering the employees' welfare, I tried to plan meals carefully and to provide them with plenty of nutritious food. As I had often seen diners eating pickled vegetables as an appetiser, I thought it a good idea to include some pickled bamboo shoots in the fried meat, especially in the hot weather of summer. This is something we from Fujian enjoy.

I discovered, however, that not everybody appreciates the delicacies of southern Fujian cooking. The moment the sour bamboo shoots were fried, they gave off a heavy odour. The next day, when the employees came for their meal, the dining hall smelled like spoiled leftover vegetables. Immediately the sound of angry voices began to fill the huge room. The employees thought I was serving them leftovers, spoiled ones at that.

A man named Mr Fung led a delegation of protesters to my office. By the time they arrived, they were very worked up. Everyone was talking at once, and tempers were flaring. One man even picked up the abacus on my desk and hit me over the head with it.

Obviously I didn't serve pickled bamboo shoots again!

Country bumpkin

During those days Brother Paul Han, a student then at the National Defense Medical College, and I worked together in the youth fellowship. As I sang in the choir at church and also led our 'singspiration', he thought of me as musically inclined. So when his elder sister was planning her wedding, he asked me if I would play the wedding march on the piano for her. Though I could play a little, I had never formally studied the piano; so I declined. 'Practice,' they insisted, 'and just do the best you can.' And that is what I did.

Paul and his sister, of course, invited me to attend the wedding feast afterward. And, as I often did, I wore a shirt my mother had made me, one of fifteen she had sewn for me. Though anything but fashionable, I wore these shirts from Shanghai to Fujian, from Fujian to Taiwan. But whenever I wore one with a necktie, the shirt collar would crumple up instead of folding down as it should, making me look like a country bumpkin. Those shirts looked especially comical when I talked, for when my Adam's apple moved up and down, my shirt collar moved up and down with it, flapping a bit like a pair of wings.

In the midst of the chatter and laughter of the wedding feast people kept looking at me, I guess wondering why I looked so frumpish. I couldn't help feeling embarrassed. Every time I talked, I felt compelled to keep pressing the collar down with my hand.

Yet I kept wearing those shirts until I wore them out – not so much because of my inclination to thriftiness, but more because my mother had made them for me. In spite of the embarrassment of looking like a country bumpkin, I could feel in those garments the warmth of her love.

I praise God for the down experiences as well as the up. All were preparation for what lay ahead.

7

Hearts Afire

The youth fellowship grows up

We could not have guessed how God would bless the Hsuchang
Street Youth Fellowship.

The Youth Fellowship had grown to more than forty when the
Mandarin Church moved out of the YMCA, leaving the assembly hall downstairs no longer in use. As we young people were
too crowded in our upstairs classrooms, we obtained permission
from the YMCA to move into the chapel downstairs.

But as forty-something people seemed lost in such a big hall,
we decided to arrange the chairs in a circle so that we could see
each other face to face and thus have a warmer, friendlier setting.
Even when our Bible study evolved into Sunday worship, we
continued to be known as the 'Youth Fellowship'.

Not very long after we moved downstairs our numbers increased
even more. Despite our name, new attendees included a number of
older people, who saw that this group of young people, in an innocent
and pure love for the Lord, were zealous in spiritual pursuits. As a
result, our numbers grew quickly to more than one hundred and fifty.

God's fire burns at our retreat

Early on, twenty-seven of our members gathered for a retreat at
Hsinchu. On the last day we held a testimonial meeting. Calling
it a 'spiritual movement', I announced that one must be moved

by the Holy Spirit before he could pray or share his testimony. For about ten minutes after the announcement nobody stood up to pray or to testify. The long silence made the atmosphere seem dull and heavy. As the minutes ticked by, I began to regret setting up this new rule. Apparently it was making things difficult for the brothers and sisters. Oh, the stress of those ten minutes!

Suddenly I heard a noise coming from a man who was half standing and half sitting, with both hands on his stomach, acting as if he wanted to speak, yet could not do so. It was summertime, and I saw that his face was red and dripping sweat. Guessing that his stomach was giving him trouble, I walked over to him and was preparing to support him, when he suddenly cried, 'God of heavens, please pour out your grace and mercy upon the filthy sinner that I am!'

About my age, the young man was a high school teacher. Why did he say that he was filthy? It came out that he and one of the female teachers in his school, who was twice his age, were involved in sexual immorality. That night, after pouring out his sin in front of God, he pleaded for the cleansing of the precious blood of Jesus Christ.

After the schoolteacher's confession, the Spirit of God continued to move powerfully among us. One by one we took turns to confess sin. The whole atmosphere was changed, for the Holy Spirit was like a hot ball of fire burning inside everybody's heart. Afterward, cleansed and renewed, we headed for home so overwhelmed with joy that we sang hymns all the way back to Taipei.

Healing comes to a devastated family

The next day at Sunday worship the atmosphere was very different from normal, almost as if we were waiting for something important to happen. Usually when the people came for worship, the hall was filled with talking and laughing. This day the people were silent, worshipping the Lord with heads bowed. As solemn as the assembly was, there was also the sense of an indescribable fire we had never before experienced.

I led the service that day, and at the end, after we had sung the Triune hymn, I dismissed the people. But they remained in their seats. I announced a second time that the congregation was free to disperse. Still the people stayed seated. I didn't understand what was happening, since the service was over.

At that moment, however, a commotion erupted in the back. I looked to see a man supported by others entering the church. Behind him came a woman carrying a child in her arms. She was pointing at the man, who was an invalid, and accusing him. I came down from the platform with the intention of telling her that her shouts and accusations were inappropriate in the church. 'Madam,' I said, 'please calm down. If there is a problem, we will try to help you, but you must calm down.'

'Look at what he has done to us!' she cried.

I saw that the woman's body as well as that of her child were covered with sores, the result of syphilis. The husband had contracted the disease, we learned, and spread it to his wife and child. I turned to the man and asked, 'Why have you come?'

'Why has he come?' his wife answered. 'His conscience wouldn't let him sleep all night. He asked me to bring him to the church in order to repent.'

'Sir,' I said, 'if you would like to repent, ask your attendants to lift you up to the stage so that you can confess your sins from there.'

'He can't,' the man's wife told me, explaining that syphilis had not only robbed him of his mobility, but of his speech as well. He was, she said, incapable of repenting verbally before the congregation.

'It doesn't matter if you can't speak,' I told him. 'If you can make any sounds at all, God will hear and will understand your heart. You can use your voice to represent your heart.'

The invalid was carried up to the stage and began to try to speak. We could not understand what he was trying to say. But it was clear that he was pouring his heart out in repentance before the Lord. He went on for about ten minutes, when suddenly he cried out in a clear voice, 'Oh God! Please pour out your grace and mercy upon me! Lord of the heavens, I know that I am a filthy sinner and deserve death for my wickedness. Not only did I sin in my own body, but my wife and child have suffered because of my sin . . .'

When the man's wife heard him, she ran up to the stage and embraced him. Both the husband and the wife were crying, and everybody gave thanks and praise to the Lord as one. While we all watched in amazement, the long-time invalid stood and walked down from the platform with his wife at his side.

Here was a case where God's grace and forgiveness was manifested in this man's physical healing. In the book of Acts we read that miraculous signs and wonders followed to confirm the message preached. When a miracle occurs even now, it confirms the validity of the word and its messenger, and it changes the life of the recipient of the miracle. We may preach about God's word of Truth, but we often lack the evidence of the reality of what it says. The miracle that day deeply shook the innermost heart of every person there, illustrating the Chinese proverb that says, 'A hundred "hearings" is incomparable to a single "seeing".' Having seen the manifestation of God's forgiveness with our very own eyes, we couldn't refrain from singing aloud, 'Our God is the true and living God.'

Later I saw the healed man at the Mandarin Church on Chungshan South Road. Not only had his own illness gone, but also that of his wife and child. He brought the child to show me. With tears flowing he said, 'My child as well as I has received God's grace.'

Broadening witness

Eventually we felt that one Sunday worship was not enough and decided to add a Sunday evening service that was evangelistic in nature. At that time the majority of those coming were female students from the teacher's college. After believing in the Lord, they began showing genuine respect to their teachers, obeying school rules, even improving in their homework. The change in them so impressed their school principal that he encouraged other students to attend the evening evangelistic meetings. He also invited us to go to the school to share the Gospel with the teachers-to-be.

Before the evening evangelistic service the students stood in the doorway and along the street to distribute Gospel tracts and to invite passers-by to come in. All young, fourteen or fifteen years old, the students combined youthful zeal with gentle naivety. Many people came to services because of the girls' charming innocence.

Of course, some of the young people were a little more forceful than prudent, almost pulling some of the passers-by in. Elderly people in particular would allow themselves to be brought in this way, and God was continually adding new believers to our number. It got so that almost every seat was filled on Sunday nights.

We were greatly encouraged by God's working in our midst. But a Sunday would come when only two of us would show up at the YMCA.

Worship during the turbulent '2-28 incident'

Tensions rose as the rights of Chinese mainlanders began clashing with the rights of native Taiwanese. On 28 February, 1947, a massacre took place that came to be known as the '2-28 Incident'. A terrifying period of chaos followed. Going outside was so dangerous that the teacher's college prohibited students from leaving campus.

If coming to Sunday worship wasn't safe for students, who lived close, how much more for the others who lived farther out! And it was even more dangerous for members of the Mandarin Church because a majority were not from Taiwan, but were mainland outsiders.

At the time our family still lived in Hsimenting, quite a long way from the church. But because I was the one in charge of the Youth Fellowship, I felt I really had to go. And so I asked my wife to remain at home to look after the kids while I went to the church alone. Feeling quite secure at home, my wife encouraged me to make a dash for it. 'Go!' she said. 'The Lord shall send an angel to protect you on the way.'

I also knew that when we walk along the path the Lord directs, we can trust him to protect us. Remembering what David declared in Psalm 91, 'He will command his angels concerning you to guard you in all your ways,' I left the shelter of home and ran from Hsimenting to Hsuchang Street. Along the way I saw people who had been beaten and killed. Had I not depended on the Lord, my courage would have failed, and I have to admit I was glad to arrive at the church.

On that Lord's day only two people came. I was one of them, and the other was Chang Kuo-hsun, who lived and worked practically next door to the church. Because Brother Chang had worked for the Lord in Kunming when he was on the mainland and was our spiritual elder, we had invited him often to come and teach us. He would later become a Baptist minister.

How did Brother Chang and I worship on that day? Well, we took heart in the words of Jesus in Matthew 18:20: 'Where two or three come together in my name, there am I in the midst of them.' If the two of us could be one in heart, we were confident that the Lord would be there with us. We followed the usual sequence of prayer, singing, and preaching, with Brother Chang doing the preaching as he was the more spiritually mature.

After worship we parted with great joy. Chang prayed for me, asking the Lord to sustain me so that I might get back home in peace. I also prayed for him, asking for God's blessing on him. When I arrived home safely, my wife could hardly stop thanking and praising the Lord.

Visitation by bicycle

As the Youth Fellowship underwent the quiet metamorphosis from young people's group to church, the needs and situations of our brothers and sisters called for home visitation. With public transportation not yet well developed, buses ran only on the main roads. And since I couldn't afford to hire pedicabs, I needed a bicycle. Even second-hand bicycles weren't cheap, however, so when I saw one thrown away, I picked it up. Its tyres were rigid, and its wheels rusty. But fortunately for me, Brother Yang was around. Today he lives in the USA, but at that time this handyman was still working in the factory of the public roads bureau. He helped me remove the rusty portions and replace them with good materials, also to replace the tyres with second-hand ones that were in better shape. As the wheels were not perfectly round, even after the repairs, riding the bike was a bit jolting, but better than walking.

That old bike saw a lot of mileage, as I used it whenever I went out for visitation. Though it took a lot of effort to pedal the wreck, I was in my twenties then and could endure it. More than that, my zeal for the Lord helped me not to feel the fatigue. Besides, my wife always knew when I came home by the bike's tell-tale squeaking and squawking!

Christmas the hard way

As Christmas was approaching at the end of the first full year of the Youth Fellowship, we began organizing a Christmas Eve celebration. We decided to sing *The Messiah* during the service. Of course, in the 1940s photocopying machines didn't exist. With only one song book, we had to copy the music onto stencils and mimeograph it. For days I copied, continuing long into the nights, until my hand swelled painfully. To this day my middle finger is larger than normal, having suffered permanent damage from wielding the stylus for so many hours. Still, zeal made the effort joy.

We also needed a Christmas tree to decorate the church. Discovering a suitable tree in the hills above Keelung, I hired a man to help me dig it up. Then he and I carried it down the hill, the hired man on the heavier root-ball end, me on the lighter tip end. Transporting the tree from the Keelung hillside to Taipei YMCA was hard, tiring work. Here again I was so in love with the Lord that I counted the sweat, knocked knuckles, and aching back as no match for my joy. That tree, by the way, after Christmas was over, was replanted in the yard of one of the sisters named Chen, where it became a long-lasting remembrance of the Youth Fellowship's first Christmas.

At this point I was not quite a year old in the Lord.

Early street preaching

Reflecting the admonitions of Romans 12, the Youth Fellowship in its early months served the Lord with keen spiritual fervour. In simple obedience to Jesus' command, 'Go and make disciples of all nations', we would go to streets crowded with people to spread the Gospel with tracts and spoken witness. Both before and after going out we spent time in prayer, asking the Lord to work in and through us to touch the hearts of people who would be willing to come to Christ.

In our post-street-evangelism prayer time, we would give thanks for the day's outcome and ask the Lord to help us continue leading people to the truth. When the outreach produced fruit that we could see, the prayer was enthusiastic, with everyone participating. However, when the night lacked visible fruit, prayer times showed people's disappointment. Acting as though we were ashamed before God, we would sit silently and heavily. Even when someone prayed, often his voice was small and limp, so that no one could hear. This, I feel now, reflected our immaturity, for real prayer is not controlled by emotions and can be voiced whatever the circumstances. Prayer that focuses on God's unchangeableness, not on what happens or doesn't happen, is the kind of prayer in which our spirits truly communicate deeply with God.

Training from God

When the Youth Fellowship first started, everyone inexperienced and lacked Bible training. Finding people who knew the Scriptures to teach us was to our little group like discovering treasure. Early on, two such men, Chang Kuo-hsun and John Wang, were part of our fellowship. But they, like others who helped after them, left because of changes in jobs and other circumstances. In the end, we had no choice but to be courageous and preach ourselves.

Actually, I believe that God allowed one gifted man after another to be removed so that I would be forced to rely on him and that I would discover preaching to be one of my spiritual gifts. With no mentors, I prayed more earnestly. I needed God so deeply that I completely submitted to him, realising that without his help, I could do nothing, as the Scripture says in John 15. I was like Jacob at the ford of Jabbok, when he held onto the angel of the Lord and said, 'I will not let you go unless you bless me.'

In fact, in those days God so ordered my life, removing one hindrance after another, that my grasp on the Lord became increasingly wholehearted, single-minded, and firm. Thus the great Potter was able gradually to mould and polish me, a formerly useless vessel.

Our first exorcism

During these early months we began discipling a group of Christian girls in the dormitory of the Central Printing Plant. Eventually we organised a family worship time to which they could invite the people to whom they had been witnessing. Through these meetings we were able to preach the Gospel and lead many people to the Lord.

Some of the Christian sisters in the dorm were so faithful in relating to their neighbours with the love of Christ that they gained a good reputation among Christians and non-Christians alike. The plant foreman, in fact, seeing the power of love in their lives, formally requested us to come to the factory on Sundays to evangelise the labourers. The truth is that we would have gone even if we hadn't been invited.

One day a security guard at the factory named Shen Te-kui suddenly lost his sanity while guarding the gate. The doctor at the hospital could not find anything physically wrong with him. His outbursts were unpredictable. Sometimes he was out of control, sometimes quite peaceful. 'Could he be possessed by an evil spirit?' somebody suggested.

When this idea got around, another person in the factory said, 'Good! These people who have come to evangelise claim that their Jesus is the God who governs all things. Not only did he preach, but he also healed diseases and cast out demons. Why not ask them to cast out Shen Te-kui's demon? If they can cast it out, that would prove that what they say is true. If they can't do it, then we don't have to believe what they say anymore.' A number of people thought the plan a good one.

When a delegation went to the dormitory of the Chiangshan Building and laid out the challenge to the Christian sisters, they hesitated. As young Christians, they had no experience driving out demons. Yet, since the word was out in the factory, they didn't see how they could decline the request.

One of them, they decided, would watch while the rest of them prayed. The observer could keep the prayers informed about Mr Shen's condition.

Going to Shen Te-kui's hospital room, one of the Christian young women stood by the patient's bed as planned, while the others knelt down and began praying. 'O Lord, please give us your grace,' led a trembling voice. 'We believe your promises because you are faithful. You came to the world not only to heal sickness but also to cast out demons. When you ordered demons to come out, they came out. Right now we beg you to cast the demon out of the body of Shen Te-kui!'

The watcher's eyes grew wide as the demon began to manifest itself in Mr Shen's body. First the bed began to shake. Then the man's face began to change colour and his features twisted in hate and rage. He bit and gnashed his teeth. So frightful was the sight of the man's contorted face that the girl watching could not utter a sound. Instead she just fled out the door.

Those praying heard the bed shake and the fleeing footsteps, but didn't know what had happened. When one of them opened her eyes and saw that their watcher was gone and how menacing the patient looked, she was terrified and grabbed the other girls. All of them were so paralysed with fear at the sight of Shen Te-kui's face that they could muster only enough strength to crawl out of the door.

The news of what happened spread quickly. 'The Christians didn't drive out the demon,' factory workers mocked, 'it was the demon who drove *them* away!' Christians became a laughing-stock at the Central Printing Plant.

The sisters, horrified at the damage to the Christian testimony their failure had caused, were soon at our front door. 'Wu Yung,' they said after telling me what happened, 'you must go and put this in order. If you won't go, we need not evangelise there anymore. Even if we do, no one will listen. And, even if people would come, they wouldn't believe!'

Only in my twenties, I was still very inexperienced in spiritual things. So this was very difficult for me. Yet I felt responsible to clean up this mess. If I didn't, these sisters could never again step inside the Chiangshan Building.

I didn't do anything immediately, except to pray earnestly. Then one morning the Lord opened my heart to receive faith and strength from him. The sun had not yet come up when I made my way to that hospital.

On my way in I met a hospital administrator who was also an elder of the Wanhua Presbyterian Church. 'Brother Wu,' he said to me, 'please don't add to the mockery.' He also had heard about the demon's driving the sisters away.

Of course, I didn't intend to worsen the situation. Forced to try to clear up this mess in order to stop the Lord's name from suffering continuing humiliation, I could not refuse to go. In spite of my inexperience, I believed as I do now that whatever the Bible has promised we can trust to be accomplished. I had read in Luke 10, 'I have given you authority to trample on snakes and scorpions and to overcome the power of the enemy; nothing will harm you.' I was also trusting in the words of Mark 16:17: 'And these signs will accompany those who believe: In my name they will drive out demons. . .' Since God had given us this authority, I expected that if I used it by faith, it would be effective. In faith, then, I hurried straight to Shen Te-kui's room.

First I shared the good news of Jesus with the patient and the way to forgiveness through his sacrifice on the cross. Knowing that sin encouraged the demon's power, I led the tormented man to confess his sin. After he had admitted his sin, I prayed, thanking the Lord for leading Mr Shen to repentance and for the promised forgiveness.

By this time I felt my courage rise. Placing my hand on the man's head, I commanded the demon in the name of Jesus to get out of his body that very instant. Immediately Mr Shen hopped out of bed and spit out some phlegm, which hit the wall with the sound of a gunshot. Then, falling to the floor, he writhed in spasms. Gradually the patient became aware, and his appearance normalised. Sure that the demon had been cast out, I hurried to tell the sisters in the Chiangshan Building. They rejoiced with me.

I was totally unprepared for the news the sisters brought a few days later. 'Brother Wu Yung,' they said, 'the demon in Shen Te-kui's body has appeared again!'

How could that demon return to Mr Shen's body? I was puzzled. Again I prayed for the demon to leave in the Lord's name, believing that this prayer would certainly be effective in the man's deliverance. It was not to be.

Later, however, the Lord helped me learn from the Scriptures that this kind of demon cannot be driven out except by prayer *and fasting*. Thus I started to fast and pray for the defeat of the enemy in Mr Shen's life.

Then one day, on my instructions, a number of the brothers and sisters brought the victim to the YMCA on Hsuchang Street. Dozens of people gathered. Everybody, including Shen Te-kui, knelt in a circle. Two sisters surnamed Ou Yang knelt one on either side of the possessed man, unafraid in their inexperience. As everybody joined in prayer for his deliverance, suddenly from his flared nostrils came the sound of a dog's bark. At the sound of the bark, the young women on either side of Mr Shen opened their eyes to look. Having looked, they were horror-stricken. Now everybody opened their eyes. They saw Shen Te-kuis face grossly distorted, his nostrils flaring, and his teeth clicking and grinding together. The young people felt panic. Though puzzled that the demon dared to come to our meeting, I deeply believed that my Lord was alive and victorious over all. 'Brothers and sisters,' I said to the terrified group, 'you don't have to be afraid, but only need to sing hymns together. I'm relying on the crucified Jesus, and I shall surely cast out the demon this evening.'

I moved to Shen Te-kui's side, placed my hands on his head and pressed downward as he struggled against me. Though his strength was great, mine was greater. His strength came from the demon, mine from the Spirit of the Lord. I would not allow the demon-controlled man to stand up. Audibly I prayed in the name of the Lord of all, the victorious Lord, the Lord who gave up his life on the cross, he who rose from the dead, the One whose name is revered in the highest, and commanded the demon to come out of Shen Te-kui and never to enter again because he had already confessed his sin and the cleansing of the precious blood was already at work in him. 'God is faithful and just,' I concluded. 'He shall surely forgive this man's sin.'

At this Shen Te-kui collapsed to the floor, his four limbs rigid and his mouth foaming in convulsion. His whole body was perspiring profusely.

'Thank the Lord!' I said. 'Thank the Lord! Because our Lord Jesus Christ has already won, let everyone sing, "Glory, Glory, Hallelujah!"' As everybody sang, Shen Te-kui gradually regained consciousness, and, as we watched, his face as well as his body returned to normal.

Then himself thanking the Lord, the delivered man explained to us that the *Kui* of his name was not good because in the complex Chinese character for *kui* was a portion that meant demon. And from that day on he changed his name to Shen Te-kun, because *kun* contains no such element.

From that day on Shen Te-kun became more and more healthy in body and mind, and he became one of our best brothers, a precious member of the body of the church. And also from that day on our evangelism at the Central Printing Plant became very fruitful as people came to listen in great numbers.

First meeting with Witness Lee

Since I directed the Youth Fellowship at Hsuchang Street, I needed to invite ministers to feed the brothers and sisters from God's word. At that time the ministry of the group called the Local Church was very progressive and highly respected. It had a large number of members. We planned to invite their leader, Brother Witness Lee, to come to preach to us. Many testified that his messages were very constructive and filled with spiritual insight.

Although Witness Lee and I did not know each other, I thought we need not be strangers since we were brothers in the Lord. Thus I went to see him at his place on Jenai Road. Telling him a little about our fellowship and something of our needs, I told him we hoped he would preach a message to build us up. Brother Witness Lee agreed to preach for us with just one word.

When it was the time for Witness Lee to come, I rode a tricycle with him from the Local Church on Jenai Road to the Hsuchang Street YMCA. On the way I said to my guest, 'I heard that you . . . want believers to leave their churches. Please don't be offended if I have a different viewpoint regarding this matter. I believe the church is like an apartment building which needs several pillars to support it. If you remove the pillars, the building will collapse. Similarly the church stands because of the variety of spiritual people who are a part of it. If these people leave, won't the church also break down? That's why, Brother Lee, I don't agree with your advocating believers to walk out of their churches. . . Since you've seen that other churches lack the spirituality that your Local Churches have, why not send some of your spiritual people to the other churches to live out their shining lives before their members? You can also share your teaching and show them your zealous worship so that they can imitate your good example. Wouldn't this help those cold churches become more pious? Isn't this better than having people leave their churches, thus removing some key pillars? Brother Lee,' I concluded, 'please don't take offence. I may be a bit immature, and my vision may be somewhat shallow, but, truly, I have uttered these words from the sincerity of my heart.'

Brother Lee said, 'You don't understand because you're still young.'

With this single sentence, he brushed the topic away, not giving any further reasons.

Later, because of the Local Church's policy of self-enclosure and rejection of others as brothers and sisters in the Lord, the group suffered serious trials.

Leprosy sufferers test our love

Members of our Youth Fellowship went everywhere preaching the Gospel: crowded streets, public gardens, factories, homes for the aged, hospitals, mental hospitals and even sanatoriums for people suffering from leprosy.

Missionaries who served the leprosy patients welcomed us warmly. Sometimes to grab opportunities when they were hottest, we couldn't leave on the same day we arrived, but stayed at the colony an extra day or two. If someone had believed in Jesus, for instance, I wanted immediately to strengthen his decision with follow-up.

One evening at supper time Lillian Dickson, a lady missionary, invited some of the leprosy patients to dine with us. We felt very uncomfortable, for to us leprosy was a dreaded disease. Even looking at the leprosy victims was unbearable for some of us, for some had their noses sunken, lips that failed to cover their teeth, or hands that had missing fingers.

Besides, the missionaries had not even arranged a hygienic dining environment for the occasion. Their not separating the leprosy sufferers from us meant that all of us would be using our chopsticks to serve ourselves from the same serving dishes. We could hardly bring ourselves to do it. Yet for us to refuse to eat with these people would show that we lacked love. That we knew.

'Perfect love drives out fear', declares 1 John 4:18. If there is fear, there is no love. We knew that. But it didn't mean eating with these people was easy. But mustering our courage and trusting the Lord for protection, we dined with them, choosing to do so to show that we did indeed love them.

Later we learned why the missionary ate with the victims of leprosy so casually. This group, having been in the colony for a long time, were freed of the leprosy virus, and were cured. But their physical deformities remained, and many of them were also still disabled psychologically. The missionary lady had the group dine with us to build up their self-confidence, hoping to prepare them to ease back into society someday. Admiring this lady's efforts, we gave her our full support and in doing so added to our own effectiveness.

How gracious the Lord was in these early years of our inexperience! He used us of the Youth Fellowship in spite of our immaturity. And if I had known what he would ask of me in the future, I might have withered. Instead in my zeal and first love I simply stumbled from one experience to another and learned of him.

Hesitation to Step Out in Faith

A decision to make

Because I was still working at the railway station to support my family, I could give only my spare time to direct the work of the Youth Fellowship. The Lord's servants, including famous evangelists Andrew Gih, Wang Shih, and Timothy Dzao, often asked me why I didn't quit my job and concentrate on serving the Lord. Even apart from their encouragement I also had the desire to concentrate on praying and preaching.

But a preaching ministry is not simply a career choice. It is not just a means of livelihood. Preaching is serving the Lord of Hosts, the Lord Jesus Christ, the One who sacrificed his life for us by dying on the cross. Our motivation for ministry must be clearly of him and for him.

But my decision to go into full-time ministry got hung up on another issue. One day while I was contemplating what the Lord might have for me, I went to see Pastor Kuo Ma-hsi of the Mandarin Church on Chungshan South Road. When I arrived, Pastor Kuo was having lunch with his kids. Besides vegetables and a meatless soup lacking in flavour or aroma, there was nothing. With little appetite, the kids dawdled, idly moving their chopsticks around in their bowls. One of them said, 'Dad, how can I eat this?'

'Never mind if you can't eat,' he said to comfort the boy. 'Today we will eat simply, and tomorrow Dad will buy some meat for you.'

My heart couldn't accept what I had seen. *If I were he and those kids were mine*, I thought, *how would I feel?*

This question created a huge barrier for me in deciding whether or not to go into full-time preaching. It was not that I wasn't willing to suffer, but I wanted to be the only one to suffer. I wasn't willing to include my children in the sacrifices I faced.

Encouragement through healing

One day during the time I was working at the railway station I went to the hospital for a check-up because I had not been feeling well and was coughing up blood. X-rays and a culture showed me to be suffering from a lung disease. I was devastated. How was I to get well? What if I transferred the disease to my wife and children?

'Is there any drug particularly effective for this sickness?' I asked the doctor.

'Streptomycin will work,' he said.

'Would one or two injections be enough?' I asked naively.

'Your sickness cannot be treated so quickly,' he said. 'In addition to having proper nutrition, you can't overwork yourself, and you must get injections for a long time.'

'What do you mean by "a long time"?' I asked.

'One to three months,' was his reply.

'Will I have to buy a lot of medicine?'

When he answered that I would, I felt numb. Where was I to get the money to buy streptomycin? If I used my salary to buy drugs, what would my children eat?

By the time I got home I could hardly speak. That night I shed many tears before the Lord. 'you not only preached the Gospel, Lord, but you healed diseases while you were on earth,' I cried. 'Now that I am sick and incapable of buying the drugs I need, I can only look to you. Please heal my disease.'

God answered in an unexpected way. After turning this problem over to him, I was surprised by the visit of a man whom I admired and who often led us in our Bible study, Mr Wang

Lien-chun. He bought for me a half-dozen streptomycin ampules for my injections. But as that medicine was used up in just a few days, it seemed almost a waste.

Yet those six ampoules of streptomycin helped turn my sickness around. By God's grace my coughing stopped, the blood no longer streaked my sputum, and a healthy colour began to return to my face. To my great joy, after taking another X-ray, the doctor said that, incredibly, the disease was already in remission.

From this incident two things stand out: the love of old Brother Wang and God's great power to heal. God used Wang's gift of streptomycin to bring healing – after only six injections, not sixty or ninety. The Lord truly bears the burdens of his own!

In a new way I saw that we need only to seek first God's righteousness in order to see him provide for all our physical and material needs. This experience of his care encouraged me to continue to pursue a full-time preaching ministry.

An envelope of love

Though God had been training me for a long time through the Youth Fellowship in Hsuchang Street, though many older spiritual leaders advised me to quit my job and dedicate myself to serving God full-time, and though I also had a great burden for the work of God, I still held back from taking the step. A lot of complicated reasons and hindrances, both seen and unseen, internal and external, made me continue to hesitate. One was uncertainty about whether or not I had the spiritual gifts from God to use in serving people. Another continued to be the hang-up I mentioned before, my reluctance to ask my children to suffer with me the poverty common in the lives of ministers. Indecision unleashed a firestorm of conflict within.

Yet God patiently worked to build up my faith.

One day after the worship service a couple came looking for me. I remember that the wife's name was Fang Tze-lin and that her husband worked in southern Taiwan in agricultural research. The two of them gave me an envelope. Since I was not a full-time minister, but only acted as the worship leader during Sunday worship, I did not know what it meant when someone gave a person an envelope. Because I thought it contained a request for a favour, I accepted the envelope without thanks and asked the giver what the matter was. When he said, 'The small amount in this envelope is from the burden that God has given us to provide for your needs,' I felt embarrassed that I had accepted someone's money without saying thanks. I apologised.

'Please do not think too much about this, Brother Wu. We were moved into doing it. I noticed that you look quite pale and need some nourishment to replenish your health so that you will have strength to serve God. Please don't neglect yourself anymore.'

I felt very strange. How precious is this kind of offering! I felt, not only the warmth of these people, but that of God's love. This demonstration of my heavenly Father's care for the smallest details of my life eventually became a significant part of my decision to enter full-time service. But God was not finished with his real-life visual aids.

The lesson of the widow

One day my wife and I went to visit a widow, a peddler who depended solely on selling things to support herself and her kids. But for many days a high fever had kept her from doing business. We went to comfort her and to give her some spiritual help.

As the bed-ridden woman was coughing constantly, we wanted to give her some water to drink to bring down her fever, so we entered her kitchen to boil some water. While it was boiling, we noticed that her food cabinet was empty. We opened her rice jar and saw that she had only a handful of rice. Realising how desperate was the woman's situation – without stores and unable to go out to sell her wares – we found our hearts heavy. What would her children eat?

When the water was sufficiently boiled, we poured it into a glass to cool. We then gave it to her to drink and said to her, 'Let us pray together.'

'Wait a minute,' my wife said to me, pulling me over to a corner. 'This woman is in a pitiful state. We must help her practical needs.'

I said, 'Yes, I feel the same way. All right, let's prepare something for her.'

We brought out 120 dollars from our pockets, all the cash we had for that month. Thinking that half of that was great enough sacrifice, I reserved sixty dollars for ourselves.

'Sixty dollars is only enough for her to buy food,' my wife objected, 'not enough to see a doctor and buy some medicine.'

'How much do you want to give her?' I asked, surprised.

'Give it all to her,' she answered.

I wasn't sure this was wise, for if we gave it all to her, then *our* pockets would be empty. However, I put all the money into the hand of this widow, and she thanked us profusely. Then, the two of us knelt beside her, and the three of us prayed together.

How sweet that time of prayer was! If a person submits to God's instructions, his spirit flows freely because there is nothing separating him from God. Having obeyed God's word in helping the woman in a practical way, we knew deeply that our prayer that day touched God, because it pleased him.

We went home with great peace and joy, only to be met by our househelper with the words, 'The kids no longer have any milk powder.'

Upon hearing her words, I began to be upset, with just a twinge of regret that we had given all of the 120 dollars to that widow. In fact, I blamed my wife for our predicament, as she had been the one to urge giving all our money to the widow.

'Why get upset?' she chided. 'The children won't die of hunger by not having milk for a day and a half. Let's use rice soup instead. They'll do fine eating that.'

It was Saturday afternoon, and the church office was closed; otherwise I would have considered taking an advance on my next month's salary. But now there was no other way but to adjust a little and let the children drink rice gruel instead of milk.

At that very moment of acceptance of the situation, I heard somebody shouting for me outside. Hurrying out into the alley, I found Brother Chang Kuo-chuan's nephew. After I had invited him into the house, he said, 'My uncle asked me to bring some money for you,' and handed me a handful of bank notes. It totalled 490 dollars – more than four times what we had given to the widow! The punishment for sin is fourfold; God's blessing and reward is also fourfold. 'He who is kind to the poor lends to the Lord,' says Proverbs 19:17, 'and he will reward him for what he has done.'

God used Brother Chang to feed us, just as he used the ravens to feed Elijah when he called him to go to the Kerith Ravine. I couldn't miss the lesson. I had experienced the reality of listening to God's instructions and of his providing for all my needs, not only in this incident, but in the earlier gift of medicine he used to heal me and in the money gift for nourishing food. It was as if God were saying, 'See, you can trust me. You can let go of your job to serve me full time. I'll take care of you and your family.'

I still did not dedicate myself to full-time ministry, however. I was unable to stop worrying about the future if I cut myself off from visible support; I lacked the faith to step out.

Land for a church

Before our Sunday evening evangelistic meetings a group of fifteen and sixteen-year-old girls continued to go into the streets and alleys to distribute Gospel tracts. Sometimes in their zeal to get people into the meeting, they used their hands, with one girl pulling a person from the front and another pushing from behind. When YMCA members saw them doing this one day, they thought this action improper, that the girls' behaviour would ruin the reputation of the YMCA. As a result the YMCA put a stop to our having evangelistic meetings on Sunday evenings.

Because we considered the main role of the church to be bearing the responsibilities God has given his body, we were frustrated. If God's name is to be hallowed by all under heaven as is urged in the Lord's Prayer, then Jesus must be preached to all the people on earth. Not only that, but as recorded in

Matthew, Mark and Luke, Jesus commanded us, just before he ascended into Heaven, to go and make disciples of all nations and to preach the gospel to all people. Since the church is the body of Christ, then all parts of the body must do what the head has in mind, including the Hsuchang Street Youth Fellowship. If a church doesn't evangeliae, it neglects God's instructions and can't satisfy God's will. Unable to evangelise, we spent Sunday evenings praying instead, asking God to give us a place where we could preach the Gospel as he commanded. With the spectre of lost souls on their hearts, some people even prayed in tears.

One day I was riding my bicycle to visit an elderly sister who lived on Chienkuo North Road. As I turned onto Nanking East Road near Chungshan North Road, I passed a funeral parlour called 'Greatest Joy'. After negotiating a three-board bridge, I came to the present location of the Nanking East Road Church. At that time Nanking East Road was very narrow with rice fields on both sides and a big ditch on the left, quite a deserted place. As I rode by the spot, I felt an inexplicable touch within me – *I can build a church in this place, the thought came, a church to become God's house and a place to feed the sheep*. Leaving my bicycle on the side of the road, I walked toward the piece of land to offer thanks and praise to God. I believed that God had already listened to my prayer according to his faithfulness.

The sense of God's touch that day was such a great joy that I didn't continue my home visitation. Instead I looked for several young brothers and took them immediately to that piece of land to give thanks and to pray together. Everybody was joyfully excited until a brother asked, 'Who gave us this piece of land?'

'No one yet,' I said, 'but because we prayed, somebody is going to give it to us.'

For the first time in almost half a day of praying and giving thanks for the land they realised that the property was not yet ours. Their disappointment was almost as real as if I had poured cold water on them. Having rejoiced for nothing tangible, they went home in despair. Although they could not be blamed under the circumstances, the principle of faith is not first to see, then to believe. It is first to be assured of God's will, his touch, his purpose, and then to give thanks by faith to see the result.

Sometime later I went to see that piece of land again. Not only was I deeply attracted to this site, but the inner assurance that God meant us to have it never faded. That day on the road I met Dr Andrew Loo, a Chinese with American citizenship, who was working for the Pocket Testament League in the United States. 'What are you looking for?' he asked.

I am looking for a piece of land to build a church,' I told him.

'You are looking for land? Do you have the means to get it?' he probed, I think sensing that I did not, he added, 'You ought to have been looking for me.'

'Look for you?' I puzzled. 'What means do you have?'

'I had a classmate from Yanching University who is now the department head of the Daily Products Management Bureau . . . He would surely be willing to help you.'

Pastor Loo took me to the Bureau and introduced me to Mr Ou Yang. 'This is my friend, Wu Yung,' Loo said. 'He has been leading a church and is hoping to build a new church. I brought him here hoping that you could help him.'

Mr Ou Yang asked us to wait for a moment, then called for Mr Lin, the head of the land management division and told him our wishes. Inviting us into his office, Mr Lin asked me, 'Where is the lot you want?'

I told him it was on Nanking East Road.

He looked at the map and said, 'All right, there is land available there.'

With excitement building in my heart, Chief Lin and I went to Nanking East Road together. After we arrived, however, he looked at the map again and said, 'I'm sorry, someone already wants this land. Another ten minutes' walk ahead there is still some four hundred square feet of available land.'

Very disappointed, I said, 'No! I had hoped I could get this precise piece of land.'

Why did I have to insist on getting that particular lot? For a number of reasons, but most importantly because I felt it was the place God wanted to give us.

My refusal to look at any other piece of land struck Chief Lin as impudence. 'You are not the king of Taiwan,' he said. 'Haven't I told you already? This land belongs to someone else. If you want another piece of land, go and see to it. If not, then it's over.' After speaking he rolled up the land map and left.

I was very disappointed and troubled. Why did I still have this clear conviction that this was the place?

Sometime later I met Dr Loo again. 'Did you get the lot you wanted?' he asked.

'Lin doesn't want to give me the land I want, and I don't want to take what he's giving.'

'Then where is the lot you wanted?' he wanted to know. So I took him to see it. As soon as he saw the precise location, he became silent. Finally he said, 'Tomorrow morning come early to my house, and we shall discuss this again.'

Although I didn't understand what he wanted to discuss, I did go to his house as we agreed. 'I own the land you want,' Dr Loo told me when we were comfortable.

I was dumbfounded. What a coincidence! How in the world did it happen that I found the owner of the very piece of land God seemed to be promising us?

'We won't hide anything from you,' he went on. 'After my wife and I prayed together this morning, we decided to give this land over to you.' Then they immediately wrote an authorisation letter for the transfer of the property and handed it to me.

Suddenly everything made sense. God had used a casual meeting to give us the very piece of land he had laid on my heart! My heart was overwhelmed with joy, and I spoke to the Lord, 'O Lord, you have answered our prayer according to your faithfulness and love. Because of this, you have helped to build up the faith of our young people once again.'

By a miracle the Nanking East Road Church had its construction site.

God calls again

I knew God was working to build up my faith. I myself hoped that I could get rid of all doubts and hesitation and courageously walk forward. Unhappily it was not so. Yet the inner burden to minister God's word was strong and not to be resisted. So I prayed, 'O God, if you really want me to come out and preach full time, then you yourself must be the one who makes the calling clear and direct.' I felt that the answer to that prayer could make me brave and answer all the turmoil in my heart.

As for Abraham, when God let him know that he wanted him to go to Caanan, the man didn't even ask God what kind of soil Canaan had. Or whether the weather was moderate. Not even what the people were like. He didn't ask anything. God asked him to go, and he went because he had an innocent faith. In the face of such faith, existing problems became nothing. Looking at Abraham's life, I prayed, 'O Lord, I am exactly this kind of man. If you reveal yourself to me and lift up my faith, then my faith will be established and my problems will be banished.'

I looked also at God's relationship to Isaiah. 'Lord,' I said, 'when you called Isaiah, you said, "Whom shall I send? And who will go for us?" O Lord, since you have made this calling for Isaiah, please give me the same calling. If a supernatural event were to happen, then I could bravely brush my personal reasoning and wisdom into a corner.'

One day, not long after I had so prayed, I went to work just like any other ordinary day and took my noon break. Just after one o'clock in the afternoon, with no one else having come back to the office yet, a man named Hsu Pao-wen, who was working at the information office of the domestic airport, came looking for my office mate, Yang Lien-chang. As Mr Yang had not yet arrived, I asked Mr Hsu to wait for a little while.

I can't wait any longer,' Mr Hsu said. 'When Mr Yang comes, just tell him I've come to ask him to make a phone call for me.' I accompanied the man to the doorway and said good-bye to him. Suddenly he turned his head toward me and said, '2 Timothy 2:15.'

As this struck me as weird, I grasped the man's hand quickly and said, 'Mr Hsu, what you have just mentioned – 2 Timothy 2:15 – is a Scripture verse.'

A puzzled look came over his face. 'I'm sorry,' he said. 'I had wanted to say good-bye to you, and I don't know why those words suddenly came out. Probably because I wasn't able to sleep well last night, my mouth murmured sounds which even I don't understand. Again I'm sorry! I'm sorry!'

I went back to my office, opened my Bible to 2 Timothy 2:15, and read: 'Do your best to present yourself to God as one approved, a workman who does not need to be ashamed and who correctly handles the word of truth.' I had God's answer – through the mouth of a stranger. I was so moved that noontime that I could not work any longer, but hurried home.

Having the calling of God, not just of people, greatly strengthened my courage. Yet, incredibly, this lift to my faith lasted only a short while, and I slipped back to my former doubts. Again I delayed my decision to walk the path of faith.

Two-sided election and calling

And so the delay went on day after day. The tasks of praying and preaching, I knew, were callings of God. They were the burdens of my heart. Yet God's calling in my life could not come to full bloom without God's sought-for response from me.

God chose Moses. But Moses also had to choose God and his way. Though considered the pharaoh's son, Moses did not live for himself or desire the pleasures of the palace. He did not care about his own future prospects in Egypt. God also predestines us to be conformed to the image of his Son and chooses a way for us. But how much God will use us depends on how willing we are to deny ourselves to do what God has foreordained.

The life of faith has two parts: one is the emotional touch, the reaching out and making contact with the Lord God; the other is the choice of the will, the decision to be used by God, to do his will. With the will a person chooses God. When someone decides to make themselves available to God, they must be willing to deny themselves. For a calling that succeeds, God's choosing of someone must be tied to them choosing God. In my case, although God had already clearly chosen me, my anxieties kept me from choosing him.

Doing God's work and doing a secular job are not the same. God's servants work among people. People are alive and have will and reason. Because people, like sheep, are often unwilling to go his way, the task of discipling is very difficult. That I knew too well. So, though God had worked wonderfully to strengthen my faith, incredibly my commitment to his calling remained unstable.

9

The Master's Responsibility

'Please come quickly and see something!' The voice was that of the Chief Director of the YMCA.

'See what?' I asked.

'Come, and you'll see.'

With curiosity pushing me, I hurried to the YMCA building. Just one look, and I knew what Mr Chung wanted me to see. I was shocked. Over half the roof was gone, and the whole assembly hall where we met for worship was in great ruin, the result of the wind and rain of a fierce typhoon the day before.

'We have already reported the damage to the Bureau of Public Works,' the Director said, 'and they will send men to inspect our place. You people can't meet here this Sunday; you must quickly make some other plans.'

At that time we had three or four hundred people attending church at the YMCA, which was not a small place. Where could we find another such place for temporary use? For a good part of the day, I felt numb at the sudden turn of events.

That evening we had our prayer meeting as usual. As we knelt to pray, we could see the stars in the sky when we lifted our heads. For a long while no one opened his mouth to pray. If someone did venture to pray, he prayed in a voice as soft as that of the mosquitoes around our heads.

Oh, Lord! Oh, Lord! What shall we do? was the cry of our hearts. That day was a Thursday, with darkness having already taken over from daylight. In two more days it would be Saturday. How could we find a place which was big enough to seat three or four hundred people for Sunday worship?

Then my wife's voice broke the heavy silence. 'Oh, Lord,' she prayed, 'I believe that you know what to do.'

Her short prayer gave my heart tremendous comfort. *Yes,* I thought, *He is Lord, and we all are only his servants. Now a natural disaster has occurred. It should not be the servants who worry. What to do is the Master's responsibility!* As I grasped the reality of the situation, I joined my wife in believing that he knew what to do and could do it. 'The one who trusts in him,' I was sure, as the Prophet Isaiah declared, 'will never be dismayed' (28:16).

My heart, which had been like a ship being tossed up and down in a big ocean, suddenly became restful and calm. The responsibility was God's, not mine.

The next day the people at the YMCA waited for government inspectors to come. Meanwhile, having wakened very early, I waited inside the broken sanctuary for word that we might be allowed to worship there that coming Sunday, in spite of the ruin.

All of a sudden an inner urge pushed me to walk out onto Hsuchang Street. As I turned onto a nearby lane, I saw a flight of stairs and decided to walk up. There in a huge open room an old man was sweeping.

'Sir,' I asked him, 'what's the function of this big hall?'

'Originally it was not a hall,' the sweeper told me. 'It was divided into many rooms for offices. When the company found a better location, it moved . . . Our boss then remodelled this place into a big open hall so that his workers could use it for a canteen.'

'Where is the person in charge of this place?' I asked.

'Downstairs. You can see him right now. His surname is Liu.'

When I found Mr Liu, I introduced myself. 'I came over from the YMCA opposite you,' I told him.

'How can I help you?' he asked.

'The typhoon which hit the day before yesterday destroyed the YMCA hall. Half the roof is gone. We have been holding our Sunday worship there, but now we can't use it any more. On

Sundays we have three to four hundred people meeting together, and we don't know where to go. I see that you have a big space upstairs. Could you lend it to us on Sunday morning?'

This Mr Liu did not ask me how long we would use the place, nor what the name of our church was, nor what was the content of our worship. He simply replied easily, 'If you want to come, just come! After all, we are neighbours. You just use our place, and you don't need to worry about anything. You can start using it this Sunday!'

I was so overjoyed that I grabbed both his hands and held them tightly to express my overwhelming thanks. Then I ran to find the YMCA Director, who hurried to tell me: 'Oh, Mr Wu, the Bureau of Public Works notified us that this place cannot be used without extensive repairs. I'm sorry.'

'It doesn't matter,' I told him excitedly, 'because God has already prepared a place for us. We can use it this very Sunday. It is not far. It's just opposite us.'

The man was astonished. 'How did you manage it?' he asked. 'You just say you want a meeting place and then you have it?'

But that is the kind of God we have. He created all things, rules all thing, and there is nothing that he does not have or cannot do.

That very Sunday we moved to the Alkali Company Building and began to have our Sunday worship there. When the brothers and sisters heard how the Lord had opened the way for us, they all joyfully gave him glory. Seeing God take responsibility for us helped us understand why Jesus said, 'My yoke is easy, and my burden is light' (Matt. 11:30).

From that time on we held our meetings at the Alkali Company Building. We worshipped there, in fact, until we built the facilities on the land God gave us on Nanking East Road. The Alkali Company Building was a constant reminder over those years of how dependable and how faithful our God is – because he took responsibility for us when the way ahead looked like a dead-end.

10

Cancer

'Dysentery' turns out to be a tumour

When Dr Andrew Gih came to Taiwan for revival meetings in 1951, I served as co-ordinator on the preparatory committee. As I was working in the railway station, I negotiated to borrow the railway's big assembly hall. Though I wasn't feeling well, the fact that those revival meetings brought great blessing to Taipei City lifted my spirits.

During the meetings a couple who were both physicians invited Dr Gih and me for dinner. While we were eating, Dr Gih noticed that my face was grey and that I looked drawn and thin. He wanted to know why.

I did not know. My abdomen felt continually uncomfortable, I told him, actually sore. I had both indigestion and severe diarrhoea, and my stools sometimes contained blood and pus. And I was continuing to lose weight day by day. By that time, in fact, I weighed only about fifty kilograms.

'It's good that Dr Wang is here,' responded Dr Gih. 'Let him check you out to see what's wrong.'

After the meal Dr Wang took me to his clinic and examined me. Suspecting my problem to be dysentery, he gave me some antibiotics.

Still not well after taking the antibiotics, I was massaging my aching abdomen one day when I felt a hard lump on my lower left side. Nervous about what I found, I went for an examination the next day in the railway hospital. An X-ray showed that a tumour had formed and fused the large bowel to the peritoneum. The doctor said that the sooner I underwent surgery the better and that only after surgery would we know for sure whether the growth was benign or malignant.

Afterward when Pastor Andrew Loo asked me about the result of the examination, he suggested that I get a second opinion and gave me the name of friend, a Dr Chang, a famous internist. When I took his advice and went to Dr Chang, the diagnosis came back exactly the same: that I had a tumor and that I should have surgery as soon as possible. I was devastated.

God's promise through my little daughter

As an employee in the railway station, I could have the surgery I needed in the railway hospital without cost to me. As I readied myself to go there for the operation, Dr Wang, a specialist at Taiwan University Hospital, asked his wife to tell me that I could go to their hospital. An elder at the Wanhua Presbyterian Church, he had been a student of the famous surgeon, Dr Kazuishi Kunio of Japan. The love that Dr Wang and his wife demonstrated was widely known. They often took care of the lonely, poor, and others without anyone else to lean on. Not only did they give these people free treatment, but included drugs as well, sometimes adding cash to the packages of medicines. They also took care of God's servants. I decided to accept Dr Wang's invitation.

I remember vividly the day I was to go into hospital – 2 May, 1951. As my wife packed my suitcase, I lay on the bed, worrying. What if the tumour proved to be malignant? What should I do? My wife was only twenty-nine years old, and the eldest of my kids was only five, the youngest but a few months old. I myself was only thirty-one. If my tumour were cancerous, I would soon be travelling the path of no return. What would my wife do in this strange land? Where would she get the strength and wherewithal to raise our children?

Also thinking of the way ahead and the vagueness of her

future, my wife was crying as she packed. Confused myself, I felt helpless to comfort her.

At that moment my not-quite-five-year-old daughter suddenly ran in from outdoors. 'Mama, don't cry!' she said, ' "A bruised reed he will not break, and a smouldering wick he will not snuff out." '

My wife, consumed with her crying, paid no attention to what the child was saying. But from my bed I heard her clearly. *How can my child be speaking such appropriate words at this moment?* I wondered.

Then she said for the second time, 'Mama, don't cry! "A bruised reed he will not break, and a smouldering wick he will not snuff out." '

My wife still was too much in tears to hear. The third time our little girl repeated these words, however, my wife heard her and immediately knelt down and embraced her. Holding the child's small frame to her bosom, my wife joyfully gave thanks to the Lord for his grace. From the bed I also seized hold of the promise and received the comfort the Lord meant to give.

We respond in faith to God's promise

When we arrived at the hospital, Dr Wang welcomed us sincerely, and I was soon settled in a very nice room.

The next morning my wife and I were up early to pray and read the Bible together as we did on any other day at home. Our reading included John 11, the story about Martha, Mary, and Lazarus. These siblings loved Jesus very much. When Lazarus got sick, the two sisters sent men to Jesus to tell him. 'The one you love is sick,' they said.

'This sickness will not end in death,' Jesus replied. 'No, it is for God's glory.' When my eyes had taken this in, I stopped because I couldn't continue any more. As both my wife and I were convinced that God had given me a very clear message, we thanked him. The God in whom Abraham believed is the one who gives life to the dead and the one who makes something out of nothing. My heart took boundless comfort. And to know that there was a purpose in all this – what an assurance!

God is in Heaven, and we can neither see him nor touch him, how can we believe? 'In the beginning was the Word, and the Word was with God, and the Word was God,' says John 1:1. When a man sees with his heart what God's word says, he has also seen God. Contact with his word is contact with God. 'Faith,' says Hebrews 11, 'is being sure of what we hope for and certain of what we do not see.'

With God's giving us the passage in John 11 that morning of my surgery and the 'bruised reed' passage from Isaiah through the mouth of our daughter the day before, I was deeply comforted. I had been looking at death; now I was looking at life.

Despair at the prognosis

While I was in surgery, a number of brothers and sisters were outside praying. In fact, two brothers among them were so intense in their concern for me that they came right into the operating room to pray. And after the surgery was over, the church folk came to the hospital to visit and to intercede. Because we are one body joined together, God's family is more important than any number of blood relatives. Thanks to the Lord for letting me experience the affection of this body life in him or in his church! Up to this day I still feel their unbounded warmth and touch every time I think about those otherwise difficult days.

The surgery was very long. Right from the beginning things did not look good. As expected the surgical team had to separate the intestines from the peritoneum. Even as they did so, they could see that the smaller bowel was speckled, as if bitten by mosquitoes. When they cut into the cardia, the opening of the oesophagus into the stomach, they found that the stomach showed signs of the invasion of cancer cells as well. Because of this, Dr Wang decided that the operation could no longer proceed and ordered his team to sew the incisions back together. The surgical team's inability to help me made them feel sad. Obviously my illness was already in its terminal phase. Neither surgery nor medicine could intervene. That third day of May was very black.

When men's efforts fail . . .

Once I was fully conscious, I immediately asked the result of the surgery and whether the tumour had been benign or malignant. Instead of an affirming answer, all I got were sad, heavy looks. Obviously the situation was truly grim. I guessed the worse.

On the third day after the operation several brothers and sisters, including Brother Chang Kuo-hsun and Sister Tu Lien-kuang, went to Dr Wang to consult with him, hoping that they could convince him to tell me the truth. Dr Wang, however, felt from a physician's standpoint that psychological suffering should not be added to my great physical suffering. Uninformed, I could not do worse than to doubt and wonder.

Brother Chang and Sister Tu did not agree. 'It is not necessarily without benefit to Brother Wu if you tell him his situation,' Brother Chang argued. 'Even though he has not walked a long road spiritually, he has at least run a short distance well. He must have confidence with regard to his faith and must have a clear understanding with regard to his entry into the spiritual realm from the physical world. This is important for his stability in the Lord's grace of salvation. Informing him will not go beyond what his spirit can endure . . . Once he understands his situation clearly, he will know that he doesn't have to focus upon men, but rather on God . . . And when you inform him of the short span of his life, he can rejoice that he shall soon see the Lord. This will give him an opportunity to prepare himself. If there's sin, he can deal with it. If he owes anybody, he can pay him back. In this way he will meet the Lord with confidence.'

'All right,' Dr Wang conceded. 'If this is what your opinion is,

I don't have any more objections . . . except we must first ask the permission of Mrs Wu.'

So they asked my wife to come to Dr Wang's house on the fourth floor of the hospital.

'Brother Wu has only one or two months to live,' Dr Wang told her once she had arrived upstairs. 'During the operation we found that the intestines were not only blocked, but that the cancer cells had spread to the entire abdominal cavity. Because of the cancer's exceedingly wide coverage, your husband couldn't have survived further surgery to remove all affected parts. We had no choice but to sew him back together. Right now we are just delaying his appointed time.'

Upon hearing this, my wife fainted. After the men had carried her to a sofa, Dr Wang left her in his mother's care and went with Brother Chang downstairs to rest.

When my wife revived, she was so overcome with grief that she wished to die. Though old Mrs Wang wanted desperately to console her, she really didn't know what to say or what not to say. Grabbing my wife with one arm, she whimpered, 'Oh, how pitiful! You are still so very young!'

Yes, my wife thought, *I am too young to become a widow, too young to lose my husband, and too young to bear the responsibility of raising a family*. At this, she could no longer control her crying.

But in these most sorrowful and despairing moments, God lovingly gave my wife a word from the epistle to the Ephesians: 'God is able to do immeasurably more than all we ask or imagine, according to his power that is at work within us.' Immediately she grabbed hold of those words, 'God is able.' With this promise as an anchor, she again remembered the Lord's earlier words: 'This sickness will not end in death', and the promise he gave through our daughter: 'A bruised reed he will not break, and a smouldering wick he will not snuff out.'

If God doesn't intend to fulfil these promises concerning my husband, my wife thought, *why would he move my child to utter these words?* Immediately she stopped crying and said to the Lord, 'Oh, Lord, since you have already granted our request for my husband's life, that's sufficient for me.' Immediately she wiped her tears and went downstairs to tell Dr Wang that she was not opposed to his informing me clearly about the truth. Because the prognosis was hopeless from a human perspective, she told him, the stage was set for us to look up to God wholeheartedly.

Between promise and perceived reality

By the sad looks of the people who streamed to my bedside I had already guessed the outcome of the surgery. When dear, gentle Dr Wang followed, however, he could not bear the thought of delivering the heavy blow of the truth. He wanted to say something, but couldn't. Several times he tried to speak out, but stopped. Finally he gazed painfully at Brother Chang and then at Sister Tu, who were also in the room. They nodded their heads toward him, and then he spoke, 'Mr Wu, we are very sorry to find after surgery that we can no longer do anything for your sickness.' He could say no more.

The emotional shock hit me like a bolt of lightning. But forcing myself to speak calmly, I asked Dr Wang, 'Does this mean the tumour is malignant?'

The surgeon simply lowered his head and left without uttering a single word.

I felt like a convict sentenced to die. My heart shook. I was like a ship lost in the midst of a big ocean. Not only afraid of walking a path which I had never walked before, I felt again an overwhelming sorrow for my wife and young children. How could a husband and father leave such a heavy burden for his wife? I raised my head to look at Bao Lian, who was hiding her head in a corner. Everyone there in the room with me was discouraged with inexpressible sorrow.

To whom could I look for encouragement? I remembered at that moment that when the Israelites were fleeing from Egypt, they were hemmed in by the Red Sea in front and the murderous Egyptians behind. Death seemed the only possible outcome. But how did Moses react in this situation? He said, 'Look!' He wanted the Israelites to look up to the God of Heaven. When I thought of this, I realised that I ought to look up to the God of Heaven because he had spoken a special word to me through my daughter: 'A bruised reed he will not break, and a smouldering wick he will not snuff out.' And he had spoken to my wife and me through John 11:4: 'This sickness will not end in death.' Faith was just within reach.

This little faith produced a wonderful effect. 'All right,' I said to the brothers and sisters gathered around my bed, 'every one of you kneel down, and let us pray together.' All ten people in the room knelt. I led them in a prayer of faith. First I gave thanks to the Lord for speaking through my daughter, promising that he would not break the bruised reed or snuff out the smouldering wick. I thanked him too for the Bible verse from John he gave the day before the operation. I closed with a promise to God, 'From now on, Lord,' I said, 'I will not look at my sickness, but only at these two precious promises.'

God's promises usually do not agree outwardly with the visible facts. Certainly that was so in my present circumstances. Based on what the doctor saw during surgery, the outcome of the disease raging in my abdomen would be certain death. Had I only visualised the 'facts' of my condition, I would have considered my going on to live impossible. But since God had promised that this sickness would not end in death, I had to make a choice – to look at the apparent reality or to look to God's promises.

The very promise from Isaiah admitted the seriousness of the situation. As the reed in the word picture was bruised to the extent that it was nearly broken, so my condition was grave, so irreparable as to defy the doctors skills in mending it. And the smouldering wick also talks of a tenuous situation. Yet the promise was that he would not snuff it out. The challenge to me was to believe God. 'Without faith,' says the book of Hebrews, 'it is impossible to please God.'

Faith tested

Peter says in his first epistle that faith must undergo testing so that it might be proved more precious than imperishable gold, that the Saviour might receive honour and glory at his appearing. Gold must be refined by fire to remove its impurities. The same way, a lot of impurities are mixed with our faith. We are always doubting, fearing, and wanting to have some obvious emotional experience before we agree to believe.

My faith was quickly tested. On the sixth day after the operation my belly began to swell. Wasn't this one of the mortal signs of a dying man? The persistent symptom emptied out my faith. All those previous divine promises seemed as nothing. Hopelessness washed over my heart like murky flood waters. Seeing brothers and sisters come to see me without speaking a word, I sensed the bleakness of my visitors' inner emotions. Thinking of their despair and contemplating my wife's soon widowhood and my children's impending fatherlessness, I fought tears continually and stumbled through the darkness of an extinguished faith.

My wife showed herself stronger and wiser than I. Setting her heart firmly, she was determined not to reveal her inner pain for fear of discouraging me.

A persons faith, I now know, does not come from within. Because we are bankrupt spiritually apart from God, he must give us the faith we need. Unless the Lord gives grace, we can never stand before him. How would God revitalise my faith in my present circumstances? I could not imagine.

The vision

I was half asleep and half awake when God gave me a vision, one especially calculated to strengthen me. I saw God commanding the Jews to enter Canaan. Those carrying the ark of the covenant walked up to the shores of the Jordan River. When their feet stepped into the water, the river parted and the water became walls on both sides so that they walked on dry land. After them millions of Jews surged across, and together they entered Canaan. Though this event happened thousands of years ago, it was now played before my eyes as if it were on a screen.

This unusual experience made me feel very excited. Though quickly over, the vision hovered in my mind for hours. As I meditated on the Biblical event, I saw that the feet of the priests carrying the ark had to first step into the water before it would separate, not the other way around. Their eyes were focused, not on the rushing water of the Jordan, but on the promise given by God. Now I understood what God wanted to teach me: I must not look at my swollen mid-section, but concentrate on what he had promised. At last my spirit cleared of the enveloping darkness. In his love God had given the vision so that my faith would be restored.

A book I read during those days also helped me. In it was a story of a servant of God who was gravely ill with a serious lung disease. Vomiting blood, the man saw his health quickly vanishing. One day the doctor brought out his X-ray and compared it to one of another person also with lung disease. 'Your X-ray and this other person's X-ray are very similar,' the doctor said. 'That other person is now dead.' When the servant of God learned that his illness was incurable and lethal, he wrote to a sister who was strong spiritually and told her everything. In reply the sister quoted Hebrews 11:27: 'By faith he left Egypt, not fearing the king's anger; he persevered because he saw him who is invisible.'

Contemplating this verse, the servant of God at last grasped what faith really was, accepting something not yet received as if it were. He got up from his bed and went to the meeting place, surprising the brothers and sisters who were gathered there. Everybody knew that his sickness was beyond remedy and that he was going to die soon. Said the minister to his gaping congregation, 'The meaning of faith is getting well when you're still sick and receiving something when you haven't yet received it.' Afterwards he did indeed get well. Reading this story gave my own faith a boost.

Planning for the church

With my faith strengthened, peace of heart followed. My emotions stabilised. Encouraged when they saw me speaking and laughing, the construction committee for the new church invited me to join them in their planning. Others on the committee were Pastor Andrew Loo, Brothers Chen Kuo-hui, Weng Chi-hsiang, and Hsiao Chen-hua.

Though the others on the committee set a time to meet in my hospital room, they did not intend to use too many hours nor to discuss too many details, fearing this would consume too much of my mental energy and thus exhaust my physical strength. That day, however, I felt strong and energetic, and I was the first to give words of encouragement. 'The church is the body of Christ,' I said. 'If the body is strong, its effectiveness will be increased, its motions fast, and its testimony will be beautiful. Such vigour will make for rapid church construction.

'When King Solomon built the holy temple,' I reminded my colleagues as I continued, 'he did not do it alone. He had 153,600 men, among them 70,000 who took charge of lifting, 80,000 who drilled out stones in the mountains, and 3,600 who acted as overseers. Because they all worked together, the temple was built. Today,' I went on, 'the construction of this church is not a personal matter, nor will it be accomplished by the members of this committee. Only when all the brothers and sisters of the congregation unanimously bear this burden together will it be smoothly carried out.'

With many more words I tried to clarify this truth and to imprint it on the hearts of committee members. The men left my hospital room committed to involve the whole congregation in making the vision of a church building on Nanking East Road a reality.

Right now, as I reminisce, I find the recollection of these great and small things from the past unendingly pleasant, overwhelming my heart with praise to God.

Taking the leap of faith

'Mrs Wu, give Mr Wu whatever he asks,' instructed the doctor, sure that my days were numbered. As I was approaching the dusk of my life, he felt my wife should help me to enjoy the few days I had left.

My wife, however, stood with me in firmly grasping the promises of God. Although I remained medically hopeless, both of us had inner peace. God became our greatest hope. Even while I was visibly degenerating each day, my heart within continued to strengthen and to rejoice in hope.

Faith must be accompanied by action. 'Faith without deeds is dead,' wrote the Apostle James. Though before I got sick, I was unable to make a decision to 'burn my bridges' to go into the ministry to which God had called, I now came to believe that God was giving me life again after facing certain death in order that he might be glorified through me – in the ministry, full time. To prove that my faith had indeed been restored, I wrote a letter of resignation to the Bureau of Railways and Transportation.

But getting no response to my letter, I sent someone to ask whether my application for resignation had been approved.

The manager, it turned out, had purposely withheld my resignation. A Christian, he had thought, *Brother Wu Yung already has incurable cancer of the bowel. Since his departure time is expected shortly, if he should resign now, he will not be able to claim his pension benefits.*

When I learned the truth, I asked the manager to come to the hospital. When he arrived, I told him of my commitment to God and begged him to let me resign no matter what the consequences. Savvy in spiritual matters, this brother left having agreed to approve my resignation. Thus I took the first step on the road to dedicating myself to serve my Lord full time.

On the eleventh day after my operation, as I was waking up from my afternoon nap, I noticed the pages turning on the Bible left on the windowsill. 'Someone is turning the pages of my Bible,' I remarked to my wife.

'No one is turning the pages of your Bible,' she corrected. 'The wind is blowing them.'

I watched while the wind continued to blow, flipping the pages this way and that. When the breeze died down, I said to my wife, 'Now that the wind has stopped, bring the Bible here and let me see the particular page to which it has opened.'

As I study the Bible, I normally use a red pen to underline words which I recognise to be significant. Now my eyes quickly picked out three portions marked in red. The passage was telling about Jesus riding into Jerusalem on a colt. The first highlighted portion read. 'Jesus went on ahead.' The second occurred after the owner of the colt questioned the disciples' right to untie the animal, when they replied, 'The Lord needs it.' The third place had to do with the untying of the beast to bring it to Jesus, so that he could ride into Jerusalem as the King he was.

I could not miss the import of these three bits of Scripture in my life. Emotionally I clung to the first one: 'Jesus went on ahead.' If Jesus would walk ahead of me, even though I would walk through the valley of the shadow of death, I would fear no evil. Then meditating on the second sentence, 'The Lord needs it,' I said to the Lord, 'O Lord, since you need me and have chosen me, even though I'm not qualified to become your instrument, please accept me and let me continue to live.'

The third underlined word was 'untying'. *God has untied me for his service*, I thought. *Since I've been released and freed, I can arise from my bed and no longer lie on it.* 'Tell Dr Wang we're going home now,' I said to my wife. 'Also ask them to borrow a car from Pastor Andrew Loo to take me home.'

When my wife had relayed my message, Dr Wang came to my room and tried to convince me not to leave. 'Please don't leave the hospital. You will be more comfortable here,' he said. 'You have water in your abdomen. It is more convenient for us to draw it out here. And here, if you feel any discomfort, I can give you an injection. If you go back home, everything will be inconvenient once your cancer has reached the critical stage.' I could see the concern on his face.

I told the kind doctor about the Scriptures I'd read earlier and shared my testimony with him. Being an elder of the church and committed to obeying God's word, he could do no less than let me check out of the hospital.

But home was no place to rest. While our two older children understood my need for quiet, the two younger ones could not contain their noisy exuberance. Happily a friend, who was the administrator of personnel affairs for the Bank of Taiwan, arranged for me to recuperate peacefully in the bank's guest house at Yangming Mountain. There, surrounded by craggy peaks and clear water, I was in for a time of many surprises.

11

Healing on Yangming Mountain

Support for a battered faith

Even a strong-willed person will lose will power and spiritual verve when they meet failure or a blow such as the prediction of impending death as was my case. John the Baptist, who pointed to Jesus and said, 'Look, the Lamb of God, who takes away the sin of the world!' weakened and began to doubt when left, seemingly forgotten, in prison. Though he had had a clear knowledge of who Jesus was, he sent someone to ask Jesus, 'Are you the One who was to come, or should we expect someone else?' Today, too, when a calamity comes, we sometimes find our faith threatened with collapse or battered by discontentment against the Lord. That certainly was true of me during my early days in the guest house up on Yangming Mountain.

Yet I received two kinds of support to my faith: One kind came directly from God through visions, revelations, movings of the heart, and his written word. The other came through the stream of brothers and sisters who came to visit me, to speak with me, and to pray with me. Together they helped my faith to grow strong and to stand firm.

Preparation for preaching

During my period of recuperation I also grew in spiritual knowledge through a number of books that Miss Ni Sung-te, the former vice dean of the Shanghai Jiangwan Theological

Seminary, sent over for me to study. As I hadn't been to formal theological seminary, it was important for me to understand clearly the truth spoken through these books so that I would avoid making errors when I began preaching God's word. Not allowing myself to be idle, I earnestly read those books, finishing all of them. This spiritual exercise was good medicine.

Healed!

On the nineteenth day of my stay on the mountain, the odour of my body was awful because I hadn't taken a good bath since my surgery. 'I want to bathe in the pool of sulfuric water today, giving myself a hot-spring bath,' I told my wife, 'to cleanse completely the scar from the operation.'

When the brothers and sisters delivered me to the hot spring pool, I asked them to leave me alone to enjoy the comfort of bathing by myself. I planned to cleanse first the trace of red antiseptic from the operation. I never thought that while I was cleansing my scarred belly that I would suddenly discover that the hardened thing on my left side was no longer there, seemingly to have disappeared without a trace! Excited, I began to shout. The brothers and sisters outside the bathroom wondered what had happened, but politely waited for me to dress and come out. When I appeared, relaxed and smiling, they were relieved, but puzzled.

'God has already freed me completely,' I told them confidently. 'He has healed me, for the tumour in my body is gone. My abdomen has regained its former suppleness. Thank God for his grace! He has done a great and marvellous thing in my body!'

Baffling 'iron-nail' revelation

One day whilst recovering, I was sound asleep taking my afternoon nap at the Yangming Mountain guest house, when suddenly I heard a voice, saying, 'Don't hammer an iron nail because on the day you do, you shall surely die.'

Instantly awake, I asked my wife, 'Who told me not to hammer an iron nail because on the day that I do, I shall surely die?'

'I didn't hear anything,' Bao Lian answered. 'You were dreaming. Go back to sleep!'

I had just closed my eyes again when the same voice repeated the warning: 'Don't hammer an iron nail, because on the day that you do, you shall surely die.'

When I again asked my wife, she said she didn't hear anything this time either. 'You are mistaken,' she said firmly.

A third time the voice came, and the third time the identical words were repeated.

We were mystified. Since we couldn't figure out a higher meaning, we tried to explain the vision's message literally. My wife, in fact, refused to let my hands touch *any* hammer or nail. Since I'm not a carpenter, this was no problem. Yet my very unhandiness with hammer and nail made a literal meaning to the thrice-given vision improbable.

An elderly sister from our home town, whose spiritual life was deeper, wider, and stronger than ours, shed the light we needed. Dropping by our house one day, she told of having a vision while praying for me. In her vision a grapevine grew so prolifically that its branches extended out over the garden walls. 'This has a meaning,' she explained. 'I believe that in the future Brother Wu will not just testify for God locally, but also abroad.'

Suddenly I understood that 'the nailing' in my vision meant that I should not nail myself down. God didn't want me to be fixed in one locality, but to be loose in his hand to be sent to other places to help people. If I were to be consistently settled in one place, my work would be dead rather than living. The meaning of the grapevine and 'the nailing' was one and the same. Both were to be taken spiritually rather than literally. Since then God has led me, not only to work in my own church, but also in other churches, and not only locally, but also abroad.

The roaring of a collapsing mountain

Another morning while I continued to recuperate on Yangming Mountain, my wife and I rose early and went outside to pray. Suddenly I heard a sound so loud that I could imagine a mountain collapsing and being thrown out into the sea. Frightened, I grabbed my wife's arm.

Having heard no sound nor felt any motion, my wife pulled away from my grasp. 'Are you insane?' she asked, upset.

'I am not insane,' I assured her. 'I really heard the sound of a collapsing mountain.'

She was not convinced. 'Though the sky has not yet brightened,' she argued, 'you can see for yourself that the mountain is still there, and the rice fields are also very much undisturbed.'

However, the sound of a mountain being thrown into the sea did not stop, but continued roaring inside my ears.

As much as I thought about what happened, I could not comprehend its meaning. Actually it was quite a long time before I fully understood. Not until I was fully healed and had gone down to the lowlands to preach did the reason for the sound of the collapsing mountain begin to be apparent.

While I was standing in the pulpit in Pingtung, the Lord very clearly moved me to read from the book of Isaiah and to speak about the sin of the Jews. 'The donkey knows his owner's manger, but Israel does not know me, says the Lord', I read. 'On one side my people observe solemn assemblies, but on the other side they do evil.' Immediately after I had explained the first sentence as 'ungratefulness', someone cried out from in front of the platform, praying earnestly: 'O Lord, forgive me because you have shed your blood and sacrificed your life for me. This grace is much higher than the mountains and much deeper than the seas. And yet I've forgotten all about this grace. I want to confess my sin to you, O Lord, my Father! You know that when I was sick, I begged you, and you did heal me and gave me back my health. But I have forgotten about it. Please forgive my sin!'

I had no sooner explained the second sentence with a description of 'two kinds of living', when another person came to the front to confess his sin of hypocrisy. He said that on the one hand he was standing inside the church singing praises and partaking of the Lord's Supper, while on the other he was using foul words against others at home and gambling for money.

Continuing to read from Isaiah chapter one, I came to the phrase, 'Wine is diluted with water', explaining it as signifying dishonesty and craftiness. At this moment another man came forward to confess, with tears rolling down his cheeks and with a voice similar to that of the mountain being thrown into the sea. Obviously the Holy Spirit was there, working in hearts, stirring up confession. Isn't this what we should expect, when in his power we ask people to confront themselves for sin, for righteousness, and for judgement?

Once a man asked Mr Moody, 'Why is it my spiritual life has never grown up?'

Moody turned to ask him, 'How long has it been since you've confessed your sins to the Lord?'

The man said, 'I've forgotten. Probably long ago.'

Moody then said, 'The reason why you don't grow spiritually is because you haven't confessed your sins for too long a time.'

I am convinced too that we must continually confess our sins. Today we confess, and tomorrow we still have to confess. Confession and repentance are together life-long activities. Upon entering a house, the Jews had to wash their feet. These feet were not washed only once, but had to be washed continually throughout the day. Because our feet walk on the roads of this world, we always get contaminated with the world's dust and filth. We must confess and turn from our sin again and again, relying on the precious blood of Jesus to wash away the contamination. Confession and repentance must go hand in hand in order for our spiritual lives to grow.

I am reminded of the story of two men who, before going to a meeting, knelt down to pray. 'May the Lord give me peace along the way,' prayed the younger of the two, 'and may I be built up upon reaching that place.' The other man, an old pastor, confessed one sin after another. Puzzled, the young man said, 'I've been doing the Lord's work for only a short time and I have nothing to confess. You have been working for the Lord for a long time – how come you still have so many sins?'

'A person can see his own situation clearer when he is nearer to the light,' explained the older man. 'If we use a 40-watt light bulb, we can see a small portion of the dust in the air. But with a 200-watt bulb, we can see that the air is filled with dust. That's why the nearer we get to the Lord, the clearer we see our dirty and evil status.'

From the time I came down healed from Yangming Mountain I continually thanked the Lord from the pulpit for rescuing my life and sparing me from the death of cancer. At the time the new church building was under construction. I was especially thankful, for I believed – and so testified – that had I died, the building process would have been hampered. One Saturday, however, when my wife and I were fasting and praying, I realised that this testimony was not right. Moses and Joshua were working together. Yet after the death of Moses, Joshua continued on and led the people into Canaan. Moses' death did not hinder the Israelites from entering the land. If God had not healed me and I had died, God would surely have raised up someone else to continue his own work. With the Holy Spirit's enlightenment, I turned to God, earnestly confessing my sin of feeling myself indispensable, as well as my lack of humility.

Later, when I went to serve in Kaohsiung, I continued to lead the brethren to walk the path of confession and repentance. At that time I was still young, with strong vocal cords, and always led the people in singing first in order to raise the spiritual atmosphere of the meeting before starting the message. One day, though I had only read a few verses of Scripture and had just begun to lead the congregation in singing, I saw people being thrust forward one by one to the front of the platform to confess their sins. What was happening reminded me of a mountain being thrust into the sea. Suddenly I understood that this was the meaning of the sound I had heard on the mountain. It was not that I was capable of anything. The people were responding, not because my mouth was eloquent nor my message touching, but because God himself was working – just as he says in the book of Zechariah, 'Not by might, nor by power, but by my Spirit.'

Disbelief exacts a price

The proprietor of the hardware store in front of the Hsuchang Street YMCA was a brother called Shen Hsiang-cheng. Next door to his store was a Western drugstore, owned by the anaesthetist during my surgery. 'The man who's always coming in and out of your church underwent an operation today, didn't he?' the drugstore owner had said to Brother Shen on the day of my surgery.

'Yes, he is our Brother Wu Yung,' answered Brother Shen.

'We are the ones who performed the surgery,' the anaesthetist said. 'Upon making the incision, we found that the cancer cells had spread throughout the entire abdomen. We could do little more than sew him back up and wait for his time.'

'Nevertheless, we thank the Lord,' said Brother Shen in a statement that must have surprised the bearer of bad news, 'because though for men the situation is hopeless, it is not for God. And because of that Christians can continue to live with hope.'

The drugstore owner grinned and said, 'If your God can keep this man alive, then I would surely go and worship in your church.'

'Do you mean that?' challenged Brother Shen.

'Of course!' the man came back.

Eventually my health obviously stopped degenerating. Colour returned to my face, my weight increased, and I even began doing God's work. On those grounds Brother Shen invited the anaesthetist to worship.

'Let's wait a bit longer,' the man said, not yet convinced of God's miracle. 'Although faith can help,' he said, 'I believe that the human body itself has some defence mechanisms. However, even if the defence mechanisms increase, they can't overcome cancer cells. Let's wait for a while. If your Jesus can truly make him live, I will surely go to worship in your church.'

Brother Shen invited the anaesthetist several times more. His answer: a smile.

After some time Brother Shen discovered that his business

neighbour was confined to the Taiwan University Hospital. What disease did he have? Cancer – in fact, a tumour in the rectum that, similar to mine, spread throughout his abdomen. He lingered for just twenty-nine days before he died. What a waste! He had seen God's miracle in me, but had been unwilling to believe.

A predestined meeting

Staying next door to us while we were up on the mountain, however, was another drugstore owner named Hsieh Po-ling, whose story turned out quite different from that of the doubting anaesthetist. From the Minghua Drug Store on Hengyang Street in Taipei, Mr Hsieh had come up to the mountain retreat to flee a dispute in his home.

One day my wife and I, arising around four a.m. as usual, went outside to pray together on the grass as we often did. In spite of our using hushed voices, in the quietness of the place the sound of our praying awakened Mr Hsieh. Peering out of the window, he could see this man and woman outside seemingly chanting some kind of scriptures. Since he could not get back to sleep, he asked an attendant to find out what we were doing.

'Oh, Boss, Mr Hsieh, don't argue with that man,' the attendant objected. 'He is going to die soon. I've heard people say that he has cancer. After opening up his stomach, they found that it was too late for surgery. And so he came here to wait for his death.'

Hearing this, Boss Hsieh was not about to argue with me. Superstitious, he believed if he quarrelled with a dying man, that man's soul would come back after he had died to deal with the still-living tormentor.

However, during the day I met the druggist several times. Each time he looked me over curiously. At noontime, when we were both eating our lunch in the guest house dining room, he continued to stare at me. I guessed that he was probably looking at me as a cancer patient soon to die, expecting to see a bitter face and evidence of a heavy heart, a man who just picked at his food. Instead he saw me relaxed and glad-hearted, eating well, and all the while chatting and laughing with my wife. I did not in the least resemble a sickly patient awaiting death.

On the second day, seeing that he was still inclined to stare at me, I went up to talk with him. 'Mister, may I know the reason why you have been watching me continually these past two days?' Embarrassed, he turned his face away from me. 'You were probably wondering,' I continued, 'why I still can relax and enjoy speaking and laughing. Is that true?' He didn't answer, but I kept on. 'There's only one reason, and that's because I have Jesus within me. If you also would have Jesus within you, you would also be relaxed and happy and enjoy speaking and laughing as I do.' Without saying more, I returned to my table to eat my meal.

That very day Mr Hsieh left to return home. After that coincidental meeting with me, he couldn't help but think why a man like him, who was healthy, couldn't be relaxed and glad like me. How could I, who was going to die, be so filled with peace and joy? What I had said about having Jesus within me had to be reasonable, he decided – how else could a dying man be happy? Confronting a Christian employee in his drugstore, he asked, 'Would you know which church is preaching about Jesus?'

Since it was the boss asking, the Christian felt awkward. Yet, he thought, since the boss took the initiative, why not? *Hurry! Grab the opportunity!* he told himself. 'Yes, there is,' he said boldly. 'Our church has an evangelistic meeting this evening, and they will introduce Jesus then. Boss, if you are willing, I could drop by tonight and accompany you to the church so that you could listen to the message.'

'Okay,' Boss Hsieh said, 'you come and fetch me tonight.' And that night Mr Hsieh went to the Jenai Baptist Church, listened to the message, and believed in Jesus.

How amazing this incident was! Not only was this man saved, but he went on to pursue his faith zealously and after only a short while was chosen to be a deacon at the church.

'Mr Wu, I presume you don't know me,' Mr Hsieh said when he phoned me sometime later. 'Nevertheless we had a predes-

tined encounter. I want to invite you to come to my house today
to lead the family worship. When the time comes, I will explain
to you this predestined relationship you and I have, and you will
understand that what God is doing is marvellously great.' How
could I not agree to come?!

When I entered his house, Mr Hsieh couldn't keep himself
from jumping up and embracing me the moment he saw me.
'Thank the Lord for his leading!' he said, then reminded me of
our encounters on Yangming Mountain.

When he had finished his testimony, I came to understand in a
new way how God tailors his ways in leading us to believe in
Jesus. Sometimes, as this case, we may not need to preach a
powerful message, but let our life preach for us. Before I became
a Christian, I could not fall asleep, but afterward, could sleep
soundly. Before I always worried, but afterwards learned not to
worry. So when this man saw me, a man promised only death, he
saw me relaxed and joyful, evidence of the Lord's indwelling and
help. The upshot was that Mr Hsieh believed in Jesus and
received his grace.

Today, if each Christian would be willing to carry the
responsibility of helping one another and letting a peaceful and
joyful life give testimony publicly, we would be surprised how
fast the Gospel would spread – certainly faster that if
we depend solely on the church to organise evangelistic
meetings!

I thank God not only for his healing up on Yangming Mountain,
but the use he made of the testimony of his working in my life.

Testimony of healing tested

In the months following our return from the mountain to take
up full-time ministry, however, God allowed the trial of my faith
not once, but repeatedly.

One night my wife dreamed of attending the women's meeting
and of seeing Sister Hsu wearing a red woollen dress and leading
the hymn, 'The Blood of Jesus Covers Me'. Then a few days later

what she dreamed played out in reality. There at the women's meeting was Sister Hsu in a red woollen dress leading the women in singing, 'The Blood of Jesus Covers Me'. *What could this mean?* she wondered, startled.

The day following my wife's return home, she and I went out together to do some home visitation. I rode the bicycle while she walked nearby. Suddenly my stomach knotted with such extreme pain that I abruptly dismounted and fell to the ground in agony. I couldn't even stand up. Alarmed, my wife rushed to my side to support me and to examine the painful area, singing as she did so, 'The Blood of Jesus Covers Me'.

All of our life must be covered by the precious blood of Jesus, I thought. *If not for the blood of Jesus, we'll be giving the evil one a foothold at every corner. Surely God must be reminding me that I must continually cleanse myself in order to become a noble vessel in his hands, fit to be used by the Lord.*

After this my belly always swelled when I went out to preach, sometimes to the point that I could hardly breathe and couldn't eat or drink. Each time this happened, I would wonder if the old cancer had come back again. Would I have to ask someone to announce that Wu Yung's sickness had attacked again and that he couldn't come to preach that night? Since I had been bold in my testimony of healing, wouldn't God's name be diminished if the cancer had returned? My own dignity didn't matter.

Again and again I was thrown into this kind of conflict and struggle. God's answer of comfort was always the same: 'With man this is impossible, but with the man who believes, all things are possible. Who is the God in whom Abraham believed? He is the God who gives life to the dead and makes something out of nothing, the God who turns the impossible into the possible.' And with each reassurance, I would depend on the Lord's grace and stand in the pulpit as if nothing were wrong.

Amazingly, once I preached, the bloating inside my stomach would be gone. After the message I could even eat and drink.

For two years I battled the pain and bloating and the

temptation to doubt. Again and again the Lord encouraged me to lean on him to maintain victory. Then gradually the pre-preaching distress disappeared. For many years now my body has remained healthy. Truly I want to thank the Lord for his amazing grace.

12

Preparing Sermons

Not everybody's way

During my stay in the mountains I was very diligent in reading the Bible and studying a few spiritual books. These became my foundation for serving the Lord. Through the teaching and illumination of the Holy Spirit I experienced new insights and was able even to grasp how to prepare a sermon, though perhaps a bit unconventionally.

A clue that my way of preparing messages was not everybody's way surfaced one Saturday when I visited a minister, his desk piled with a mountain of books. His face was rigid and anxious. Although I knew the reason he was anxious, I deliberately asked him, 'What are you busy with?'

'Tomorrow is Sunday, and I am preparing my sermon,' he said tautly. 'How can I feed the congregation without a sermon?'

'What are all these books on your desk?' I pursued.

'I was thinking of getting some sermon ideas from these books,' he answered. 'How else will I come up with my sermon?'

'Don't be angry if I say this,' I said boldly, 'but I don't think this is the proper way to prepare a sermon. This method is difficult and tiresome, like searching for a needle in a haystack. Skimming through all these books just makes your head spin, and you still can't find the sermon you need. If you keep this up, you will surely wear yourself out and probably dread preaching.'

I think the last statement rang bells, though he was probably still doubtful. 'What then do you think is the best way to prepare a sermon?' he asked curiously.

'By using only the Bible,' was my reply.

'What about the topic of the sermon?'

'The topic, outline, and contents – all these can be found in the Bible, without your having to use outside references,' I assured him.

As the pastor seemed puzzled, I went a step further and gave him an illustration. 'We can start with a small portion of the Bible. For example, 1 Thessalonians 1:7 says: "Be an example to all the believers." This can be a good topic, and the outline can be found in the whole chapter. Verse 3 concludes: "your work produced by faith and your labour prompted by love and your endurance inspired by hope in our Lord Jesus Christ." Isn't this verse a ready-made outline? Faith is one part of the outline, love is another, and then hope. As you can see,' I said, 'you already have the topic plus the outline. And as for the content, you can also find that in the same chapter. What is the content of faith? It is to depart from idol worship and serve the true and living God.'

I doubt if the minister was expecting a whole sermon from me. But he got it. 'Let's look at Paul's thanksgiving for the Christians in this chapter and throughout his letter,' I suggested. 'His letters to the Romans, Corinthians, and Galatians all speak of thanksgiving. If we look at the details of Paul's thanksgiving, notice that it has two parts: for the Christians in Rome, he thanked God that their faith was being reported all over the world, thus glorifying God. For the Christians in Corinth, he thanks God that they are blessed in Christ.

'During our childhood days we received much from our parents,' I went on, applying the Scripture. 'But as we grow up, they in turn receive much care from us. It is disappointing for our parents if we have to depend on them for the rest of our lives. It is similar with our Father in Heaven. In coming to know him and becoming new Christians, we received much from Christ. Then as we start to grow, we need to give our ourselves to God. If after being Christians for eight to ten years, if we remain blessed without giving of what we have to God, will he not be disappointed?

'The words "Saviour" and "Lord" are not the same. Being our Saviour, God saves us from eternal destruction by giving us eternal life – this is what we receive from God. But his being our *Lord* is not the same thing. When Paul met Christ on the way to Damascus, he asked, "Who are you, Lord? What do you want me to do?" This response to who God is, is what we can give to him. While it is natural when we are new Christians to consider Jesus primarily as our Saviour, after we are Christians for three to five years, we should be considering him as Lord. Many Christians never move from one relationship to the other.

'Some would probably argue, "Who said that I never considered him as Lord? When I pray, do I not call him Lord?" Yes, but we call him Lord too often only with our lips, not with our heart, not with our obedience and service.'

I told the minister finally, 'See, through this short scriptural reference, I have found the topic, outline, and contents. True, with these few words, the scope is not broad, but it is very abundant, and you don't need to spend a lot of time poring over those books.'

Happily the minister grasped my point, seeing that he didn't need to scour stacks of books to find his sermons, much less to fall into panic and fear.

I am grateful for those weeks of retreat in the mountains in which I could concentrate on digging through and studying the Scriptures one chapter at a time, comparing scripture with scripture. How important these hours in God's word were to me and my hearers in the years to follow! How much delving deeply into the treasures of the Scriptures has enriched my life and ministry! Surely the cancer that drove me to that retreat was part of God's perfect plan for me.

Preaching to professors

I learned some important lessons in the dynamics of sermon preparation very early in my development as a Christian worker, during the years of my association with the Youth Fellowship. The learning adventure began when the general secretary of the YMCA said, 'You have a phone call, Wu Yung.'

The call was from Brother Chu Sheng-pai from the Petroleum Company. 'I'm relieved to have found you,' he said.

'Why?' I asked.

'Our general manager's younger brother is Professor Chin of the National Taiwan Normal University. His wife is a Christian. On his birthday he invited some professors from the university over for cake. As they wanted to invite a minister to preach to them, the general manager, knowing that I was a Christian, entrusted this thing to me. However, I forgot all about it! When I remembered a little while ago, I realised you're the only one I could ask to speak.'

'When is the party?' I asked.

'Two o'clock,' he said, 'this afternoon!'

I looked at my wristwatch. It was already past eleven – not quite three hours between then and the gathering.

'I was hoping you could solve this difficult problem for me,' he pleaded. 'If you can't find anyone else to preach, then you had better do it yourself!'

'How can I do it?' At that time I rarely preached. I was not a minister.

'You are young,' he said, 'and have heard a lot of messages. Besides, you have preached before in the adult Sunday School. Just give one or two examples with testimony, and that should be enough.'

'Brother Chu,' I said, 'professors are different from other people. We can't just wing it. Those people are very educated; we must consider this seriously.'

'I know that,' he pleaded, 'but I can't wait any longer. It's impossible to find a minister, and so my only alternative is to invite you.'

'I really can't do it,' I insisted.

'Brother Wu, you regularly bear a variety of responsibilities within the church. If brothers and sisters in the church have any favour to ask of you, you always ignore the hardship and do it because you like to help them solve their problems. No one is unaware of your zeal. Everybody admires your willingness to help others . . .'

At the time I was still young, and those beautiful compliments about me tilted the halo over my head in his direction. Sensing that I did not altogether decline, he quickly said, 'All right, thank you! Now please get a pen so that I can tell you the address.'

I felt I had no alternative but to get a pen. Giving me the address, he added, 'Please be there early. Thanks!'

I still wanted to say something, but he had already hung up the phone. Now I could only rush back and tell my wife.

'How could you agree?' my wife asked impatiently. 'What these people wanted was someone who could preach among the college professors. How dare you get the address and plan to speak?!'

'I knew it was wrong . . . but what could I do?' I answered weakly.

'Preaching requires prayer,' Bao Lian said. 'The Bible mentions "praying and preaching" and not "preaching and praying". Since you are going to preach, you must quickly go to pray.'

'Pray first?' I objected. 'Look at the time! I have only a little more than an hour before I have to get dressed and go, and that is not enough time for me to prepare a lesson. Where can I find time to pray?'

'You ought to pray in order to get a message to preach,' she insisted.

'No, I must prepare first,' I argued, opening my Bible to the book of Matthew. I found nothing to preach on. I proceeded to flip through Luke. It also was empty. I still had found nothing by the time I was at the end of John. The more I turned pages, the more anxious my heart became. With anxiety came fear, and with fear, confusion.

Seeing my agitation, my wife pleaded with me again: 'Look, other people pray before preaching. Pray first so that you can have a message to preach!'

By this time I was too anxious to do anything but pray. And before long I had a Bible verse. I had written down only a few notes when I noticed it was almost 1:30. I had to go.

With my notes in my pocket, I rode my bicycle to Hoping East Road and Chingtien Street. Upon reaching the doorway of Professor Chin's house, I rang the doorbell. A housekeeper came out and asked, 'Whom are you looking for?'

'Professor Chin.'

'What for?'

Not daring to say that I was coming to preach, I said, 'Tell him to come, and he will know.'

'Okay. Please wait for a moment,' the housekeeper said.

When the professor did not recognise me, he asked, 'For whom are you looking?'

'Professor Chin.'

'I am he,' he said.

'Are you the one who is having a birthday party and has invited some professors from the university and a minister to preach for the celebration?'

'Yes,' he said.

'Someone invited me to come to speak,' I said half apologetically.

The professor looked puzzled. He saw that I was of slight build, probably just over twenty years old, and that I had ridden there on an old and dilapidated bicycle. He gazed at me from head to foot. I guessed that he couldn't believe what he saw. But because I'd already come, he had no option but to invite me in.

Upon entering the living room, I saw that more than thirty college professors had found seats around the room. All were over fifty years old, most of them bald. All appeared very educated. The more I looked, the more fearful I became. So I just bowed my head and prayed.

When invited to speak, I stood and followed the dictates of my heart in delivering the message that God had given me. And God spoke. More than one person confessed being moved by what I said. By relying on prayer and the mercy of the Lord, and by getting my message from him, I came through the challenge of preaching at short notice all right. The situation had not turned into failure at all; I had not made a fool of myself. Thanks indeed to the Lord!

Preaching, I have learned, does not depend on one's own ability, eloquence, or education, even on adequate preparation time, so much as it depends on having a message from God and his blessing. 'Not by might, nor by power, but by My Spirit, says the Lord' (Zech. 4:6). The experience at Professor Chin's house was both amazing and significant for me in the discovery of the dynamics of Christian ministry.

The Holy Spirit-altered sermon

Sometimes the Holy Spirit moves the preacher to say something unplanned. I had such an experience one day during a conference. Suddenly during my sermon my mind was drawn to Jeremiah 8:20: 'The harvest is past, the summer is ended, and we are not saved.' The verse had no relevance to what I had chosen to speak about. Why then did I repeat these words again and again until the congregation was astonished? I did not know. But I knew that if the intrusion were from the Holy Spirit, it would never be irrelevant to what he was doing.

After I finished preaching, I received a note from someone in the congregation. The note said, 'What you said a while ago concerning "the harvest is past, the summer has ended, and we are not saved" is true of me, for I am not yet saved. Can I invite you to my hotel after the service? I have an important matter that requires your help and prayer.'

When I went to his quarters at the hotel and rang the doorbell, he came to the door. When he saw me, he fell down on his knees. Surprised, I asked him what the matter was. He broke down in tears and said, 'I asked you to come here tonight because I have to deal with my sin now.' When he went on to confess that he had a mistress and that his mistress was one of the members of their church, his wife, who was sitting beside him, was shocked. Though the infidelity had been going on for years, had he not confessed, she would not have known about his unfaithfulness and would have continued to come and go with the other woman in church.

The broken man asked me to pray for him. And on that day he dealt with his sin completely. Because he held a position in the church, his sin had been contaminating the church and damaging the Lord's work. Not only was the Holy Spirit unable to work freely because of it, his marriage had come under stress as well. But now because of the wonderful working of the Spirit in the man's heart, the penitent man was not only saved from his sin, but the Spirit was free to work in new ways within the church and within this man's home.

Normally a preacher will diligently prepare before going to the pulpit, committing what they have prepared to the Lord. But always we are to admit humbly that the effectiveness of a sermon is never dependent on what one has prepared, nor one's ability to deliver a speech, or even knowledge learned at school. Zechariah 4:6 declares: 'Not by might, nor by power, but by my Spirit, says the Lord Almighty.'

13

The Church on Nanking East Road

Seed sermon and the piece of gold

After my retreat on Yangming Mountain and my healing, I offered to work full time in the ministry of the word of God, to serve with other brothers and sisters in the Youth Fellowship. The first thing I wanted to do was to finish the construction of the church building on Nanking East Road. The piece of land had been transferred to us by Dr Andrew Loo, and the church building committee had applied for the necessary documents to move ahead with the construction project. The way was open.

But we did not have the funds to move ahead. Believing we needed to be united as a congregation in commitment to the building's construction, I prayed for an opportunity to promote the project so that the brothers and sisters might catch the vision and respond to the need.

When the opportunity came, God gave me as the topic for my message a question from Chronicles: 'Today, who is willing to give himself for the Lord?' Having spent much time in prayer, I felt the power of God as I preached. Even I was moved by his presence. After I finished preaching, I was very eager to know how the congregation would respond.

How do you evaluate a sermon? There must be unity between the pulpit and the congregation. The preacher himself and the hearers must both be touched by what is preached. If the preacher is not touched by what is preached, how can he expect others to be touched?

I remember once when I preached in Hong Kong, a man known as Elder Lin asked me after I finished preaching, 'How do you feel? Are you pleased with your sermon?' When I told him I was pleased, he said, 'I knew that you were pleased because I was also.'

But this day, after I had preached to stir up commitment in the church building project, no one like Elder Lin came to ask whether I was pleased or not. So to evaluate my sermon, I thought it practical to count the offerings since construction projects require a lot of money. Surely that would tell me whether my preaching was effective or not.

So after the service, when everybody had left, we counted the offering. To my great disappointment, it was only slightly more than what was usually given. I concluded that since the offering was not what I had hoped for, my sermon was not good enough.

Suddenly the wife of a military policeman came to me and said, 'Brother Wu, I was touched by your sermon today.' I was comforted – at least one person was touched!

Within minutes the same woman was back with the same message.

'Thank you,' I said, 'but it's late, and you should go home now.' She turned to go, but was soon back again, saying the same thing.

'Sister,' I said, 'I believe that you were really touched by the sermon. I never doubted it.'

Then she said, 'Yes, I was not only touched, but I felt the need to be concerned with this project. And yet I just don't have anything to offer.'

I said to her, 'Sister, it does not matter how much you give, for God is not concerned with how much we give, but rather that we give what we can.' I told her the story in the Bible about people who went to the temple to give their offerings. The rich gave large amounts, while a poor widow offered only two small copper coins. Jesus said that the woman had given more than all the others, because she gave out of her poverty, having put in all she owned and all she had to live on. 'God views things differently from us,' I told her. 'We give more attention to the amount of money, but God gives more attention to our motives. If God moves you to give, just give what you can give, and that will be just fine.'

'Thank you,' she said and went away. But not for long, for she came back again and said, 'Brother Wu, God really wants me to give my offering.' Then she took something from her pocket and placed it on the table without looking at it and left without looking back.

As I picked up what was on the table, I was surprised to find that it was a piece of gold. I believe it was all of her savings. The fact that she didn't dare look back, perhaps afraid that she would change her mind, made me sure that she treasured that piece of gold, perhaps even had a sentimental attachment to it. Tears welled in my eyes as I looked at it because the giver was like the widow of whom Jesus spoke who gave all she had. That day I was really comforted because God had moved in the heart of that woman.

The giving of that gold piece, in fact, was the first step on a long journey.

The next Sunday, as the leader during the worship service, I told the congregation of the woman's gift and showed them the piece of gold, reminding my hearers of Jesus' praise for the widow who had given all she had. Although the piece of gold was not much when compared to the amount needed for the building project, before the throne of God it was considered much. The lesson got through to the people's hearts, for when the offering that morning was counted, it amounted to a total of forty thousand New Taiwan dollars (approximately one thousand US dollars)! When I announced the amount, the congregation knelt down on their knees and praised the Lord.

By faith we start construction

Our next step was to announce a public bidding in the newspapers. A number of construction companies bid for the project, but the contract was finally awarded to the Lien Hua

Construction Company. Once he had the bid, Brother Hsiao Ting-kun, manager of the company and devoted Christian, asked us, 'How much money do you have right now?'

'Only forty thousand,' we told him.

'But the project is going to cost two hundred and ten thousand – forty thousand is barely one-fifth of that!' he noted incredulously.

We were aware of our financial weakness, for the majority of us were students and public servants. If the construction went by phases, and we were unable to pay the bill at any point, the project would be jeopardised. And any delay would just push up the costs.

When Brother Hsiao asked what we were going to do about our meagre resources, I told him, 'Our church building project proceeds fully from the Lord. As the place where we are meeting now for our fellowship is not the best for evangelistic purposes, our brothers and sisters prayed that God would provide a place where we could freely share the Gospel. After we prayed,' I went on, 'I happened to pass through Nanking East Road, and God told me that he would use this land to build a church. Moreover, through my sermon God moved the heart of a woman to donate a piece of gold, and this encouraged all the brothers and sisters to give additional offerings which amounted to the forty thousand dollars. Through this experience we believe that God is in total control. And since God started this project, we believe that he will complete it.'

'All right,' responded Brother Hsiao, 'I'll donate twenty thousand more, and that will leave us with a balance of one hundred and ninety thousand. We'll use the first forty thousand to buy steel bars and other important materials before the price goes up.'

Thus the construction of the church began. At each phase, praise God, we were able to pay the expenses. In fact, at no time was the project ever delayed. The whole construction went smoothly, finishing in June 1952.

Surely God remains our Jehovah-Jireh. As long as we do things according to his own heart, he will faithfully provide till the very end.

Laying the foundation of the church

Construction of the building is easier than building up the people inside the church. In the end choosing not to transfer the Hsuchang Street Fellowship to the new church, we started the Nanking East Road Church from scratch, viewing the project as church planting. We simply expanded from one church to two.

But we put the Hsuchang Street Fellowship people to work. First we selected seventy people from the Fellowship who were willing to assist and to do the pioneer work necessary to bring the congregation of the Nanking East Road Church into existence. Within the area of the then still half-built church building these seventy went from door to door, shared the Gospel with everyone they met, and invited people to attend the church services.

Beyond that, how does one start a work like this? As in the book of Ezra the Israelites began building the temple by building the altar, so we started with prayer. When the exterior structure of the building was almost finished, we started a prayer meeting in the shell since there we were protected from the heat of the sun and the wet of the rain. The prayer meeting and the construction went on simultaneously.

One prayer meeting night a strong typhoon hit. Violent wind and turbulent rain uprooted trees and overturned cars. Most people would have cancelled a prayer meeting. Not these folks! In the fervency of their hearts members of the church-planting team deemed that while other types of services can be cancelled or postponed, prayer meetings could not. On that wild night everyone attended. Though we didn't have chairs and had to sit on the floor, we fellowshipped together with joy. The sound of the wind did not frighten the group nor dampen their zeal. Though at times it threatened to drown out the sound of our voices, we simply increased our volume.

After the meeting we discovered that the streets were flooded and that public transportation was not running. How were we to get home? Without cars, we formed a chain and headed for home hand in hand. At that time we were a little young and a little impervious to the realities of the danger.

Disaster struck almost immediately. As we stepped out of the church building, a gust of wind lifted Brother Lin Hsui-ming's hat off his head. When he let go of my hand to make a grab for his hat, the wind blew him into a deep ditch. The water current was so strong that Brother Lin was quickly being swept away. Everyone was terrified. Fortunately someone quickly reached down and pulled the victim to safety.

How good it was that a fervency of spirit united us! That's what held us together in difficult circumstances and helped us be effective in ministry.

Not long after, the building was complete except for a door, a kitchen, and a rest room in the building itself and a wall between us and the street. For our thanksgiving service about five hundred people squeezed into the church and raised their hearts and voices in jubilant praise for what God had done.

At that service was a man in the construction business whose family name was Sun. Noting the lack of the door, kitchen, and rest room, Mr Sun committed himself to helping in their installation. His response to God's prompting illustrated again that when work is according to God's own heart, he will move people to take part in accomplishing his work according to their abilities.

We follow Paul in choosing elders

Having had our inaugural ceremony, we remembered that after the Apostle Paul established churches anywhere, he appointed elders. Our brothers and sisters felt that we also needed to appoint elders to oversee the new church.

But who could be an elder? All of us were very young – most of us in our early thirties. In fact, there were no elderly people among us.

Searching the Scriptures, we came to the conclusion that the word 'elder' as is used in the Bible does not indicate age so much as the spiritual maturity of a person. Those chosen should be seasoned in spiritual matters, able to cope with the various problems and needs of the sheep.

Okay, but what do elders do? From Acts, chapter fourteen, we gathered that elders are overseers, supervisors. They decide between what is and what is not, what is right and what is wrong, what can be and what cannot be.

But why do we need supervisors? In the Bible we saw that the church is a body, which needs every member to co-operate with and supplement one another. But we also had learned that many members are unwilling to take responsibility for their part. In fact, when Nehemiah in the Old Testament needed people to guard the city, he found only a few people brave and willing enough to serve. His solution: to force people to participate by having them draw lots. So, we decided, the church needs supervisors, or overseers, to urge believers to take part in the ministry. Many people would otherwise be spiritually lost if we wait for people to volunteer.

Having studied the matter fully, we now had to decide whom to chose as elders. Three people were nominated: John Wang, Wang Chang-kan, and myself. With the whole body of the church participating, we were ordained. This was the birth of the Nanking East Road Church. It was June 1952. I was thirty-two.

14

Standing Against Wrong

What to do about a fellow believer's sin is always a problem for a minister of the Gospel. The Bible tells the story of Eli, a priest of Israel, who, though he himself did not commit sin, tolerated sin. God reproached Eli for failing to find fault with his two sons, who were acting wickedly in the temple of the Lord. Early I became convinced that it is not enough that we don't sin ourselves, but that we must not tolerate it in others who are bearers of the Lord's name as well.

The Bible says, 'If you see a sheep fall into a pit, you must not pretend not to see.' The same holds true, I believe, with someone who has sinned. If we fail to try to help them out of their pit, we will have a share in their sin. We must 'speak the truth in love', as Paul says in Ephesians 4:15, when we see flagrant disregard of God's standards.

Rebuking a brother's adultery

Once when a church invited me to speak at one of their revival meetings, a certain brother received me as a guest in his house. While there I found out that my host was having an illicit relationship with one of the sisters.

What was I to do? If because of his hospitality towards me I had pretended not to know about it, I felt I would be failing as a servant of God. I was in a difficult position.

But one night I stayed up late to wait for the brother to come home. He tiptoed in around midnight. Seeing me, he smiled and asked, 'Why aren't you asleep, Elder Wu?'

'I was waiting for you,' I told him.

'Is it anything so important that it can't wait until tomorrow?'

'No, it can't wait. I need to clarify something with you.'

I told him everything I knew. He stood there quietly throughout my recitation, then said, 'Besides having Sarah, Abraham also had Hagar. Abraham was a man of God. And if he was allowed to have two wives, there is no reason why I can't follow suit.'

The Bible recorded some good things for us to take as examples, I told him. But it also recorded some bad things for us to take as warnings. We cannot take another woman in addition to our wife, just because Abraham took Hagar in addition to Sarah. God makes his standards clear in the Bible. Right at the beginning he created one Adam and one Eve as a pattern.

Again my host said to me, 'Elder Wu, you are not the only one who is aware of my situation. I consulted with an elderly minister, who is my senior mentor in spiritual matters. Since I am the president of the Board of Deacons, I asked the man if I should resign from my post because of my involvement. He advised me not to resign, fearing that I would cause problems for the ministry and become indifferent myself to the work of God. With this over my head, he felt I would not be able to remain zealous as I have until now.'

I said, 'This is not right. The Bible says that when Uzzah reached out toward the ark of God that the oxen had nearly upset and took hold of it, God struck him down right then and there. The ark should have been carried on poles on men's shoulders, but instead Uzzah used a cart. The ark of God was merely touched by a disobedient hand. If God did not tolerate that, how much less will he tolerate your using the hands of an offender in participating in his work?'

Obviously not agreeing with my opinion, my host said, 'That's enough. Let's not talk about it again. Let's go to bed!'

What happened to this brother in coming days? His company closed down, and his debts piled up so much that maintaining his basic daily needs became a struggle.

I still believe that we must not pretend that we do not see when we observe others committing sin. We must not only preach God's word, but defend the faith by guarding the purity of God's flock.

Drawing the line between truth and error

At a breakfast service a noble and prestigious elder said from the podium, 'Ten years ago I had a wish which I didn't expect to happen, but it came to pass.'

Sensing that the speaker was full of joy, I sat up and listened. What was it that gave him such pleasure?

'Protestant Christians and Catholics have been separated for a long time,' he said. 'but now there's a trend in Taiwan for Christians and Catholics to come together, without any division between the two. Everybody has a common belief toward one Lord, one God and Holy Spirit, standing together, working side by side for the gospel. This is the most joyful thing to my heart as a Christian.'

I strongly disagreed with his viewpoint. To remain silent would suggest that I was in agreement with him. If I should go to church and a brother or sister would ask me about my agreement with him, how could I answer?

Why did I oppose the unification of Protestant Christians and Catholics? Simply because I had been in Rome and in Catholic churches and had observed people there worshipping idols: statues of Jesus, of Mary, and of the various apostles. If Christians and Catholics were united, idolatry and the worship of the true God would be united. That would violate the Bible's admonitions that we keep ourselves separate and holy and avoid worshipping idols of any kind. Not able to remain silent at that breakfast meeting, I stood up and spoke to the crowd, not only expressing my disagreement, but my strong opposition to what had been shared.

Another time when I was in Japan and staying with Brother Wang Chih, I found out that a certain pastor had left his ministry and had become a priest. My host and I decided to visit him. 'We would have no responsibility if we didn't know about his situation,' I told my companion. 'But since we are aware of it, I feel we must go and see him.'

Fortunately when we arrived at the priests' residence, the administrator allowed our visit. Upon seeing us, our friend was awkward, as we had served together in the past. 'You have two great sins, and one of them is idolatry,' I challenged him. 'One of the commandments says, "Do not worship any idols." This is common knowledge among Christians. Pastors especially should know that.'

'I don't!' he answered defensively. 'When have I worshipped idols?'

'When you pray, do you not kneel in front of a statue of Mary?'

'Of course,' he said.

'Why do you need to kneel before the statue of Mary?'

'Protestant Christians pray in front of nothing, which makes it difficult for the mind to concentrate. With an object in front of us while we pray, our minds find it easier to keep focused. I kneel in front of the statue of Mary, not to worship her, but to help my mind concentrate while I pray.'

His words were an excuse. Surely to kneel is to worship. Already our friend, I felt, had been brainwashed. Brother Wang and I left the Catholic residence feeling grief and sadness for the man. We had done our best to admonish him; now it was up to him as to whether or not he chose to listen.

On another occasion I had to take a stand against blurring distinctions between Protestant Christians and Catholics. A large church with branches all over Taiwan was approaching its one hundredth anniversary. I was involved because at the time I was helping to manage the Taipei branch, hoping that through this ministry the kingdom of God would be spread throughout the land as we encouraged believers to go out to share the good news. I also hoped to encourage churches to unite and to work hand in hand for the sake of the Gospel. The commemoration day was nearing when someone told me that the programme included a speech by a Roman Catholic priest.

Immediately I became anxious. If I had a part in this matter, it was the same as participating with people in idolatry. I could not do it. So I wrote a letter to the committee, announcing my resignation from all my responsibilities.

Agitated, the head of the committee came to me. 'The commemoration day is very near,' he complained. 'If you suddenly resign, it will be a hindrance to the committee.'

'Yes,' I agreed, 'resigning at this stage is usually not the best thing to do. But since you invited a Catholic priest to speak and I am a member of the presiding committee, I would have to work with him. That would involve me in compromise. I believe that Catholics worship idols, and I do not want to have any part in it.'

The committee predicted that if I resigned so close to the commemoration day, people would ask me the reason, and if I told them, others would also take leave as well. In order to guard the whole programme from disaster, they were forced to write me a letter. I have preserved this letter until now. It reads in part: 'Because of the work, the co-operation, and the safety of the whole committee, we accept your opinion. We the committee agree that no Catholic priest will be invited to speak . . .'

Why did I take such a stand at that time? Though some might judge me to be very obstinate, I was trying only to defend the faith. We should not easily compromise, nor be careless in regard to the truth, because the Bible teaches that light and darkness cannot be united. Believers and non-believers should not be yoked together. As God hates idolatry, how can idolatry and the worship of the true God be put together?

A Christian funeral for a Christian general

One of the touchiest matters of principle arose over the funeral of a general who was a very pious and zealous Christian. As he lay dying, he grasped my hand and the hand of his wife and uttered his final words to her. 'I want Brother Wu to take complete charge of my funeral affairs,' he told her. 'You must abide by what Brother Wu arranges for my funeral service. You must remember what I have said to you.' His wife nodded her head as she wept, accepting what her husband had said.

After the general died, the government organised a committee to plan and oversee his funeral because of his high position and academic status as a graduate of one of the military academies in the United States. After the committee had planned the usual excessive and pretentious ceremonies, they showed it to me and asked for my opinion.

I said, 'I don't have any comment.'

Surprised, they asked me again, 'You don't have any comment?'

'Because I didn't have any part in this arrangement, why then should I make any comments?' I came back.

'Fine,' they said. 'Since you do not have any comments, then we'll push through with the plan.'

But it wasn't fine. Soon the wife of the general came to me and said, 'Brother Wu, before my husband died, did he not hold my hand and yours and make his last wish? You are the only person who can decide matters concerning his funeral affairs. Why did you say you had no comment when the committee came to ask you after they had arranged everything?'

I explained to her that since I was not related to her husband, it was not my place to offer comments. 'You are his wife,' I told her. 'Only you have the right to make any comments.'

'Your opinion is . . .?'

'It's very simple. The government arranged the funeral according to their official customs. If you ask me, I think it should be arranged according to the customs of Christians. As these two customs are totally different, how can they be put together?'

'Oh, I see,' she said. 'What do you want to do then?'

'I'll do it according to the customs of the church,' I said.

After talking with me, the general's wife went to the government officials and told them just what I had said. The government people said, 'It's no problem. He can proceed with what he has in mind for the funeral service. We can wait until after his funeral service, and then we'll proceed with the public memorial service. Or we can hold the public memorial service first, and then he can proceed with his plan.'

The general's wife thought this a good plan. So the committee sent a representative to me, who said, 'The general's wife told us about the situation, and we are willing to compromise. We can hold the public memorial service; then you can have your style of funeral service immediately afterward. That way we can both attain our goals . . . correct?'

'If you are going to proceed with the public memorial service, then I will not proceed with mine. If I do mine, then you should not proceed with yours. However, you can come and attend the funeral service.'

Understandably they were unhappy upon hearing what I had said because, although the general was a Christian, he was also a ranking government official. Then I told them, 'I understand how you feel. That is why the first time when you came to me, I said I didn't have any comments. Since you consider my opinion inappropriate, you will have to do whatever you wish. It does not have anything to do with me.'

Afterwards the general's wife came to me again. If I didn't take part, she said, how could she be true to her husband's wishes?

'I cannot fight for a Christian funeral,' I told her. 'Only you can. You are the only one who can speak up, because I am not your husband's brother nor his relative. If you want to be fair to your husband, then you must go and speak up.'

Finally realising that I was right, she went to the government officials and said, 'It won't do if Brother Wu will not attend the funeral service.'

At last the government officials saw that the problem concerning the general's faith was a serious one and could not be compromised. After discussion, they asked the general's wife: 'Can all the civil and military officials stand at attention in front of the casket, to express our grief for his decease?'

When the widow came to me and asked me, I told her that it was all right. Thus the matter was decided. Before the funeral service all the civil and military officials came and stood at attention in front of the deceased in silent tribute. We started the all Christian funeral right after they left.

Dispute over doctrine

The man advertised as speaker for a youth meeting in Taipei was a man who at an earlier international gathering had said, 'Each of you can pray to your God. Now let us pray . . .' What his introduction to prayer suggested was, 'My god is god, your god is god, their god is god.' This is polytheism. That the God we worship is the only true God is the unshakeable foundation of our faith. I was therefore unhappy to hear that the man was coming to Taipei. And, since checking his advertisements for the meetings did nothing to allay my suspicions, I told the young people of our church not to attend any meetings in which he was the speaker.

The young people didn't think as I did, however. Convinced that the most important work of the church was evangelism, they thought that as long as the gospel was being shared, I was wrong to oppose the effort. In fact, they thought I was mistaken in thinking that the invited speaker's doctrine was off the mark and doubted my reasoning in stopping them from attending the meetings. I therefore proposed a face-to-face meeting with this minister to find out more about his doctrine.

Agreeable, the young people arranged an appointment between the speaker and me at the Nanking East Road Church. We held our meeting in a hall open to the public so that anyone who wanted to might clearly hear our conversation.

When the speaker came to the church at the appointed time, he said to me, 'Brother Wu, your scope of ministry is different from the scope of my ministry, but we serve the same Lord.'

Although his words were very good, I pointed out rather bluntly that he had compromised, for the truth permits no ambiguity. His was a 'nationalistic' theology. There is nothing wrong with being a nationalist; the Bible is very nationalistic concerning Israel. Paul remembered his Jewish brothers in tears for three years. Moses refused to enjoy life in the palace, but rather chose to suffer with his Jewish brothers. While conceding these things, I said to him, 'However, you inappropriately have bent Christianity to conform to Chinese culture. If every country bent Christianity to its own culture, then the Bible would be distorted. The truth of the Bible is one thing; one's national culture is another thing.'

I continued: 'During one of your youth meetings, you said, "Everyone, pray to your own god." If our God is God, and their god is god, are we not promoting polytheism? The One in whom we believe is the one and only true God; therefore I think that you have some problem with your doctrine.

'For another thing,' I went on, 'in one of your speaking engagements you used an example: "Heaven is like a huge mountain," you said, "and though there are lots of ways to go up, there is a way which is easier and would save us a lot of trouble – a short cut – and that is by believing in Jesus Christ." Your example greatly hurts the faith. The book of Acts clearly says, "Salvation is found in no one else, for there is no other name under heaven given to men by which we must be saved." Whoever wants to be saved must believe in Jesus. Your stand is like the Rockefeller Church in New York. They have a statue of Laotze, a statue of Sakyamuni, and a statue of Jesus. They believe that through Jesus, Laotze, Sakyamuni, and Mohammed we can be saved. Is this any different to what the Unification Church teaches? This is an absolute violation of the truth in the Bible.

'One more thing,' I said, 'in one of your books you mentioned something about funerals. You said that in the West people put up a picture of the deceased, so why can't the Chinese put up an ancestral tablet? In the West people use fresh flowers. Why, then, can't Chinese use fruits and other foodstuffs? I think that in the West people put a picture up to remember the person who has passed away. The Chinese put up an ancestral tablet in order to elevate him as a god. In the West they use flowers as ornaments. The Chinese use fruits and other foodstuffs as an offering. The meaning and significance is totally different. I believe that you have seriously deviated from the Bible.'

After I had finished my speech, he replied concerning my first point. 'I am very sorry for inadvertently blurting that out. Certainly thoughtless speech by itself is not a grave sin. But comments that affect the very truth of our faith cannot be taken lightly. As for the problems concerning Christianity and the Chinese culture, particularly concerning the use of pictures, fresh flowers, and foodstuffs at funerals,' he continued, 'if I have the chance, I would like to correct what I have written.'

The man was admitting that he was wrong. A few years later, as this brother and I recalled this incident, although he had committed a mistake concerning the truth, I commended his willingness to sit down and discuss things with me in public. I believe that this discussion helped him a lot in sorting out the truth. I don't have any prejudice or ill will towards him, but I believe we need to be vigilant, seeking to have a clear understanding of Biblical truth and its foundations, so as not to be swayed from it.

Looking after the sanctity of the house of God

One evening I went to the church and discovered many strangers without much clothing sitting in the pulpit area, playing and singing Beijing opera. I knew I could not let their behaviour go unchallenged. Inquiring, I found out that the group were frontline soldiers temporarily on duty in the city. Some were staying at a school, others were put up in a temple, and these were assigned to our church.

Politely I approached the group. 'Fellow soldiers,' I said, 'we can live in peace and go on with our lives because you are in the front lines protecting our land, and I am very grateful and full of admiration. I am in charge of this church, however, and this place is the temple of God, where we worship, and it is not a stage for operas nor a place for people to live. I would like to ask you to move instead to my place, which is in front of the church.

I can arrange for my family to live temporarily at a friend's house.'

The soldiers were not at all pleased. 'Hey, man,' retorted one of them, 'are you trying to set us up by inviting us to move to your place so that you can sue us for trespassing on private property? How should we take this kind of offence?'

'I didn't mean that,' I said firmly. 'But you cannot stay in this church and use it as a stage for operas. Since I want you to leave this place, I must find you another place to move to. I want you to move to my place, though I admit it is a bit small. Anyway, what is the difference to you whether you stay in this place or at my place?'

Emotions flared, and one of the soldiers took his rifle and pushed it against my chest. 'If you speak again, I'll kill you,' he said.

There's no use in killing me,' I said more bravely than I felt. 'Since I am in charge of overseeing this church, I have the right to defend its sanctity. No matter what, you must all leave this place.'

I went quickly to the soldiers' headquarters to negotiate with their superiors, who proved very reasonable. Immediately they ordered the soldiers to leave the church, and the confrontation was over.

What I did was not meant to be disrespectful to the military. But I felt it my responsibility to guard the house of God, to keep it holy. Set apart for the worship and proclamation of the Lord God Almighty, it cannot be used for secular purposes.

In taking the unpopular stance against wrong in all of these cases, I was being loyal to God. I feel that while preaching is important, preventing the erosion of truth and standards is important too.

15

Back to Singapore

God does the impossible

In the autumn of 1952 I received a phone call from Dick Hillis, founder of the Orient Crusades (OC International). He wondered if I would be interested in meeting Dr Ford Canfield, a friend visiting from Singapore, where he was a director at Overseas Missionary Fellowship's international headquarters. Of course I wanted to meet him, because my parents were still in Singapore. As I had not visited home since I was sent into exile thirteen years before, I thought it would be marvellous if this old missionary could help me go back to Singapore.

Before I went to meet Dr Canfield I spent the morning praying and searching the Scriptures, and during that quiet time in the Lord's presence, God gave me his word very clearly in answer to my prayer. The passage I read told about a father who brought his demon-possessed son to Jesus. After explaining how the demon had tormented the boy and robbed him of his speech, the father said to Jesus, 'If you can do anything, please have mercy on us!'

Jesus said to him, 'Everything is possible for him who believes.'

Immediately the boy's father exclaimed, 'I do believe; help me overcome my unbelief!'

After I saw the import of these verses, I was like a person who had found a treasure. I hurried over to the headquarters of Orient Crusades on Nanking East Road, where Dick Hillis introduced me to Dr Canfield. 'I am going back to Singapore tomorrow,' the missionary told me after we got somewhat acquainted, 'and your family is there. Is there anything I can do to help?'

'I left for China many years ago,' I answered. 'I first went to Shanghai and then to Fujian. From Fujian I came to Taiwan. I haven't seen my parents since I left Singapore. If I could go back to see them, that would be the best thing I could do.'

'Do you need my help in processing your papers for Singapore?' he offered.

'Yes, please.'

He said, 'No problem. Just submit your application. I will be your guarantor so that you can come.'

'But Dr Canfield,' I said, 'my status is different from other people's.'

'A different status? What do you mean?' he asked kindly.

'Living in Singapore, you might know that Singapore has had two historical pasts . . . There was one incident when the whole city was on strike. Another time all the overseas Chinese went to the streets to welcome the ambassador to China, and when the government came to deal with the disrupted traffic, the crowd had to disperse. When some were put in jail, many of the rest of the overseas Chinese went to the police station to demand the release of those people. Unfortunately I was involved in these two incidents, prompting the government to issue a decree for my deportation. According to British law, when a person is deported, he is not to be allowed to enter a British colony for the rest of his life. They are very strict on this.'

After hearing what I said, Dr Canfield frowned and said. 'So, since this is their policy and you are in their records, getting you into Singapore isn't going to be easy to accomplish.' A cloud of worry cast its shadow on my heart. But then Dr Canfield continued, 'With man it is not possible, but with God everything is possible.'

At that my faith leaped. 'Dr Canfield,' I said smiling, 'before I came to see you this morning, I prayed to God, and he gave me that very same message.'

'Then that's good. I'll go to Singapore, and you keep on

praying. Let us see if God will give me an opportunity to ask for clemency and that the Singaporean government might forgive you so that you can visit your parents and be united with your family.'

'Thank you,' I said. 'I will cling to these verses every day and pray that God will give you the opportunity. Since God gave me this promise, he will fulfil it.'

Then we bid each other good-bye.

Not long after Dr Canfield returned to Singapore, he went to see the head of the Immigration Department, who was a Christian. In his duties as a member of the Overseas Missionary Fellowship, Dr Canfield often had occasion to meet with this man and so felt free to speak with him on my account. 'I have a friend in Taiwan,' he said, 'who once lived in Singapore. His parents, sister, and brother are still living here. He wishes to come home to Singapore to visit with his family.'

'No problem,' said the official. 'You just be his guarantor, and we approve his papers immediately.'

'But my friend is a very special case,' said Dr Canfield. 'His name is Wu Yung.'

After hearing my name, the man was perplexed and said to Dr Canfield, 'I'm sorry, but he was deported by an emergency decree, and according to British law, he cannot be allowed to enter a British colony for the rest of his life.'

Though disappointed, the elderly missionary persisted, 'He is different now. He has become a Christian and is in charge of a church. If he were allowed to come back to Singapore, wouldn't this be a good testimony to the young people as to the glory of God's work? This could help them in their spiritual life. Can you think of a way, another approach, we could try?'

'This is an impossibility,' the immigration head said. 'Our only option would be for the governor to give him a special permit.'

Dr Canfield decided to approach the governor. His opportunity came when the heads of local organisations were invited to attend a tea party at the governor's residence. When the way opened for conversation, the soft-spoken missionary told the governor about my case. The governor frowned when he heard it. Although he could give me a special permit to come to Singapore, using this privilege was not that simple. In response, Dr Canfield gave him a detailed account of my spiritual condition, status, work, and my good relationship with foreigners. Relieved, the governor said, 'If your friend can find two foreigners in Taiwan who are willing to be his guarantors, then I will give him a special permit to come to Singapore.'

Dr Canfield smiled his gratefulness, but inside thought, *With man it is impossible, but with God all things are possible!*

Immediately upon returning to the OMF office, the missionary telegraphed me, telling me that the governor would grant me a special permit if I could find two foreigners to be my guarantors.

No problem! I thought. And I was right. Dick Hillis of Orient Crusades and Pastor James Dickson of the Presbyterian Church each gladly wrote letters of guarantee for me, which I forwarded to Dr Canfield in Singapore. After receiving the two letters, Dr Canfield went to the governor as he promised and applied for my permit, which was eventually granted. The impossible had been accomplished. How thankful I was for God's faithfulness to his promise!

A fearful but safe return

I prepared myself for the trip back home with a heart full of indescribable joy. Not only did I long to see my family again after so many long years of separation, but I earnestly desired to lead them to Christ.

I had come from Singapore to Taiwan via China by land and sea. My return trip was to be by plane. There being no direct flights between Taiwan and Singapore in 1953, I had to get a connecting flight in Bangkok, Thailand. On our way to Songkhla, between Bangkok and Penang, Malaysia, our two-propeller plane began to malfunction. Though I saw that one of the propellers had stopped spinning, since this was my first time to fly, I assumed that one propeller automatically stops to take a break while the other one continues to propel the aircraft. However, the situation worsened when the other engine broke down as well.

Unable to control their fears, the stewardesses cried out. Seeing the stewardesses' agitation, the passengers concluded that there was no hope and also cried out in despair. In the palpable terror of the moment I also began to lose control of myself. Suddenly I remembered that I belonged to God and that I should give my life into his hand. As I prayed, God gave me his promise through Psalm 23, 'Even though I walk through the valley of the shadow of death, I will fear no evil, for you are with me.' Immediately the fear and tension in my heart vanished like smoke, and the peace of God which surpasses understanding filled my heart.

In spite of the danger of disaster, our plane glided down and landed safely on a plain, and eventually we landed in Singapore little the worse for wear.

What did I feel as I walked away from the plane across the Singapore Airport tarmac? I had mixed emotions, to tell the truth – excited, but anxious. Only people who have experienced coming back after many years of separation can understand.

Suddenly I remembered the scene at the dock thirteen years before, with my parents crying in distress, not knowing if we would ever meet again in this life. In that black hour I never expected that through the mercy of God, we would meet again in this way.

I felt as if I were in a dream. Ten of my family members were lined up on the far side of the rail. Although they were quite far away still, I could see my mother crying for joy at seeing her son face to face again. As I walked toward them, we could see each other more clearly. I cannot describe the expression on our faces. It seemed impossible that we could be seeing each other again, and yet it was happening. My parents looked at me, and I looked at them. My brothers and sisters looked at me, and I looked at them. After twenty minutes of being absorbed in each other, we realised that we ought to be heading home.

That evening my family arranged a dinner party, inviting all our friends and relatives for a happy reunion. The whole scene was like the son's homecoming in the parable of the Prodigal Son recorded in the Gospel of Luke.

Immediately in trouble with the government

Before coming to Singapore, I had made arrangements to preach at a series of meetings in a village. In order to boost attendance, my sponsor had put a story in the newspaper describing my past. It said that I had had a problem with the law when I was young and that I had been expelled from the country.

Unfortunately the story attracted the attention of the Singaporean government. And when I arrived, they confronted me with this newspaper article. 'We let you come back to Singapore because the governor gave you special approval. Now the article in the paper makes potential trouble for us. Because of your announced return, others who have the same record as you do may think that they can also return to Singapore.'

I pleaded innocence. In no way was I involved in putting the article into the newspaper. The sponsoring church had done it to attract people to the meeting.

Nevertheless these officials required me to send in every sermon for approval before I could preach it from the pulpit. So, for a time, all of my sermons had to go through this approval process.

Tales of brutality

I had not been in Singapore long before I began to hear of the terrible events that had taken place after Singapore fell into the hands of the Japanese. After hostilities broke out in the Pacific the British had established a naval port in Singapore, to take their stand against the Japanese. The British expected to defend Singapore from the sea. Instead the Japanese invaded from the north, from Malaya, and attacked the defending British with such severity that the whole Malayan Peninsula soon fell into their hands.

Poised in Johor at Malaya's southern tip, across the Malay Strait from Singapore, the Japanese ordered the Singaporean government to surrender, demanding that all of the hundred thousand British troops line up on the race course until the commanding officer arrived to receive their surrender. At this point a group of Chinese gangsters, who had organised an independent army, said to the British government, 'If you don't want to fight, then we the Chinese will fight for you.' The beleaguered British authorities agreed to let them try, providing them with arms and ammunition.

When the Japanese army, who had come across by sea because the bridge between Johor and Singapore had been destroyed, pulled ashore, the Chinese gangsters raised their flag and charged toward them. Surprised, the Japanese immediately retreated.

But when the Japanese learned that the men mounting the resistance did not constitute the Chinese army, but rather a gang of local hoodlums without any particular organization or military training, they pushed through with their invasion of Singapore, slaughtering many people along the way and leaving the streets littered with dead bodies.

Singaporean Chinese had a reputation for resistance to the Japanese. The invaders were quite aware of their monetary support to the mainland Chinese government for arms and munitions, also of the anti-Japanese rallies and destruction of Japanese businesses in the past months. To solidify their rule, the Japanese conquerors divided Singapore into four districts and employed a Chinese traitor in each one. District by district the Japanese lined up Singaporean Chinese, separating out all who wore eye-glasses and all who were deemed suspicious. Then they asked all who had one hundred thousand dollars to raise their hands. Some of the gentry and rich people thought that if they admitted they had that much money, they might be considered good citizens. Assuming the Japanese would not harm them, many raised their hands and were ordered to stand to one side. Then all those who had been sorted out were loaded into trucks and hauled away.

Those wearing eye-glasses were singled out because the Japanese believed them to be the well-educated and therefore most likely to resist Japanese rule. Those who had one hundred thousand dollars might well provide monetary support for Chinese determined to fight the imperial army.

These people the Japanese transported to the seashore, where they were ordered to dig a ditch. Thinking they were digging a trench for defence, the captives dug as they were told. Afterwards, however, they were lined up in front of the ditch and shot with machine guns. About one hundred thousand Singaporean Chinese were thus slaughtered at one time. It was a terrible loss to the tiny colony, since those killed were mostly intellectuals, gentry, and rich people.

One of those killed was a classmate of mine. He was nearsighted because he was very studious, and he was an only child. His mother died of grief, leaving his father all alone. During my visit these many years later, I often saw the father holding a walking stick and a worn-out bag, walking aimlessly, calling out for his son, 'Ah-Hu, where are you? Father is looking for you. Please come home!' It was very sad to hear him call. I understand that he did not stop calling for his son until the day he died.

Seeing him, I thought of God, how he keeps calling our name in Heaven for us to return to him. Is this not what he longs for?

My family accepts the Lord

My main purpose in coming to Singapore, of course, was to see my family, with the hope that I could lead them to the Lord. They had heard my testimony about the cancer and how God had healed me from it. They were very grateful to God for saving me from death. I also testified how my life was before I met the Lord, how God convicted me of my sins and of my indebtedness to my family. My parents were greatly moved by my testimony and listened as I carefully shared the gospel with them.

The Bible frequently mentions families in connection with

God's saving grace. In the Old Testament it is Noah's family that enters the ark, and Abraham's entire family who are circumcised, not just Abraham. In the New Testament Cornelius and all his household were led to Jesus Christ through Peter's witness. Moreover, Paul said to the jailer, 'Believe in the Lord Jesus Christ, and you will be saved, you and your family.' Obviously the heart of God is for a family to be a unit in faith, so that the whole family will be saved. If the family of every person who believes would come as well, the church would be greatly increased. Today God needs families in this world, for there is mutual love and care among family members. If some are weak, then the others will care for them. If we have strong and spiritually healthy families, the families can help the church by sharing some of the responsibilities that now fall on a handful of people in the ministry.

God greatly blessed my testimony to my own family, and within a very short time all had come to faith. Not only was my own wish fulfilled, but I believe God's heart was also satisfied.

Opportunity to preach

As only a few Taiwanese Christians and fewer native Singaporeans knew me, openings to preach were hard to come by. As a minister I felt lost without this outlet.

'You must look for people who are well accepted in the church and who can recommend you as a preacher,' advised Mr Hsueh, a friend. To help me, he introduced me to Rev. Calvin Chao, the dean of the Singapore Bible Seminary, hoping that he might be able to recommend me to various churches in Singapore. Because he didn't know me very well, Rev. Chao was a bit apprehensive. He said to Mr Hsueh, 'Why not let Mr Wu come and preach to us? Then we'll decide if we can recommend him or not.'

I turned down the offer, for I felt that spiritual matters cannot be solved or measured with human methods. If God was going to use me, then he himself would give me the opportunity to preach for his glory.

But refusing to adopt any human methods to get invited to pulpits to preach meant that I remained at home much of each day, quite ill at ease with the inactivity and without the income I normally received from preaching engagements.

However, God opened a door for me unexpectedly when a group of churches in Singapore found themselves without a foreign evangelist to conduct a series of evangelistic meetings they had organised. Because it is true that 'a prophet is not without honour except in his hometown,' the organisers were nonplussed when one of their speakers, a man from Indonesia, sent a telegram to inform them that he was sick and could not come to the meeting. They were frustrated because they were not willing to invite a native speaker to substitute for him. Anyway, who would come to speak on such short notice?

With only two days left before the meetings were to start, the organising committee did not know what to do. Someone then proposed me, 'a young minister from Taiwan who is thirty-two years old and whom God has healed from cancer' as a substitute, adding that I was currently visiting in Singapore. When no one commented, the one proposing the idea said, 'Look, even if he doesn't preach, we could just let him share his testimony.'

With no alternative, the committee sent someone to invite me. I accepted because I thought that, as I had not recommended myself, this was a God-given opportunity.

On the second day of the meeting not only the church was full, but an overflow crowd filled both the courtyard and the adjacent playground as well. Recognising what a great opportunity we had on our hands, the MC came to me and asked, 'Can we extend the meeting for a few more days? What a waste if we conclude the meeting today!'

As I could see no reason not to proceed, I willingly accepted the offer, and the meeting was conducted for many days. On the last day there was a spirit of excitement, a sense that God was doing things in our midst, and the meeting concluded with an atmosphere of fervency.

As I left, I expected to be given a travel allowance or a love gift for conducting the series of meetings, which was the usual practice. However, no one gave me anything. No, that isn't exactly true – the church maintenance person gave me twenty eggs!

My brother, who had come with me, and I went home silently. I was feeling very down. Having spent all my savings for this trip to Singapore, I didn't even have money to buy a gift for my parents as a token of respect. As the eldest son, I seemed very poor and miserable. I had been hoping that conducting those meetings would help provide money for my family. All I had to offer were twenty chicken eggs.

Unable to bear the awkward silence, my brother asked, 'How do you pastors make a living?'

How should I answer him? I grumbled silently, then answered piously, 'Brother, since it is God's work, then God will provide for me.' True, but frankly I was offended. There was no glow on my face. I did believe, deep in my heart, that God is faithful and trustworthy, but this night that belief was buried in embarrassment and self-pity.

A surprise invitation to stay in Singapore

Since I didn't have money, I seldom went out. Nevertheless after my exposure in the evangelistic meetings, my reputation spread quickly, and I received an invitation to speak to Jubilee Church, a Presbyterian congregation. After I concluded my sermon, someone handed me an envelope – an offering more generous that I had received in my whole life. God had made up for my not receiving anything at the evangelistic meetings with a love gift far exceeding the standard amount! What I had said to my brother was true: God called me, God uses me, and God will be responsible for me, though sometimes his provision is delayed in order to test my faith.

I gave a portion of the love gift to my parents and bought some articles for everyday use. My heart was full of joy. God had not failed me.

Not long after this, when the pastor of Jubilee Church was invited to join the Chinese Gospel Center in New York, he resigned from the church and left with no minister to replace him. As the church leaders were discussing their problem, Elder Ting of the church proposed me to take over as pastor. He listed certain criteria he felt Jubilee Church required in a pastor and showed how I satisfied each of them perfectly. First, I was thirty-two years old, not too young and not too old. Older men were stubborn, he pointed out, and young men lacked experience. Second, because I grew up in Singapore, I would be sensitive to their customs and traditions, could get along with the local people, and would easily readapt to the climate. Third, I was originally from Xiamen and spoke a dialect identical with that spoken in the church, making it easy for us to forge strong relationships and to work together. Fourth, since I had personally experienced being 'raised from the dead' when God healed my cancer, surely he must have a special plan for me. The proposal was unanimously approved by the church leaders, and Elder Ting was asked to inform me of their offer.

The church not only had good reasons to call me, but I had good reasons why I should accept their offer. Frankly, I was very happy because such a position would mean I could be near my family in Singapore. Second, I could see advantages for my children's education. From every point of view the offer was a very good opportunity, and I expected to take it. Nevertheless I said to Elder Ting: 'I am a servant of God, so I cannot say I'll come when asked to come or go when asked to go. Let me first ask the Lord about this. If God allows me to accept your offer, then I will certainly do as he tells me. Please give me some time to pray about this, and then I will be able to give you an answer.'

Elder Ting happily agreed, convinced also that this should be the attitude of a servant of God.

God's leading disappoints my father

I began asking for God to confirm the rightness of accepting the call to Jubilee Church, fully expecting a positive answer. Instead God's answer was Luke 14:26: 'If anyone comes to me and does not hate his own father and mother, his wife and children, he cannot be my disciple.'

Why did I come to Singapore? Because of my parents. Why did I want to stay in Singapore? Because of my children. For these reasons Luke 14:26 spoke very clearly that God did not want me to stay. I could do nothing but inform Elder Ting of God's leading.

Disappointed, Elder Ting and other church leaders asked my father, who was very happy at the thought of my staying in Singapore, to talk me out of my decision. Confident that he could change my mind, my father told Elder Ting, 'Don't worry; I can convince him to stay.'

Hence Father asked my brother to tell me that I should be home for lunch, promising snail on the menu. Having loved snail since I was a child, I happily went home.

The meal was already prepared when I reached the house. One after another I lifted the lids on the serving dishes, discovering that all four dishes contained snail meat, including the soup. I was impressed that Father had remembered my childhood likes and dislikes.

Father sat down after I did. His first words were, 'Do you know something? I'm very happy.'

I said, 'Of course, you're happy, since we are reunited after being separated for such a long period.'

He said, 'My happiness is because of my future.'

'What kind of happiness is in store for you in the future?' I asked curiously.

'My happiness is in you.'

'Father, please tell me how I can make you happy. I am willing to risk my life just to make you happy.' I meant what I said.

'There's no need for you to risk your life,' he said. 'My

happiness is very simple. I wish that you would take care of me the rest of my life.'

I said, 'Father, if you want me to take care of you the rest of your life, that's no problem. You can stay with me in Taiwan . . .'

'That would be unreasonable,' he replied. 'Your father bore seven children, all of whom live in Singapore – except you. If I go to Taiwan with you, it would not be fair to your brothers and sisters. You ought to stay here and be with the whole family – that is reasonable.'

Then I said, 'I would like to have the opportunity to stay. Yet times are far different now, unlike back in the old days. Coming to Singapore is not very easy.'

'There is an opportunity,' countered the ageing man across the table. 'The problem is whether you are willing to accept it.'

I tensed up. *Had Elder Ting said something to my father?*

My father must have guessed what I was thinking because he told me frankly, 'Mr Ting came to see me. I have already assured him that you would stay on in Singapore no matter what. If you stay on, then you will have the chance to take care of me and your mother. You can also be with your brothers and sisters.'

I felt caught in the middle. If I agreed to stay on, how could I face God? If I decided not to stay on, how could I face my father? God is greater, but that does not mean that our fathers are unimportant. As the battle raged inside me, a verse suddenly came to my mind: 'If you love your parents more than me, you are not worthy to be my disciple.' I had no choice but to harden my heart and say to my father, 'Father, I'm sorry, but I have already asked God about this and, unfortunately, he will not allow me to stay.'

Upon hearing this pronouncement, my father threw down the bowl of rice he had in his hand, stood up, and went to lock himself in his room, weeping bitterly. Hearing my seventy-year-old father crying because of me was unbearable, like the relentless slashing of a knife. Sweet words and phrases could not compensate for my decision not to stay. Words cannot describe my father's obvious disappointment and hurt.

My father dies

Not long after the altercation with my father I went to Terengganu, Malaysia, for a speaking engagement. On the last day of the meetings, when I came out from the shower, standing before me was the church pastor, the elders and deacons. I thought it strange. Surely they weren't waiting outside the shower room just to thank me. Looking at the serious expressions on their faces made me wonder if I had said something wrong during the meetings.

As I was guessing, the pastor came forward and embraced me, then took a piece of paper out of his pocket and handed it to me. A telegram from my brother, it said: 'Father's funeral, come quick.' I left for Singapore immediately.

When I got home, my family and relatives were all in the living room. Although they saw me come in, they did not speak to me.

'Do you know how your father died?' my mother asked eventually.

'Brother told me that because Father felt congested, he went to his room to take a rest. Later, Brother discovered that Father was having breathing problems, and when he went in to check on him, Father's eyes were rolled back and his breathing was shallow. So he called the doctor. But when the doctor came, Father had already died.'

Then Mother said, 'Your father didn't have a heart problem. I don't understand why he suddenly died.'

Though she didn't say it outright, I knew deep within me what she was trying to imply – that my father had died not of illness, but of a broken heart. Many people believed that. And it was I who made him sorrowful by rejecting his demand. He was hurt and disappointed. I caused him grief as a child, and now I had grieved him to death.

I believe we will understand God's way in this only when we get to heaven. There is no way I can put forth an answer that will satisfy everyone's questions. The Bible does not teach us not to love our parents. On the contrary, God's word promises blessings to him who honours his father and mother and cursing

on him who does not. Yet because we must obey God rather
than people, we sometimes experience, as I did, conflict between
loving God and loving our parents. Even now I still do not know
what really happened to my father or how culpable I am, but his
death left a deep wound in my heart.

16

Full-Time Witness

Christians commonly divide their lives into what they perceive to be the spiritual part and the non-spiritual, everyday part. We also classify some Christians as being in ministry full-time or part-time. Scripture and experience make it clear to me that both ways of thinking corrupt the witness of God's people.

Too busy at church

The family living across from the church provides an example. One day when I knocked at their door, someone inside asked who I was. I answered that I was looking for Mrs XX. He asked, 'Where are you from?'

I replied, 'I come from the church opposite you.'

'Church? Humph!' came the response from inside in a very rough voice. 'My wife's not home!'

Right away I knew that this man had a prejudice against the church. When I continued knocking, he said, 'Did I not tell you that she is not at home?'

'Yes. If Mrs XX is not home, is Mr XX at home?' I persisted.

'Why are you looking for me?' challenged the man as he came to open the door.

'Because your wife has been attending our church for many years, but I've never visited you. I'm very sorry about it; that's why I came especially to visit you today.'

'Come in,' he invited reluctantly.

I stepped inside and sat down in the living room. Immediately I understood why this man became angry when he heard me mention church. It was then almost eleven o'clock in the morning, yet the floor had not yet been swept, and the room was untidy. And from where I sat I could see that the bed was not made in the bedroom. Overall I got the impression of disorderliness.

We Chinese call our wives the inner person. The man in Chinese culture is responsible for matters outside the house, while the woman is responsible for matters inside the house, including housework. This man's wife was so occupied with church business from morning till night that she neglected her duties at home. No wonder her husband developed deep prejudice against the church!

Many people believe that such activities as reading the Bible and praying are spiritual, while mundane chores around home or fulfilling duties for a company or an organisation are worldly and unspiritual. They take this from the Scripture that says, 'Set your affections on things above, not on things on the earth' (Col. 3:2 KJV). They reason that because 'things above' are more important than 'things on the earth', taking care of housework, rearing children, or doing business or office work – 'things on the earth' – can be done carelessly or haphazardly, with left-over time. That is not what the Scriptures teach. Carelessness always leaves a bad impression among unbelievers. Our Lord says that whatever we do, we should do it to the glory of God and not to give offence to people, either in or out of the church, that unbelievers 'may be saved' (1 Cor. 10:31–33).

I believe that all activities of Christians ought to reflect spiritual realities. Although a mother's looking after a child may seem mundane, if it is done in order to do one's best for the Lord, then it is of profit and has spiritual value and witness. If a tradesman is trustworthy and practical and if the products he sells are of good quality and reasonably priced, he is glorifying God. If a Christian servant working in someone's home is hardworking and efficient and does not steal things, he reveals God's work in his heart.

Unappreciated factory workers

Once a factory manager asked me, 'Do you know what kind of people I cannot hire to work in my factory?'

'Probably those who loaf on the job, who are treacherous and dishonest,' I said with a laugh.

'Wrong! Wrong!' he said.

'Then what kind of people?'

'If I tell you, please don't get angry.'

'I won't get angry,' I said. 'Please tell me.'

'Christians!' he said.

I was surprised, because I believed Christians would be honest and loyal in doing their duties. How could they have earned such a bad reputation?

'Elder Wu,' he replied, 'you ministers care only for spiritual things, not for worldly things. Christian workers in my factory tend to open their Bibles during work time, and once they open them, they aren't aware of anything else. If my office were full of such Christians, my factory would have to close down after a very short while.'

Such behaviour causes people to be prejudiced against Christians. Believers who are truly spiritual gear all their activities toward fulfilling their obligations and in so doing glorify the name of the Lord.

Full-time or part-time?

Ministers who give up their original jobs to become preachers go into full-time ministry, we say, and those who work for government or do business and make use of their free time to participate in church work are in part-time ministry. Let's look at this kind of thinking; I think these definitions require a second look.

If ministers do not have a real calling from God or stumble after being called, they cannot possibly be serving God, but they are serving themselves. They are simply working for their living;

the ministry is their rice bowl. We can hardly call this full-time ministry.

Moreover, if pastors love fishing and spend a great deal of time at the seaside fishing, but do not have enough time to pray, to preach the word, and to shepherd their flock, how can this be considered full-time ministry? Though our bodies need time to rest, if people heed bodily needs while paying little attention to spiritual work, they can hardly classify themselves as a full-time minister of the Gospel.

In contrast, if two people fulfill their own duties well, if mothers take good care of their children, and if servants do their job well, they can consider the time spent on their chores as the same as the time they spend for God in ministry, because they glorify God in whatever they do. How are Christian mothers supposed to look after their children? How are Christian servants supposed to serve their master? The Lord through the epistles of Paul teaches us a great deal about these things. If we really practice them, even if we are just looking after children, making meals, or serving our masters, we are serving the Lord full-time. In short, we are to be full-time Christians, always witnessing by our lives the truth of the redeeming, sanctifying work of God within us.

An example of a full-time Christian

A bus driver I met at one o'clock in the morning a number of years ago illustrates what I would call a full-time Christian. I had preached at Hsinchu and was headed home on the ten o'clock evening Taipei train, when the conductor announced that, because of an accident near Yingke, the train could not continue. Tickets would be refunded in Taipei, but passengers had to find their own way to Taipei.

As passengers reluctantly filed off the train, it was nearly midnight. The best way to Taipei, of course, was by taxi. But with few taxis and many passengers, the price of a taxi, normally ten dollars, skyrocketed to eighty dollars. People who did not mind paying the exorbitant fare took off. Others, like me, unwilling to pay the high price, stood around waiting, hungry, cold, and frustrated.

When by one o'clock in the morning taxis were still unable to meet all the demands, I headed off to another street to see if I could find a taxi driver who had not learned of the price hikes. At that hour not a taxi was in sight. As I stood there helplessly, a bus with a sign that said 'Taipei XX Factory' came towards me. Stopping it, I asked the driver, 'Sir, may I ask whether you are going to Taipei?'

'Yes,' he answered.

'May I ride with you?' I asked.

'Sure!' he said. 'My bus is empty. Get on!'

'Sir, it's not just me,' I said, 'there's a whole group of people at the station who also need a ride.'

'Okay,' he said without hesitation. 'Tell them to come and fill up the seats.'

Running back to the station, I shouted, 'If anyone wants a cheap ride, please follow me right away!'

Many people scrambled after me, and within minutes the bus was full. When we were about to pull away, someone thought to ask, 'Mr Driver, how much should each person pay?'

'Since I was driving an empty bus back to Taipei, I feel uneasy talking about money,' he answered. When the people insisted the man name his price, he said, 'I am embarrassed to say it, but if each of you would pay ten dollars, that would be great. I am very greedy.'

'How can this be considered greedy?' someone objected. 'Those taxi drivers are charging *eighty* dollars per person!'

Before we reached Taipei, at a place called Sanchung, a passenger called out, 'Mr Driver, can you let me off? My house is here.'

The driver stopped the bus and waited while the man tried to find ten dollars in his pocket. He searched in vain.

'Enough!' said the driver. 'Ten dollars isn't much, and it's already late. Quick, just go home!'

Apologising, the man asked for the driver's name and address, promising to send the ten dollars the next day.

'Friend,' the driver said, 'don't trouble yourself about the ten dollars. Please go home quickly. Your family is no doubt anxious about you.'

As the passenger thanked the driver and got off the bus, a man who knew me said to me, 'Elder, I think this driver is a Christian . . . I'll ask him.' Then, hurrying up to the driver and patting him on the shoulder, he inquired, 'Mr Driver, sir, please tell me, are you a Christian?'

'How did you guess?' the man answered.

'You look like a Christian!' the passenger answered.

'How can you say I look like a Christian?' he retorted. 'A Christian is a Christian.'

True, I thought. *Christians should not only show themselves Christian-like when they are attending church or reading the Bible. They should be Christian, letting others identify their status from the details of their daily lives.*

What that driver said in the early hours of the morning is really a great challenge to us. If we are Christians, then we are to be thoroughly Christ-like all the time, not just look like Christians superficially. Only by doing this can we satisfy the heart of God and glorify his name. Our testimony is more than spoken words; it is demonstrated by our behaviour in everyday life. Every Christian should be a living Bible, thoroughly manifesting God's word. Only in this way can we truly attract others to follow the Lord and avoid being labelled Pharisees and causing the name of the Lord to be profaned by the unbelieving.

17

Consequences of Misjudgement

What we think may not be necessarily so. What seems to be good may not be good, and what seems bad may not be. We are all extremely limited and imperfect. We simply cannot be one hundred per cent correct all the time.

Misjudgements happen in everyday life and sometimes result in little more than embarrassment. One day, for instance, I had made an appointment with Miss Kathleen Heath of the Overseas Missionary Fellowship to meet me at our house. Unfortunately something urgent came up at a church member's house, and I had to go and handle the situation. But as Miss Heath was coming all the way from southern Taiwan, I requested my sister's help to entertain the missionary when she arrived. 'I have bought some dessert already,' I said, 'and the coffee is right there.'

'Don't worry,' my sister assured me, 'I'll take care of it.'

When Miss Heath came, this sister apologised for my absence, explaining that my wife and I would return within an hour. As Miss Heath sat down to wait, my sister placed the dessert in front of her, then brought her a cup of coffee.

When Miss Heath took a grateful sip of the coffee, my sister was surprised and puzzled to see her smile turn noticeably to a frown.

'I'm very sorry,' Miss Heath said, distressed, 'but I can't drink salted coffee.'

My sister had mistaken salt for sugar!

Sugar is white. Salt is also white. But substituting one for the other causes problems. So does impulsive judgement in bigger matters. Our assessment of people should not be done by just observing the outside. Just as we can confuse sugar and salt, because both are white and granular, so we can confuse right and wrong. We must be careful in making judgements, looking always to God, who alone can judge human hearts because he alone is omniscient. Moreover, God's way and will are far higher than our way and will. We are just too slow to know or grasp spiritual things very certainly.

The incident of mistaking salt for sugar was a small matter. But, because we all know that misjudgements can have serious consequences, it ought to teach us how humbly, carefully, and fearfully we should guard our own judgements, words, and actions. One such misjudgement, in fact, nearly destroyed our son.

Having a house inside a church, such as we have had, has its good points. It has been convenient for brothers and sisters to seek my help, and I have been able to care for people living in the vicinity more thoroughly than if we lived at a distance. But living at the church has its bad points as well, one of them being lack of privacy, especially for our children.

Ministers should be an example for their sheep, even be their model witness. The Bible says that ministers must first know how to look after their own home before they can look after God's church; they must first be able to teach their own family before they can teach their sheep. For this reason most brothers and sisters do not use plain glasses to look at their ministers; they use magnifying glasses to judge their ministers, expecting them in every way to transcend worldliness and to attain holiness.

If ministers alone were held to such high standards, it might not create very big problems. But when people hold ministers' children to equally high standards, it can create serious tensions. Children are inherently immature and often impulsive. When they are happy, they bounce and jump; but when they are unhappy, they might cry and yell. Our children had no way to differentiate between church and home. When we would have our meetings, the brothers and sisters sometimes complained that the place was too noisy. They would say to the children, 'We are praying and reading the Bible. Your shouting and yelling are disturbing our quiet.' Such words inevitably aroused the children's feelings of rebellion and dissatisfaction.

The most damaging criticism and misjudgement involved my eldest son. He and our neighbours' child were tussling, dragging and pulling each other here and there. Soon my second son joined in, holding the other child in the middle. Though the three of them were playing very happily, a brother from the church happened to pass by at that moment, and without observing carefully, made straight for the neighbours' home to report that Brother Wu Yung's children were attacking their son.

Now this family had only this one beloved son, who to them was more precious than anything. Of course, then, when they heard that our sons were beating him up, they were terrified. Immediately the child's mother picked the phone and called my wife. 'Mrs Wu,' she wailed, 'your children are beating my child to death.'

My wife was shocked and asked for more information.

'Two of your children joined together to beat up my child,' the woman repeated.

'Really?' my wife asked incredulously.

'Mr XX just walked by there and saw it with his own eyes.'

'I'm very sorry,' my wife said. 'I'll go to find out what's happened, and if there's trouble, I'll bring my two children to your house to apologise.'

My wife then opened the window and called the two children to come upstairs. She didn't ask what they had been doing, just gave them a good scolding: 'You shouldn't be like this. Your father is a minister. How could you beat up another child?'

Mystified, our eldest son said finally, 'Mom, what are you talking about? I don't understand.'

'You don't understand?' my wife retorted sharply. 'You two beat up our neighbour's child. Just now someone walked by and saw it with his own eyes.'

'Mom, we don't need to defend ourselves,' our big boy replied. 'We'll ask our playmate to come here, and you can ask him yourself.' With that he went downstairs to bring the neighbour's child upstairs.

The neighbour's boy said, 'Mommy Wu, we weren't fighting! We were just playing. We were *not* fighting!'

There the matter ended – for the adults. But inside the children's hearts a knot remained. For them the matter was not over. Though they had always treated the adults in the church with great respect, when they met the brother who had reported that they had been fighting, they expressed their disapproval of him. Uncomfortable with the children's 'special treatment' of him, the brother later, during a discussion at summer camp, complained of their lack of courtesy. 'We adults learn from adults. Children learn from children,' he said. 'We have no objection to Brother Wu and Mrs Wu setting examples for us adults. But if Brother Wu's children are an example from which our children learn, we may object . . . because they don't know courtesy. How can we let our children learn their children's impolite ways?'

As this brother went on and on expressing his dissatisfaction, my wife naturally felt ashamed and wished for a hole in the ground to hide in.

Afterwards someone told my children, 'The communists in mainland China have criticism meetings, and today Christians are also having them.'

'To criticise what?' the children wanted to know.

'You!' the informer said. 'They said that you are discourteous to people.'

The injustice of the brother's misjudgement, his failure to apologise, his accusation of discourtesy and now his demand for personal courtesy made my eldest son deeply resentful. *My father teaches many beautiful principles*, he mused angrily. *But they don't make much of an impact on the people who hear him, because the people don't receive them.* And from that day on he judged my work to be worthless.

Not only so, but the boy burned with indignation at the hardship that living inside the church brought him. His schoolwork suffered drastically. His temper became so untamed that he would overturn a whole table of food if he were unhappy. When he came home after school, he oftentimes sat expressionless for ten minutes or more, with his eyes staring unblinkingly at the wall. Anxious for our son, we as parents tried everything we could think of to delight and change him. We were soon at our wits' end.

As the date for our junior summer camp approached, our seething son refused to register. 'Why don't you want to go?' my wife probed. 'You are a minister's child. If you don't attend, who will?'

'To attend would be meaningless for me,' he insisted.

My wife could not help crying. And as tears do have the power to shake a person's heart, my son reluctantly consented to attend, but with the comment, 'Even so, I cannot take in God's word.'

When time for summer camp came, my wife insisted that our rebellious son sit on the first row 'so that you can see clearly and hear better'.

At the first meeting of camp I was the speaker. As I looked down from the pulpit, my son was sitting there on the first row, with his hands on the seat and his eyes on the playground outside. When I saw my own boy acting out his disinterest, how did I feel? I think only those who have had the same experience can understand the inner turmoil.

The second day was the same. I felt stricken.

As the camp neared its end, I almost wept openly at seeing the continued ungodly look of my son. Silently I cried out to God, *Oh, Lord, if you cannot move my son's heart tonight, then tomorrow night I will not have the courage to climb into the pulpit.* As I said this, tears fell. I realized afresh how abnormal my son was, both spiritually and dispositionally. I wanted to help yet was unable to. I did not know what to do or what could be done. When it was time to speak that night, I wiped my tears, reached out for the strength and comfort God offered me, and went up to the pulpit.

After I spoke, I gave an altar call. The first person to come to the front was my son. He ran to the front and fell down, holding a chair. There he wept loudly and said, 'O God, my heart is filled with dissatisfaction and deep hatred. I feel that my father's work is worthless and his preaching is completely useless. I have no strength to rid myself of this thinking. I am being bound and oppressed. Tonight you must deliver me. If you don't deliver me, that means you won't deliver my father.'

The boy cried incessantly. The sound of his crying moved the whole meeting, causing the other children to cry as well. As I saw this situation from the pulpit, I prayed agonisingly, earnestly. Suddenly God answered my prayer and set my son free.

From this experience, I can see that, while living inside the church had its negative side, the loving Lord took care of us in spite of it and gave us sufficient grace. He himself untied our bonds and released our burdens. Although he used incidents like this to try us, he deeply cared for us in our weaknesses and did not allow the attacks of Satan to exceed our capacity to bear them.

18

Hand-me-downs: the Problem of Clothes

'That outfit was my son's,' said the sister proudly. 'My, how perfectly it fits you! How good it looks on you!' The woman's gift and words were meant kindly. But my son's reaction was to run home and change the offending clothes.

'Why?' we asked him.

'Because this clothing is not ours,' he replied indignantly. His self-respect had taken a blow, his pride hurt.

I too had problems with hand-me-downs. Particularly when I first began in the ministry, one elderly sister went out of her way to care for me and to pray for me. Her encouragement was really needed in those days. In our inexperience and youth, we were tempted to retreat when encountering frustration and to get discouraged when difficulties blocked our way. But the clothes our dear supporter salvaged for me became a source of embarrassment.

'Don't throw away your unwanted clothes,' she told her son. 'Give them to me; I can use them.' So her son, who was the manager of a car company and who wore imported clothing, gave her what he didn't want. Then she gave them all to me, hoping that I could use them. What she didn't consider was whether the clothes would fit me or not. Her son was over six feet tall; I am only five feet seven inches.

Though the clothes the elderly sister gave me were too big, because I valued their quality, I asked my wife to remake them to fit me. The result was a strange, imperfect fit. Even so, I was thankful and judged that the good material neutralised the imperfections.

When I went to Japan to preach the first time, Mr Chou

Hsien-sung brought a group of people to meet me at the airport. Embarrassed at the suit I was wearing, he said to me quietly, 'Brother Wu, let's not go to the hotel right away.'

'Then where should we go?' I asked.

'To the tailor. We'll first make you two suits.'

'But there is no need,' I objected. 'I brought enough clothing.'

'Really?' he asked. 'Do they all look like what you are wearing?'

'Yes . . . they are all made of British material and are very good.'

'British material is British material,' he said, 'but the look doesn't pass. Since we are participating in an international event, our appearance has to be more sophisticated.' So convinced of this was he that he took me to a tailor's shop and ordered two suits to be made for me. He even paid additional fees for quick service.

The elderly lady who gave me her son's suits also gave me her son's shoes. Trouble is that my feet are particularly small. I generally wear size seven; the shoes I was given were at least size nine. When I put the hand-me-down footwear on, I was like a child wearing adults' shoes. They slid incessantly.

But the materials were of the very best quality. Not wearing them seemed like a waste; so I put on thick socks and stuffed cloth in the toes of the shoes. One time I was on my way to preach on Hsiamen Street. Being in a hurry, I jumped on a bus that was already moving. On the bus, though, I discovered that one of my shoes did not jump with me. Happily the ticket lady was very kind and asked the driver to stop the bus so that I could get off and find my shoe. As I put my errant shoe on, I could feel the amused stares of fellow passengers, and I felt myself flush with embarrassment.

But the hardship of the hand-me-downs went further. When I was young, I always preached the message of the cross – to suffer with Christ, to die to self for his sake. Some of my hearers began to think that my words contradicted my acts. While most of the people wore local materials, they saw me wearing high-class clothing. While they wore shoes within a certain price range, my imported shoes cost a good deal more. Could this be called suffering for the Lord and bearing his cross? It was easy for me to speak, they said, but difficult to act. They had no way of knowing that these foreign goods caused me great shame and embarrassment.

When these criticisms came back to my ears, I felt mistreated and indignant. Being still young, I hadn't yet learned to deal with gossip, and I lost my perspective easily. I was so angry, in fact, that I decided to quit, to give up my ministerial career!

Had I followed through with my inclination at that time, I would not have walked to the end of the path to which the Lord had called me. Thank God for Miss Ni Sung-te, who when she heard that I wanted to leave, immediately sent a message: 'Oh, Brother, you must learn from Paul to endure labour pains because giving birth is painful. You are a minister now, and you are in the position of giving birth spiritually. When a mother gives birth to a baby, she cannot escape suffering; likewise if a minister wants to spread the word successfully, suffering is something he must go through.'

When I took in Miss Ni's words, I came to my senses and felt ashamed of myself and unworthy to be the Lord's servant. Earnestly I prayed, recommitting myself to God and discarding any thoughts of leaving the ministry. Had it not been for Miss Ni's faithfulness in rebuking and challenging me, I really don't know what would have become of me. I covet such a encourager for every minister of the gospel in times of hardness and suffering, over the little things such as clothes, shoes, and misunderstanding in general.

19

Dealing with my Own Personality

The problem of being an extrovert

Early in my role as pastor my extrovert personality gave me trouble. The fact that any unhappiness I felt inside showed outside by the expression on my face put strain on working relationships. Suddenly colleagues did not treat me as amicably and genuinely lovingly as before.

In response my wife and I set aside Saturdays to fast and pray. As we spent time before God in openness, he revealed to me that my personality was what was causing the friction in my work. It was a problem that I could not resolve by methodical changes, nor could I use my good points to hide my weak ones. Somehow, I decided, I would need to change my response to what I didn't approve of. I would need to be patient, not letting disapproval show on my face. And for a while I was able to reduce the number of interpersonal clashes.

But very apparently God was not satisfied with my superficial change. One Saturday during our time apart I prayed, 'O Lord, I thank you that because I have already learned the lesson, I no longer have to show my unhappiness on my face, and because of this my interpersonal difficulties have greatly decreased.'

Then God reminded me that although I could manage to hide my feelings in front of people, I did not pass muster before God. What he required was *truthfulness*, and what is truthfulness? It is the outside being consistent with the inside. If the outside is not consistent with the inside, that is hypocrisy, double-facedness. As God's light revealed my sin, I was very afraid and earnestly pleaded with God for his forgiveness.

Letting my inner unhappiness show on the outside was far better than living a lie. Success in interpersonal relations, God showed me, does not mean I must concentrate on hiding defects in my character. I must interact with others truthfully, with the inside consistent with the outside. If I am right with God, my relationships with others will be right. And being right with God does not come from our capacity to do good, but from his working in us 'to will and to act according to his good purpose' (Phil. 2:13 NIV).

John the Baptist once said, 'He [Jesus] must increase, but I must decrease.' We must allow God continually to increase within us as we continually decrease within ourselves. We should pursue his prosperity, not plan our own decrease. When God is strengthened within me, I am weakened within myself.

How can God be strengthened, or increased, within me? Through spiritual devotion. I must immerse myself in his word, absorbing it day by day. Then I shall experience God being strengthened within. Thus allowing Jesus to increase within me, I will decrease, and God's power will tackle the aberrations of unsanctified personality. Only as we let Christ prosper within our lives day after day can we truly live out the meek and humble pattern of his life.

The problem of self-pity

Sometimes many small irritations can build anger and self-pity into a barrier to God's blessing. An opportunity once to preach in Tainan became such an occasion. The train that was scheduled to arrive after six o'clock in the morning arrived before five. Because of my early arrival, the pastor of the church could not meet me. I had to find my own way to the church. In response to my ringing the doorbell, the pastor came down to open the door. 'Brother Wu Yung, you've come!' he said.

Yes, I thought, *if I hadn't come, how could I be standing here?*

Already, obviously, a bad mood was showing its ugliness in my heart.

'Come up quickly. I'll prepare a room for you,' he said and led the way upstairs. As he showed me the room I would be using, he asked, 'Have you had breakfast?'

It is not yet six o'clock, I grumbled silently, *how could I have had my breakfast?* Out loud I said, 'No, not yet.'

'Fine,' he said, 'I'll prepare your breakfast at seven. Wash your face and rest in the mean time.'

At seven o'clock my breakfast appeared. Now we Fukienians and Taiwanese like to eat *congee* with cucumbers in soy sauce, salted eggs, and dried meat. That morning the *congee* came with a small fish on a side dish. As I am disgusted by the smell of fish, I ate just the *congee* and did not touch the fish. Surprisingly, fish accompanied the *congee* again the next morning. So it went for the length of my stay.

The church had arranged three meetings a day: a devotional in the morning, a revival service for Christians in the afternoon, and an evangelistic meeting in the evening. Mostly women came during the daytime, and they brought their small children with them. As the little ones made a lot of noise, I had to speak extra loudly in order for everyone to hear. The strain made me very tired mentally. But when I tried to rest between meetings, I was bitten by red ants. The combination of a heavy workload and not eating or resting well left me indescribably exhausted.

As on the last night I was supposed to return to Taipei, I said to the pastor, 'Oh, Pastor, I'm afraid if we don't purchase the ticket for a sleeping berth early, we won't get it.'

'No problem,' he said. 'Please don't worry; I will buy it for you.'

'Tomorrow morning when I arrive in Taipei, I have to preach at the Baptist church at Huaining Street,' I told him. 'If I can rest well on the train, I won't be overtired.'

'Don't worry,' he assured me, 'I'll certainly be able to buy the ticket for you.'

Before night fell he gave me the ticket. One look told me that it was a ticket for a seat, not for a sleeping berth, which meant that I would have to sit up all night. *How could this church make me suffer like this?* I fretted. In fact, the more I thought about it, the more I pitied myself, because I loved myself very much.

Before the meeting on the last night I knelt down to pray. But my heart was churning with anger, an anger that grew more and more as I thought about the ticket. How could I go in front of the congregation with this anger burning inside? As much as I tried, I could not suppress the self-pity and sense of injustice within me, even after praying half a day. I had always admonished people to die to self and to rise with the Lord, for it is only when death takes place that resurrection can happen. Preaching to others was easy; applying it to myself was another story. Though I used much of God's word to preach to myself during the day's prayer time, I could take nothing in.

Finally, in desperation, I prayed, 'Oh, Lord, I really cannot overcome myself.' Once those words had come from my mouth, something very wonderful happened – the self-love, self-pity, and the feelings of injustice and anger vanished. I thought of Jesus Christ, who long ago said on the cross, 'It is finished', and then the curtain of the temple ripped, not from the bottom upwards, but from the top downwards. According to Bible expositors, that curtain was as thick as a man's hand. How could it rip in half in one mighty rip from top to bottom? The strength came from above and moved downward, not from bottom to top. The same is true if we want to overcome our flesh: we must never depend upon our own strength, but on the strength that comes from above.

That night, thank the Lord, after all my self-pity and anger disappeared, my heart overflowed with joy and the glory of Christ. That welling up of the presence of Christ within enabled me to walk up to the pulpit to deliver my final sermon with power.

The problem of worry

Having faced many threats to my physical well-being with faith and found God faithful, I should have been strong in faith when

I contracted hepatitis. Oh that it were so!

My condition deteriorated rapidly. My liver function index, which should have read below forty, rose from slightly above forty to over one hundred, then to over two hundred, later to four hundred, to six hundred, and finally to almost nine hundred. When President Wong of the Pingtung Christian Hospital examined me and realised the seriousness of what was happening in my body, he arranged to move me, with the help of a Brother Ho, to Veterans' General Hospital.

When a brother came unexpectedly to visit and teared up when he saw me, I was convinced that he must have heard that my illness was very serious. His reaction planted a seed of worry in my heart, and sadness welled up as I faced the possibilities.
I found out later why the brother looked so sad. Over the doorway of the room in which I had been placed temporarily because I didn't have insurance was a sign: 'Terminal Ward'! So, though my condition was not all that serious, I began to feel very anxious. If I continued getting worse, I fretted, I would certainly develop cirrhosis of the liver or liver cancer.

'Yesterday's experience cannot be today's resource', goes a proverb. Though I had had many great spiritual experiences, I could not depend on them to live the present. The book of Lamentations tells us that God's compassion is 'new every morning' (3:22,23). Since they are new every morning, we need to experience their realities every day. Had I not experienced God's mercy and care often in the past? Had God not miraculously healed my cancer? Even so, I lacked faith. I was nervous, scared, and troubled. I was weak.

20

A Head-on Blow

Occasionally an unsettling blow comes when least expected. Such was the case the day I accepted an invitation to have a meal with an elderly couple who were people of some position and whose daughter attended our church and served with us.

When I knocked at the door of this family's fine home, a servant came to open it. I followed her to the living room. I sat down and waited for a long while, puzzled at why the master of the house did not appear. A full twenty minutes had passed before the servant returned and said, 'Sir, our master asks that you come to eat in the dining room.'

I followed the servant into the dining room, where I found the elderly couple and their daughter already in their chairs at the table. The old man asked me to sit down. As I did so, I wondered if this family always treated its guests this way.

I did not enjoy that meal. Not that the food wasn't good; it was delicious. But the atmosphere was as cold as a stone tomb. Neither the host or the hostess talked all through the meal. Restless and uneasy, I wished I were elsewhere.

After what seemed a long time, the master of the house said, 'Mr Wu, does our daughter attend your church?'

'Yes,' I replied.

'Do you people believe that my daughter is a real Christian?'

'A real Christian,' I said.

'According to you, my daughter is a real Christian. Is she considered a good Christian?'

'She is also considered a good Christian,' I said.

'Now I want to ask you a question,' he said in a surprising turn in the interrogation. 'What happens when one believes in Jesus? And what happens when one does not believe in Jesus?'

Had the man not asked, I would have been embarrassed to confront him with the answer. But since he had asked, I jumped at the opportunity to witness to him. I said, 'Those who believe in Jesus will be saved. Those who don't believe in Jesus will perish.'

'What happens when you are saved?' he asked. 'What happens when you perish?'

Never before had anyone asked me such a leading question. 'To be saved means going to be with God,' I answered simply; 'not to be saved means going to hell.'

'Are your words true?' he challenged.

'My words are true. The Bible records this truth very clearly.'

'Well, since you truly believe that one who doesn't believe in Jesus would perish and go to hell, and only those who believe in Jesus go to be with God' – and here's where he dropped his verbal bomb – 'please don't blame me for saying that you who believe in Jesus are simply selfish people, completely without conscience!'

Surprised and off-balance, I put down my chopsticks and tried to express my counter-arguments, perplexity, and rejection of his judgement of Christians. But the old gentleman stopped me. He wasn't through.

'I knew when I said those words, you would not be happy,' he said. 'But I say what I said not without reason . . . This daughter of mine, you say, is really a good Christian. We are her blood parents, and she is our child. According to her, she has believed in the Lord for five or six years already, but during these five or six years she has never once mentioned to us that believing in Jesus or not believing in Jesus would make such a drastic difference! If believing in Jesus takes her to heaven, then it will be just her alone who goes there. If not believing in Jesus means one goes to hell, then she has just let us two old people go to hell. You see, I said nothing wrong. Aren't you believers in Jesus who do not quickly and clearly tell us the importance of believing

Jesus just selfish people, completely without conscience?'

What he said was true. Reeling as from a blow, I could find no words to respond to his logic.

The Bible likewise condemns us if we do not spread the good news of God's way of salvation. In fact, the Apostle Paul said, 'Woe is me if I preach not the gospel!'

I think also of Jesus' story of the rich man and Lazarus. Lazarus went to be in Abraham's bosom, but the rich man suffered in hell, being burned in fire. As he lifted his head and saw Abraham, he said to him, 'Father Abraham, have mercy on me and send Lazarus, that he may dip the tip of his finger in water and cool my tongue.' From this we can see that the rich man suffered tremendously in the fire. If we don't witness to our own relatives, to our neighbours, to our friends and colleagues, one day we'll be in heaven, and all those whose lives intermingled with ours who never heard the gospel from us and who die without the Saviour will go to hell. Then if they in hell could see us, and we in heaven could see them suffering in the fire, how would we feel? If our own flesh and blood would raise their voices to accuse and scold us, how could we bear it?

I will not soon forget the encounter with the old gentleman or the point he made.

21

Living with No Fixed Salary

Gas-tank guidance

Many ministers receive from their churches a fixed salary. Other ministers must look totally to God for the supply of their needs. As each of these two methods of provision has its advantages, we cannot say that one is good while the other is bad.

To me life is very a practical thing, about which I should ask the Lord to give me his guidance. Living arrangements are best only if they are drafted according to the Lord's revealed plan. As we sought his will, God used 1 Kings 17 to teach me what his plan was for us. In that passage he told Elijah to go to the Kerith Ravine and there fed him by ravens as he promised.

In response to what we believed God wanted for us, we decided to live simply looking to God for his provision. At the time we were ten in our home, besides guests. Inevitably, though God proved faithful, an unfixed salary caused some anxious moments.

Sometime later, after discussion, the church decided to set up a system to provide for its ministers, designating a monthly living allowance, plus extra amounts for such needs as the children's education. Then when a number of brothers and sisters came to our house to give us a few months' financial provision, I found myself in an awkward position. If I refused the money, I would seem ungrateful for their love and concern. If I accepted it, I would be going against the specific guidance God had given me. I told the bearers of the money that because of their love, I would seek the Lord's guidance concerning this matter, and once I knew God's mind, I would give them an answer.

I was sure that God would show us the way we should take. When Joshua was leading the Israelites in the conquest of Canaan, and they won the battle at Jericho, but lost the battle at Ai, Joshua turned to God for the reason. God's answer was that somebody among them had taken forbidden articles. Once they had found the guilty one and stoned him, God returned to their aid, and they defeated the people of Ai. I believed therefore that if we took this matter before God and asked him to give an answer, he would do so.

We prayed for one week, but failed to find an answer. After two weeks there was still no word from God.

One day the gas company called us to inquire about our gas consumption. At the time gas was sold in tanks. After one tankful was used up, we were supposed to buy a new one. 'Mrs Wu, according to our record book,' said the company representative, 'your house uses a tankful every twelve to fourteen days, but this time it's already been seventeen or eighteen days. Why haven't you exchanged your empty tank for a new one?'

'Let me go and ask our cook,' my wife answered. Our family had hired a sister to cook our meals, because morning visitation left us no time to prepare lunch.

'How is our gas supply?' my wife asked the cook.

'When I cooked yesterday, the gas was almost insufficient to make a fire,' the cook answered. 'But after I gave the tank a couple of shakes, it started again, and even now the fire is still going strong.'

Back on the phone, then, my wife repeated the cook's explanation to the gas company, satisfying their curiosity.

Three or four weeks later the gas company called again. 'Mrs Wu, why haven't you changed your gas yet?'

'Because the gas still burns very strong,' she said. 'Maybe it's because you had added extra gas to the tank that it has lasted until now.'

Impossible, the gas company representative told her, because the amount of gas the tank holds is fixed, and its consumption time is also fixed.

'But we are still using your gas,' my wife said. 'Why it has lasted so long I don't know.'

The gas company decided that we must have changed companies. If so, we needed to return the old tank to them. So when they delivered gas to our neighbour, they took the time to check our house. To their surprise, the tank we were using belonged to their company. Curious, a senior company officer asked his mother, a member of our church, about our inexhaustible gas supply. As she did not know about it, he asked her to take him to our kitchen to have a look. After six weeks the tank was still supplying us with fuel for cooking. After nearly three months we began to realize that God was using this tank of gas to give us his answer that we could trust him for his supply. But we had to be sure.

In discussing the matter with my wife, I reminded her how God first called Gideon and how Gideon believed that the Lord would take the responsibility for everything if the plan proposed was from him. This attitude, I feel to this day, is commendable among God's servants. To make sure the calling was from God, Gideon prayed, 'O God, I will place a fleece on the grass. If tomorrow morning there is dew on the fleece but the grass around the fleece is dry, then I will know that you are sending me.' The next morning the fleece was wet, the grass dry. He said to God again, 'O God, if tomorrow morning there is no dew on the fleece, but there is dew on the grass, then that will be evidence that you are sending me.' The next morning the fleece was dry, the grass wet. Gideon knew clearly that God had indeed chosen him to deliver the people of Israel from the Midianites.

If Gideon could pray this way, we knew we could too; so we prayed that if the gas ran out the next day, we would take it that God was speaking to us through the gas tank – 'do not accept a fixed salary, but look totally to me for the supply of your need'. The next morning there was no more gas, and we knew that God wanted us to continue depending on him. So we returned the unopened package of money to the church.

The hard side

Though living without a fixed salary has been God's good way for us, it has had its hard moments. We have had times of affluence, of course, but also times of poverty. God uses both to train his servants. Life without a set income indeed helped our faith enormously. Despite the nasty side of some of what God asked us to go through, we can testify to joy and peace.

The hardest part of doing without, when that was God's way for us, was in its impact on our children. My wife particularly was sensitive to this. When my daughter was attending Jinling Girl's High School, a good brother on staff, Mr Hu Yuan-kung, told my wife that since I was a pastor, my daughter should apply for financial assistance. Afraid that word would get out that our daughter was receiving 'charity' and cause this spiritually tender girl emotional stress, my wife did not follow through on Mr Hu's suggestion, though we are to this day grateful for his kind offer.

Very 'picky' about food when he was young, our eldest son never ate his meals well, though his mother tried every means to force him to eat more. During the time we were struggling with this problem Miss Kathleen Heath of the Overseas Missionary Fellowship was coming regularly to lead a Bible study in our church. She was really a gift from the Lord, for she laid a firm biblical foundation for the developing congregation and was highly respected among the brothers and sisters. Since this foreign missionary knew so much about spiritual things, my wife reasoned that she must know something about health. So she consulted Miss Heath about our son's picky eating habits.

'Mrs Wu, what kinds of food does your child like to eat?' she asked in response to my wife's tale of frustration.

'His favourite food is dried meat,' my wife answered.

'Then it's very simple,' responded Miss Heath. 'Try to use dried meat to get him to eat more.'

My wife said no more.

'How'd it go?' I asked her later.

'Miss Heath suggested that I buy some dried meat, so I didn't continue our discussion,' she said.

I understood why: we were too poor to buy dried meat. Our faces showed the pain we felt.

Limited funds also meant that we did not buy our furniture, but made do with what the brothers and sisters gave us. We also made do with the space provided for us. One day a sister in visiting our house discovered that our bed was a single bed. The truth was that the room was too small to hold a double bed as well as a baby cot.

'Do the two of you sleep on this single bed,' our visitor wanted to know.

'Oh, yes!' we replied.

'You two love each other,' the sister concluded brightly. 'That's why you sleep on such a small bed.'

We forced a smile.

When our eldest son followed our eldest daughter to America, she took over much of the responsibility of looking after him, though not his school costs. One day she wrote, 'Dad, I think I had better get married.'

Why did she want to get married, when she wasn't even quite twenty-one years old? She wanted to lighten our load, especially that of paying the costs of our son's college education. Why at this point? The day before when our son was in the cafeteria line, the person in charge of meals came up to him and said, 'I'm sorry, but you haven't paid your meal money, so you can't eat lunch this noon.' He had to put down his tray and walk away in embarrassment. But that wasn't all. On that very same day his dormitory manager told him to strip his bed, put the bedding outside the door, and sleep elsewhere that night because his room and board had not been paid. That night, because the school was far from where his sister lived, he slept in a broken-down car. He called his sister, though, to tell her what had happened. His call prompted her letter to us.

Knowing that our inability to pay on time caused our children such hardship was very painful. Yet we had to trust that God had permitted this shortage of funds and to believe that the suffering was beneficial for us as the Scriptures teach.

The sweet-sour side

Dr Wang, the doctor who operated on me, and his wife, always showed concern for my family, often sending us fish, meat, and other good food to add to our meals. Our children never forgot their kindness. Years later, during one of the times our children invited Mrs Wang for a meal when she passed through Los Angeles, one of our now-grown-up children said, 'Mommy Wang, when we were young, we were always very happy whenever we heard you were coming because that meant we would have good food to eat that day. You never came to our house empty-handed.' The comment brought tears to Mrs Wang's eyes.

Happily living on an unfixed salary was not always hard. We didn't always have to eat frugally or do without. Yet when we did, God allowed it so that we could enter into deeper life experiences and to understand other people's sufferings more fully. Even our great high priest Jesus came to earth to taste the sufferings of humankind.

Sometimes the Lord surprises us with abundance. Once when I had a stopover in Japan, a brother came to the airport to see me and handed me an envelope. 'Don't open the letter until you board the plane,' he instructed. Inside, when I opened the envelope, I found a cheque for over forty thousand American dollars. A note accompanied it: 'Wu Yung, you are getting older and older, and you should consider your future needs. Today I am moved by God to give you this cheque, hoping that you can use it after you retire.' I thanked God for that cheque, but I invested most of the money in the Lord's work, keeping only a small portion for myself.

God refines our faith through both poverty and riches. He desires us to be like the Apostle Paul, who said, 'I have learned to be content in whatever circumstances I am. I know how to get along with humble means, and I also know how to live in prosperity; in any and every circumstance I have learned the secret of being filled and going hungry, both of having abundance and suffering need' (Phil. 4:11,12). In short, God always expects those he has called to be his servants to be content and, by prayer and supplication with thanksgiving, to ask God and to look unto him. In fact, this is a lesson I believe every child of God should learn and relearn throughout their lives.

22

Lessons in Love

The Bible makes much of love. Paul prayed for the Ephesian church that they might be able to 'apprehend the breadth and length and height and depth of the immeasurable love of the Lord'. In 1 Corinthians he wrote that the love of Christ constrained him. Love was what kept Paul running along his spiritual path despite hunger, cold, difficulty, and danger. God's love for the world cost him the life of his son. John 3:16 declares: 'For God so loved the world that He gave His only begotten Son, that whosoever believes in Him should not perish, but have eternal life' (KJV). Love took Jesus from the throne to a manger and from life to death on a cross.

Love motivates us to give others our time, effort, and our substance. The power of love is immeasurable. Let me illustrate this.

Love removes fear

One of the brothers in our church served a fairly well-to-do family who had brought him from Shanghai to Taipei to be their cook. Not long after he believed, a disease took his life. Without notifying the church or registering his name, the family he served simply placed his corpse in a funeral parlour. When a sister in our church who was from the man's hometown discovered the facts, she took a suit to the funeral parlour, hoping to wash and dress the man's body so that it would look presentable for the funeral. But to find his body, she had to go from corpse to corpse, looking carefully into each face. She lifted the cloths over the faces of twenty bodies before she found the remains of this brother in Christ. I realised that it was love that overcame her natural fear of the dead as she peered at body after body in that morgue.

Love puts others over self

A brother in our church was given a sum of money upon his discharge from military service. With interest at the bank not keeping up with inflation and the amount too little to start up a business, the man was at a loss at what to do with his funds. At the time another brother in our church was starting a business and seeking financial resources. Informing members of the church of this investment opportunity, he told them the interest on their money would be double that of the bank. So this ex-military brother put his money into the company, believing that his investment was safe with a fellow Christian. Unfortunately, the man beginning the company, lacking business skills, lost the money, and heavy debts forced him to declare bankruptcy. The military man was among the investors who suffered loss. Trying to be of comfort, I said to him, 'I can understand your inner feelings. What are you going to do now?'

To my surprise, he said, 'I'm in sorrow, but this brother from the trade company is in much deeper sorrow.' His concern for another over himself was love at work.

Love takes time to establish

Possibly because of my work, I didn't establish a good relationship with my youngest daughter. Too little time spent with my children, in fact, formed an invisible gap between us. Whenever I would enter a room where my youngest girl played, she would run away. Her behaviour made me feel deeply sad, and I wondered what other people would think. I thought hard for a way to resolve this problem, a way to bridge the gap between her and me. One day, as I was going to attend a wedding, I asked my little girl, 'Would you like to see a bride?'

Of course! No child would miss a chance to watch a bride.

'It's already eight o'clock now,' I said, 'and the wedding starts at nine o'clock, so you must get changed very quickly.'

I had just returned from the Philippines, where the brothers and sisters had given me some children's clothing. I chose something pretty for my daughter to put on, and she was pleased. The next thing to do was to comb her hair. Though I had never done that before, I took the trouble because I wanted to build my relationship with her. It took me a long time. By the time I had created two braids to my satisfaction, I had worked up a noticeable sweat. Then as I was crouching down to put my daughter's shoes on, my wife came back from market. Just one call from my wife, and the child pulled her foot from the shoe I was trying to wiggle on and ran to Mommy without giving me further thought. As I remained still crouching there, a flood of wistfulness assailed my heart.

An hour's effort could not match the relationship of love built up over the months and years. How could I dream of so quickly building up my daughter's love for me by doing just one favour for her? It was impossible.

The love between our children and my mother-in-law was perhaps as strong as between them and their mother. Because my wife more often than not accompanied me in visitation, my mother-in-law was often left at home to look after the children. Years later, when she passed away, the fact that all our children came home from abroad to attend her funeral was evidence of the strong emotional ties between grandchildren and grandmother. How they grieved in their loss!

Love is a precious bond. To weave it to its maximum strength takes time and care.

Love makes people one

There is forgiveness in love. Once Peter felt himself magnanimous for suggesting that he forgive people seven times.

'Seventy-seven times!' Jesus told him. Seventy-seven-times love is perfect love, a love that forgives and keeps forgiving.

The incident between me and my youngest daughter served as a warning – and not only concerning relationships in my family, but in the church. We can build up a church only if different parts of the church body co-operate with each other. If the parts can work together without hindrance, the body of believers can have a marked effect on all.

But how should the parts of the body function together? A good illustration is the fitting together of the framework of the Tabernacle. God told Moses to have workmen craft rings on each plank and fasteners to join them together. In the church the fasteners which hold the church together are fashioned of love. Only the material of love can join many different people together to make one body. As important as love is, however, it cannot be established in a day. It takes months and years of careful nurturing to bring it to maturity.

Love serves

In our church was a family with the surname of Wu. One day the husband, a manager of a factory, hurt his hand in a machine. His wound was washed with antiseptic, smeared with ointment, and bandaged up. On that same day the man had to go to Japan to examine and accept a machine. On his second day in Japan he began burning up with a fever, which he thought to be the beginning of flu. But when medication failed to bring down the fever, he consulted a doctor, who diagnosed a tetanus infection. The man immediately telegraphed his wife in Taipei, who hurriedly made arrangements to go to Japan to look after him that afternoon. Sadly she arrived at the hospital only in time to see him breathe his last.

Her husband's death struck the woman like a bolt of lightning. The future looked totally grim. How could she raise her two children – one four or five, the other a toddler – alone? The more she thought of the impossibility of what lay ahead, the more she grieved and the deeper she sank into depression and thoughts of suicide. If she took her own life, she reasoned, her brother could look after her orphaned children.

Brother Hu Yuan-kung of our church, who lived next door, told us about her tragedy, hoping that we would go to comfort the distraught young widow. More than willing to go, my wife hoped that she could win her with comfort from God. But the little mother was so torn with grief that she wanted only to die. She wanted none of other people's counsel. My wife could only cry with her.

'My saddest moment is when the sun sets,' the woman told my wife one day. She explained that her husband usually returned home from work at sunset, as did the children from school. Then as a family they enjoyed the warmth of togetherness and laughter. Now at sunset her children returned home, but not her husband. The pain of her loss was thus reinforced daily as the sun dipped below the horizon and withdrew its light.

From that time on my wife always went to visit the family at sunset.

One day Widow Wu said to my wife, 'I can't believe that there are still sympathetic people like you on earth. Now that I feel somewhat better, you don't always have to be with me at sunset.' Having said this, she went to her room to get something for my wife. She pressed a small container into my wife's hand, saying: 'Since I met someone who sympathises with me so much and who makes me feel comforted, I decided not to commit suicide.' In my wife's hand were the sleeping pills with which the woman had planned to take her own life. Love had won.

Later the woman attended Jenai Baptist Church and pursued spiritual things as part of that body of believers, eventually becoming a deaconess. How wonderful the strength of love is when let to flourish over time! It can help people overcome their deepest grief and lead them from death to life, from darkness to light. How much we need to ask God to help us use this greatest and most beautiful gift!

Once I needed to take a grandson, who was just a few months old, from Singapore to America. After a short time being content, the baby began to fret for his mother. As the hours of confinement in the droning plane dragged on, he cried continually. Not only so, but he wet my clothes. With all my other clothes inaccessible in my checked luggage, I had no way to change. People sitting near me could smell the odour of urine and must have wondered if I wet my pants. Trouble was, I could find no words to explain myself. The experience was hard. But why did I do this without complaint? I loved my grandson, and because I did, I did not feel any burden. And when we serve the Lord and other people with the love that is shed abroad in our hearts by the Holy Spirit, our experience will be similar. Serving, though inconvenient and costly, will be no burden.

23

A Strong Church

The problem of succession

Once after I had preached in Keelung, the pastor of the church offered to take me home. When I objected, he told me that he had something on his heart, some sort of knot that he couldn't seem to untie, and he was hoping that I could help him with a solution. During the ride back he told me his story.

His father was a pastor, eighty-three years old. Every time the old man preached, he needed someone to help him to the pulpit and back. During his sermon he swayed for lack of strength, and his voice was too low to be heard distinctly. At times his mind wandered, leaving him unable to connect what he had said with what he was going to say. Yet people in the congregation continually praised him for being faithful and steadfast in his post.

The son confessed to being disquieted by these praises heaped on his father.

I smiled. 'I think the reason for your disquiet,' I told him frankly, 'is that your father has stayed too long in the pulpit, preventing others from taking his place.'

He smiled with surprise and relief. 'That is what I think,' he said, 'but I didn't expect that you would feel the same way.'

Older people not wanting to step aside to make room for younger folk has long been a problem in Chinese churches. It is one reason young people don't want to give themselves full time for the Lord. It also makes it hard to promote a ministry that

needs youthful vitality and direction. Churches become lifeless
and lacking in energy, and in the end the older people take their
ministries to the coffin with them.

When Moses died, his work didn't die with him because God
chose Joshua to take his place. Moses brought the people of
Israel out of Egypt, and Joshua brought the people into Canaan.
And today young people must not be prevented from taking over
the ministry by older spiritual leaders who refuse to step aside.

Does this mean that old ministers should stay at home and do
nothing? Of course not. Minister should serve God for the rest
of their lives. Retirement means stepping back behind the scenes,
much like what is recorded in Exodus 17, where Joshua was
fighting the Amalekites at the foot of the mountain, while Moses
sat on the mountainside holding his hands and staff up in prayer,
supporting Joshua. Through the support, teaching, and direction
of older people, younger people will have the courage to go into
full-time ministry.

Knowing that age doesn't spare our bodies and minds, older
people who want to prevent their ministries from dying should
prepare for a successor. These they should train before the time
of their retirement, so that God's work will not suffer.

But besides not seeing the need to step aside to make room for
younger people, older ministers don't give up their pulpits
because many churches make no provision for the twilight years
of their leaders. Some who are feeble and want to retire sometimes can't, especially those who don't have children, because
they don't have the means to retire. It is a problem churches need
to address.

The problem of 'ten-thousand-year' deacons

Another problem is the term for deacons. In politics we talk
about the 'ten-thousand-year congress' – in which members
arrive by wheelchair, leaning on canes, and accompanied by
nurses, then sleep during sessions. Such a situation should not
exist in the body of Christ. A church should be like a flowing

river, like a life growing in vigour. Since the church is a body composed of members, each member should function so that the whole will function properly. If there exists a 'ten-thousand-year' board of deacons, newer, younger members will not have a chance to be trained. For this reason I advocate a two-year term for deacons, followed by a break, so that others can fill in.

These days I also emphasise group ministry, because, alone, a person is limited. If we work as a group, with each person pulling their weight, we can develop a ministry that will grow large and strong. Each member should participate in the ministry of the church, 'being fitted and held together by that which every joint supplies, according the proper working of each individual part . . . for the building up of itself in love' (Eph. 4:16). Put this verse into practice, and the result will be a glorious church, a light and a witness that will attract people to Christ.

Strengthening through small groups

At one point I felt our church was weak despite its growth, wondering what I could do to strengthen it. Eventually I selected several people who were willing to give themselves to the Lord and encouraged each of them to choose eleven or twelve people with whom to start a small group. Naturally they chose people they knew, people with whom they could work together towards spiritual growth. The small groups met every other week for Bible study, sharing, and prayer. People could share anything from problems concerning the Bible to problems in their work, family, and spiritual lives. But we placed a time limit for every part of the meeting so that our time together would not become shallow and dull, but vital and worthwhile.

Each group was in charge of a ministry in the church. 'A' group would take care of the cleaning of the church. 'B' group would be in charge of all weddings and funerals. 'C' group would take care of newcomers to the church. 'E' group would follow up new converts and members. Every six months the groups would switch responsibilities. When a small group grew to fifteen or twenty, they could divide. As the number of groups expanded, the church grew in organisational strength and spiritual vitality. And when Campus Crusade for Christ was promoting its evangelistic campaign called 'I Found It', our church was able, through the small groups, to support them completely and effectively.

Working as a whole church

I learned something about working as a whole church through two evangelistic crusades. When Billy Graham came to Taipei, more than a hundred churches, including mine, came to help with the preparatory work. As it is customary for Billy Graham to meet with the leaders of the country in which he plans to hold an evangelistic crusade, we invited Madam Chiang, the wife of President Chiang Kai-shek, a devoted Christian, to be our consultant. For that crusade an overflow crowd of nine thousand people squeezed into the Armed Forces Athletic Field. My heart overflowed with joy at the crusade's success.

Some time later a group of churches planned their own evangelistic meetings. They didn't invite any well-known speakers like Billy Graham, but planned to use their own pastors. Just the same they borrowed the Armed Forces Athletic Field as we had. I was a little concerned. We had had a hundred churches helping; they were a small group. What if only a few people came? Wouldn't they look foolish?

I needn't have worried. On the first day of their meeting all the seats at the athletic field were taken, and the organisers had to borrow the auditorium of the nearby First Girls' High School, setting up a sound system to broadcast the services to all the people there. And when the high school auditorium filled up, they also borrowed the New Park Concert Hall for the overflow. The meetings went on for three days, with crowds of fourteen or fifteen thousand each day!

I was baffled. How were these people able to conduct an evangelistic meeting larger than ours?

I found out why. Although in name we had more than a hundred churches co-operating, only a few pastors and elders actually did the work. As for this other group, their entire congregations came to help. What a difference! When the whole body of a church works, the possibilities are limitless.

Managing unity

For the whole body to work, there must be unity. But with personalities, views, and opinions tending to clash within a congregation, how can a church hang on to unity? We can't avoid arguments and misunderstandings. We have to accommodate one another, yielding to one another. Yet we can't use voting as a way to solve problems; that asks the minority to submit to the majority.

I believe that what we need is not to arrive at the same opinion, but to have the same aspiration. Unity is to have the mind of Christ. If we insist on having the same opinions, unity becomes impossible. If we let the mind of Christ be our mind, seeking his kingdom, we can achieve unity and harmony. God must have the last word.

True and effective leadership

True, the effectiveness of church work does not lie in one person. Yet teams of people working together do need effective leadership. But how do we find good leaders? In the church true leaders are not only those people who have the gifts and positions of leadership, but, more importantly, who have earned the respect, love, and loyalty of the local body of believers. Thus the support comes from the grassroots.

Let me illustrate. As a pastor, I hope that I am loved. I cannot beg my congregation to love me or demand that they come to listen to me. People have to choose to love me and to listen to me deliver my sermons. I qualify as a leader, not so much because of my position, education (or lack thereof), capabilities, or talents, but because of the touch of God on my life. My authority is bestowed by the Lord, not by my own might or cleverness.

A person's position and possessions should not be of their own grasping. When Lot stood before Abraham and asked for his piece of land, Abraham said, 'Let us not quarrel; if you go to the left, I will go to the right.' In the end, while Lot lost everything, Abraham received God's promise: 'Lift up your eyes and look towards the north, south, east and west; whatever your eyes see will be yours; I will give them to you and to your descendants.' A person whose hands do not let go will in the end find himself empty-handed, and the person who does not cling to what can be seen will in the end be abundantly blessed of the Lord, more than they can ever imagine. We should not aspire to be a spiritual leader or work hard to that end, but wait on God to designate us to it.

God gave Moses authority and power. Why? Moses was not selfish. He did not think of his own welfare, but of other people's benefit. For the sake of the people of Israel he left his life as an Egyptian prince and was willing to submit himself to the hardship of being with his people. Later, when the Lord Jehovah threatened to destroy the Israelites because they had worshipped the golden calf, Moses went to the Lord and begged, 'Lord, if You do not forgive them, then let my name be wiped out from the book of life.' Moses was willing to sacrifice himself for his people. God's power and authority are given to those who do not think of themselves above his people.

Consider David. He too was a leader, and many people followed him. Why? During the time when he was not yet king, he did not have political power, but was only a wanderer. He did not have riches; in fact, both of his hands were empty. Yet he was able to attract people to follow him. I believe this attraction was his spiritual life. Church leaders need to have good spiritual health, a spiritual vigour that springs from their relationship with God. Then, as David did, they must build relationships with the people, relationships of love and respect. If we have a life that brings joy to the Lord, if we live holy and diligent lives, we will earn the right of leadership that God has chosen us for. Such spiritual leadership will produce an effective ministry team and work that is stable, balanced, and unwaveringly God-ward.

I believe good people produce good works. Spiritual people produce spiritual work, and one who follows God's heart produces a godly work. If the church considers only different methods and systems and puts emphasis on the work itself, ignoring people, I am afraid that the work produced will be wood, hay, and stubble.

24

Signs and Wonders

The book of Acts frequently tells of signs and wonders. But each mention is linked with the glorifying of God's word. Today signs and wonders still testify to the truth of God's gracious word and thus increase the effectiveness of the preached word on the hearers. A number of such pairings I will never forget.

Healing of a mental patient

One day a psychiatrist from the National Taiwan University Hospital, also a deacon of the Wanhua Presbyterian Church, called me on the phone because he had a patient whose condition had continued to deteriorate, though in and out of hospital for years. Originally this patient was a business manager of a successful foreign firm. When he suggested to the boss that the firm should craft a system of control over its growing number of employees, the boss assigned him to draft such a plan and later appointed him to carry it out.

Other workers, however, became disgruntled and jealous of the business manager and joined together to put obstacles in his path. They tried by every means to embarrass and thwart him. Unsuccessful, therefore, in carrying out his plans, he became depressed and unable to sleep. While at first his life remained manageable, eventually he suffered a nervous breakdown.

Unable to regain control, he finally collapsed and was hospitalised as a schizophrenic. Life for him became a hopeless daze. On one occasion he bought pesticide and tried to get his wife and children to swallow quantities of it with him to commit suicide as a family. When out of hospital, he sometimes would disappear for days at a time, sleeping in air-raid shelters.

The doctor who contacted me knew the limitations of medication to stabilise this patient and as a Christian was concerned.

'If your medical practice cannot help him,' I responded to his plea for help, 'what can I do for him?'

'I understand your reluctance, Elder Wu,' he said, 'but we want to change his treatment to one that is more spiritually based. Through Bible reading and prayer we hope God will stretch out his hand to deliver this man and his family from their sorrow.'

After I had agreed to try to help the patient, the doctor brought him to my house. This Mr Chen was about forty years old, quite handsome and refined.

Following a bit of small-talk, I came straight to the point: 'Men today live with a great deal of internal discord. As high as their ideals and goals may be, they often find they are unable to carry them out. The only solution, really,' I told the man before me, 'is to find an alternate source of strength – so that a man can do what he knows he should do.'

'Yes, my ambitions have always been quite high,' replied Mr Chen, 'but my strength is inadequate to manage them. What shall I do?'

'Let me introduce you to a source of strength outside yourself. Atoms and nuclear explosive reactions are sources of energy; but what is the source of strength which created atoms and the power of nuclear reactions? It is God!'

Aware that Mr Chen was an intellectual, I told him about God, using material from an article by a great scientist in the then current Reader's Digest. The author noted that the distance of the sun from the earth is sixty-three million miles. Any closer, the earth would be too hot, and any further away, too cold. Why this exactitude? Who arranged and designed it? 'God,' this great scientist answered. 'There can be no other explanation.'

I also explained to the gracious man, so carefully listening, that cultures around the world acknowledge that all things proceed from a single source. The Chinese call this source 'heaven'; Muslims call him 'Allah'; and Christians, 'Jehovah', the Lord God. Though the Chinese in early millenniums knew of a 'Lord who resided in heaven', they did not know this God on a personal level. The Greeks worshiped an 'unknown god', and many other cultures crafted gods from wood, stone, and gold. Though humankind's understanding of him had become corrupted, the true heavenly God condescended to become a man almost two thousand years ago. God used himself in the flesh to manifest himself to humanity and to provide a sacrifice for our sin. This 'seeable' God is Jesus, and this Jesus is the source of strength. If people trust him, they will draw strength from him; all they have to do is to ask, I encouraged.

'If Jesus and Christianity are this good, then I should believe also,' the former business manager said. And soon we were praying together. Before he returned to the hospital with the doctor that day the man put his trust in the Saviour and became a new creation.

Not long afterwards the patient was cured. I met Mr Chen later at a church at which I was speaking. How great and gracious is the Lord to heal a man with such a history of mental illness!

Healing of uterine cancer

Brothers and sisters of our church doing hospital evangelism met a Mrs Huang, suffering from uterine cancer. When they shared the gospel with her, she accepted Christ. But with her tumour malignant and growing rapidly, the doctor sent her home to die among family and friends.

During one of our visits to her home we talked with her about faith, using Hebrews 11. Faith is like seeing what cannot be seen, we told her; it is as though one has already gained something that one has not yet gained. When Mrs Huang heard what we preached to her, she responded with a simple, strong faith. She found herself free from fear, worry, and depression. And as her spirits lifted, she discovered that she was able to get around better and to help out with some of the household chores. By and by, when she went back to the hospital for a check-up, doctors found her cancer completely gone.

How did Mrs Huang get well? There was no mistake in her diagnosis. Her cancer was already beyond hope of a cure via any of the current methods of treatment, whether by surgery, radiation, and/or chemotherapy. Because she believed and trusted the Lord Jesus, the deadly disease left her body. God simply chose to answer her prayer for healing.

Healing of a child's brain tumour

A little boy in our church, the only son of Lin Kang-shi and his wife of Fujian Province, suddenly developed a fever. Within a short time the child could walk no more than a few steps before falling, and he complained that he couldn't see clearly. An examination revealed that one of his eyes was almost blind. The doctors at the local hospital, realising that the boy needed better care than they could provide at their small facility, urged his mother to take the child to the National Taiwan University Hospital.

At University Hospital an X-ray showed a brain tumour pressing on the optical nerve. Determined to be growing after a wait and see period, the tumour threatened not only the boy's eyesight, but his life. The mother asked the doctor what the success rate was for the proposed operation.

'There is perhaps a 50 per cent chance of curing him and a 50 per cent chance of failure,' he said.

The prognosis left the mother in turmoil. How could she subject her only son to the trauma of surgery when there was such a slim chance of help?

'You must make up your mind quickly,' the doctor pressed her, 'because we can't go ahead with the operation without your consent.'

Unable to bring herself to sign the consent form, Mrs Lin went home and gave my wife a call, explaining the situation to her and asking my wife if she thought the boy should have the operation or not. My wife didn't know what to say. What if she advised her to go through with the operation and the boy suffered post-operative complications or worse? On the other hand, what if the tumour kept growing?

Finally my wife said to the distraught mother, 'Oh, sister, let's ask the Lord! Many people in the Bible asked the Lord, and he gave them answers. Prayer is asking. Ask the Lord, and he will surely give you an answer.'

'How shall I ask the Lord?' the mother asked uncertainly.

'Since this is a special need, you have to use special prayer,' my wife told her, 'which means prayer with fasting.'

The woman did fast and pray. God answered with a Bible verse: 'I am the Lord that heals you' (Ex. 15:26). She felt clearly that God himself was speaking to her through this verse. Immediately she called up my wife to thank her for her prayers and advice and to tell her what she had decided. That same day she checked her son out of the hospital.

Of course, in most people's eyes, Mrs Lin's behaviour was foolish, endangering her son's life. In fact, as she was leaving the hospital with the little boy, the chief doctor stopped her and said, 'I've never seen a parent's heart as hard as yours. Even though the operation has only a 50 per cent chance of success, why aren't you going for it. If you deny your child this chance, he won't even have one per cent of hope. Are you just going to leave and give up?'

Mrs Lin's heart was not hard at all. Instead it was full of hope and trust in a God who, because of his omnipotence, had a 100 per cent chance of success.

The very next day this dear trusting mother found that her boy could see from both eyes. After two days the fever was gone. And when they went back to the hospital for a check-up sometime later, a new X-ray showed the tumour completely gone.

God's miracle in me brings a surprising visitor

One day as we were eating supper, an unexpected visitor was ushered into our small dining room. As neither he nor the person standing behind him said anything, I stood up and asked what business brought them to our home.

The man before me grinned, then leaned over and whispered in my ear, 'I am Chang Hsuch-liang'. This was the young marshall who captured President Chiang Kai-shek in the famous 1935 Xi'an Incident.'

I couldn't believe my ears. This was the much renowned Marshall Chang of the Northeast – coming to *our* house! 'Marshall Chang,' I said, 'we didn't expect your presence in our home. What can I do for you?'

'I have just come to your house to visit,' he replied.

I took the gentleman to our second-floor living room and poured him a cup of tea. I saw that the person who was with him still followed him. Again I asked, 'Marshall Chang, since you have come to our home, do you have something to tell us?'

'Not really,' he replied. 'It's just that I heard many people talk about you.'

'About me? What did they say?'

'I heard people say that you once had cancer, and when the doctor opened you up, he found that the cancer was too advanced to operate further; so he sewed you back up. But because you trusted God for his healing, your disease was cured. This is what other people have told me; so today I wanted to come see for myself.'

For this man the testimony of God's healing of my cancer spoke loudly of God's power.

While Marshall Chang was already a believer, signs and wonders have also been known to shake up the deep-rooted indifference of some intellectuals to the point of bringing them to faith in Jesus Christ. Just as 2 Corinthians 10:3–5 says, 'For though we walk in the flesh, we do not war according to the flesh, for the weapons of our warfare are not of the flesh, but divinely powerful for the destruction of fortresses. We are destroying speculations and every lofty thing raised up against the knowledge of God, and we are taking every thought captive to the obedience of Christ.'

Having been God's servant for so many years, I am deeply convinced that delivering unbelievers from the power of Satan is something we can't accomplish by our own fleshly effort; we need to pray seriously for the power of God to be at work before we attempt evangelism. As God is merciful and since the gap between unbelief and belief is so great, he often sends signs and wonders to manifest his glory, giving credence to the word we preach and tearing down walls of resistance in people's hearts.

Healing of a wound

One day a military man asked me to visit a good friend of his who was suffering from skin cancer, because he had no time to go. 'When you see my friend, just tell him that I asked you to see him,' the man instructed.

Judging it to be a good opportunity for evangelism, I was glad to go. When I walked into the sick man's hospital room, I introduced myself and told the patient that his friend had asked me to visit with him and that I was a minister and wanted to talk with him about the Lord.

Immediately he cut me off, saying, 'If you want to talk about the gospel with me, please don't even open your mouth.'

Seeing his hostility to the word, I changed my style and talked with him about life, about the ultimate limits of the universe, and the end of the journey of life.

'You don't have to talk with me about all this,' he said. 'A military man like me takes death like going home.'

Though I was tempted to continue talking, he threatened to call the nurse and charge me with disrupting the peace of the ward and have me thrown out. Not wanting him to think that pastors were inconsiderate, I closed our conversation and turned to go away. The bed opposite him also held a patient, and I addressed him. 'Sir,' I said, 'he doesn't want to hear the gospel. What about you?'

When he nodded to me and said, 'I want it! I want it!' I shared with him some simple truths about Christianity, leaving him with this verse: 'With man it is impossible, but with God all things are possible.'

'What's more,' I said, 'all things are possible for those who believe.' Then I asked him, 'Do you believe these words?'

To my surprise, he said, 'I believe! I believe! Please pray for me!'

I then prayed for him, and after that I said farewell and went away. I did not ask his name.

A few months later I received a telephone call from someone within the National Defence Ministry. Said the caller, 'My surname is Hsu. I hate to bother you, but I have to call. If you have time now, would you please come to my office? I want to tell you my experience after you preached to me a few months ago.'

Of course I would go. Ministers are like doctors – if the patient wants you to go, you must go. Hence I went to his office.

At the door stood a military officer, not tall, but of high rank. He came forward to shake hands with me and invited me into his office to sit down. 'I'm not sure you remember me,' he said, 'but a few months ago you went to the hospital to visit a patient with skin cancer. When you tried to preach to him, he asked you not to open your mouth. When you tried to talk to him about life, he said that he looked upon death like going home. Do you remember?'

'Of course, I remember. Ministers who preach often meet with refusal.'

'Later you turned and began talking to the patient on the other bed. "This man doesn't want to hear the gospel," you said. "What about you?" And that patient said, "I want it! I want it!" Do you remember?'

'I remember this too.'

'Do you know who that person is?'

'I don't know,' I said.

'That person was me!' he said and went on to introduce himself as Hsu Lang-hsien, the head of his department. 'My condition was not originally serious,' he told me. 'I had an appendectomy, but after the operation the wound would not heal . . . When you came to see me, I had already been in the hospital for months . . . So I was very downhearted. I didn't expect your visit at that time, and you said something like this, "With man it is impossible, but all things are possible for those who believe." Then when you asked me, "Do you believe these words?" I said I believed. Then you prayed for me and left. I immediately called my subordinates to check me out of the hospital because I wanted to go to America to do inspections. I just wrapped my stomach tightly and left Taiwan for America.

'After I had arrived in America, our military hospital sent an official letter, together with my case history, to the American authority, hoping that during my stay in America I could be cured in the American hospitals. After the American military people received the official letter, they requested me to go to their hospital for a check-up.

'At this point I wasn't sure what to do,' he said. 'If I went for the check-up, would that not be putting down the Chinese military in the eyes of the Americans? . . . Yet if I didn't go for the check-up, I would lose the opportunity to get further help. While I was struggling between these two options, I suddenly thought of your words, "With man it's impossible, but all things are possible for those who believe." With these words as encouragement, I decided not to go. I made the decision because I believed. If I hadn't believed, I wouldn't have gotten out of bed to go ten thousand miles to America.

'Later,' he said, smiling, 'when I unwrapped the bandages around my midsection, I discovered that my wound had healed completely. The reason I asked you to come today is to tell you my testimony.'

Eventually the man wrote a small pamphlet telling of God's miracle in his body.

On whom does God perform signs and wonders? On those who believe. Our faith is like a key, capable of opening the treasure in Heaven and taking out what we need. Faith is precious, a blessing God mercifully bestows upon us.

Healing of my daughter's rheumatoid arthritis

When my second daughter Sharon was studying in Jinling Girls' High School, she was frequently ill and missed quite a lot of school. A doctor's examination found that her tonsils were quite swollen. As these glands are part of our body's defence system, when they aren't functioning well, viruses can attack easily. The doctor recommended the tonsils be removed.

For several months after the operation Sharon had no flu. But, in the midst of our relief, she came back from school one day complaining, 'Mom, I can't bend my legs.'

'Let's have a look,' we told her. As she lifted her skirt, we could see that one of her knees was very swollen. 'Did you fall doing exercises?' we asked. 'Or did you bump your knee on something?'

She said she hadn't. Since we had no idea why her knee was so swollen and stiff, we took her to see an orthopaedist at Taiwan University Hospital, and there we were told that her problem was arthritis. The orthopaedist inserted a needle to extract the fluid, and the swelling gradually disappeared. But the prognosis was not encouraging, though medicine and therapy would help.

Not long after our visit to the doctor, the knee joint in Sharon's other leg also became swollen, also the joints in her hands. Pain became constant, increasing dramatically with each change of weather. Over time our daughter's health grew worse, and her spirits sank. Rheumatoid arthritis specialists could do nothing for her. Our hearts broke to see her go down physically and become more and more dejected.

One day when the Taiwanese speaking section of our church was holding an evangelistic meeting, I shared the gospel of Jesus Christ, asking at the end that all those who had decided to believe in Jesus to raise their left hands. The first person to raise a hand was my daughter. *Why is she raising her hand now?* I wondered. *When she was nine years old, she very clearly came to know the Lord.* But then I realised that raising her hand one more time could not hurt as it could only strengthen her faith. When I invited all those who had raised their hands to come to the front, Sharon came, asking me to pray for her healing.

In agony of heart for my suffering daughter, I said to her, 'Your earthly father can do nothing, but your heavenly Father is full of power. We earthly fathers can do so little. We will ask our heavenly Father to have mercy on us.' I told her to kneel down, and then I asked everybody else to stand. I prayed against my daughter's rheumatism in the name of Jesus, pleading for God's mercy and for the Lord to manifest his glory by delivering my girl from this disease. I prayed loudly, asking the Lord's strength to work in her so that the rheumatism would disappear from her body.

After my prayer my daughter stood up from the floor. In that instant, the rheumatism completely left her. Now she is the mother of two children, and she has been well for decades. We will never cease praising God for the miracle he performed in our own family.

Healing of a spiritually lame husband

One morning while my family was having its devotions, a sister came to our home. Even before she reached the door we heard her crying. 'Brother Wu, you must help me!' she kept saying.

When she had calmed down, she told us that her husband had treated her poorly for years, and now she wanted a divorce.

I was surprised that she would come to a pastor for help with dissolving her marriage. But I managed to ask, 'Why do you need to divorce your husband?' She was not young, somewhere around sixty, with grown children and grandchildren. Obviously this marriage had already lasted a few decades. 'You are not some young couple, but a couple with many years behind you. Surely you can think of a better alternative,' I said.

'I'm seeking a divorce because I'm beyond my endurance,' she responded. 'My husband has built a magnificent house for his mistress, and I can't take his infidelity any more. I have no alternative but to ask you to help me with a divorce.'

'You have endured so many years,' I said. 'You don't have many more years to endure.'

'I've endured for thirty-eight years, and I have no more endurance left,' she insisted.

Thirty-eight years? My wife had just been reading John 5 where Jesus told a person who had been lame for thirty-eight years to stand up and walk. When this sister mentioned thirty-eight years, my wife's eyes brightened. 'Thirty-eight years!' my wife said. 'I've just been reading about how a person who had been lame for thirty-eight years could stand up and walk. If Jesus could cause a person who had been lame for thirty-eight years to stand up and walk, surely he can cause a person who has been heartless for thirty-eight years to repent.'

God's word was revealed to me through the words of my wife, and my faith soared. 'What my wife said is correct,' I said. 'A person who had been lame for thirty-eight years was able to be cured, and your husband, who has been in sin for thirty-eight years, can in the same way receive healing and forgiveness. Please give me your husband's phone number – I want to call him now and try to see him.'

I called immediately and introduced myself.

'What's the matter?' he asked.

I told him I wanted to have lunch with him. As his heart understood the reason for my invitation, he said nothing for quite a long time.

'Let's do it this way,' I said. 'Let's just meet at the First Restaurant, right opposite the church, and I'll treat you to a simple buffet lunch.'

As usually it is the brothers and sisters who invite the minister out for meals, he must have felt a little surprised, because he answered, 'I'm embarrassed that you should invite me. Let me invite you instead.'

'Let's forget about who invites whom,' I countered. 'Let's meet at twelve o'clock.' He agreed and hung up.

After I got off the phone I advised his wife to go home, and I would let her know how things went. I prayed with her before she left.

That day at noon the woman's husband was waiting for me at the First Restaurant. Rising to shake hands with me he said, 'My old wife went to look for you, didn't she?' As he talked, his lower chin quivered, and his hands were cold from nervousness.

'Let's sit down!' I said. We went first to get our food, and after saying grace, we started to eat. 'Since you know that your wife came to speak to me,' I said, 'what do you have to say concerning this matter?'

'Today before God and his servant, what can I say? I deserve to die. I shouldn't have done what I did. I am blessed with many children and grandchildren, and I have made them all unhappy by living a life which displeases God. Before we met today I had already made up my mind to live a new life and to free myself from my past affairs.'

'How then are you going to free yourself?' I asked him.

'Oh, Brother Wu, you should know that it is actually very easy to get rid of this kind of woman, because all she really wants is money. Today I'll write her a cheque and get rid of her.'

'Is it that simple?' I asked.

'In this relationship there is little place for affection. The main thing is money. Yes, money can dissolve this kind of an affair.'

'Okay, then, when are you going to do it?'

'This very afternoon. . . I feel that I have no choice but to finish this affair.'

After we finished eating, he asked me if I would go home with him after he ended things with his mistress. I told him I would be happy to, and we arranged for him to come to my home when he was finished.

Sometime after five o'clock the man came to my house.

'How did it go?' I asked. 'Have you finished your affairs?'

'It's all finished. Now may I ask you to escort me home?'

When we arrived at his house, I said to his wife, 'Today I give a person who was lame for thirty-eight years back to you whole.'

The Lord was glorified in this healing every bit as much as with a physical healing.

Driving out a one-eyed demon

One night a Mr Yang, who worked for a large construction company, stayed out late playing mahjongg. On a street corner on his way home he suddenly felt oppressed, and as he turned his head, he saw a person with one eye laughing at him, not a friendly laugh, but one that was horrible and fierce. Mr Yang was so scared that he took off like a shot. But the one-eyed man chased him all the way home. Mr Yang dashed inside his front door and slammed it shut. Though his wife came downstairs, ready to scold him for waking her, when she saw her husband, she knew he had had a bad fright.

Speechless, Mr Yang kept pointing behind him. But when his wife opened the door, she couldn't see a thing. Thinking that perhaps the one-eyed man had gone away, Mr Yang turned his head to see. No, he was still there.

Was this experience some kind of hallucination? Or was the one-eyed man really there? I don't know. In any case, when the construction worker went up to his room, the pursuer followed, sitting by the bed, and would not go.

That night Mr Yang developed such a high fever that his family sent him to the hospital. A blood test revealed no increase in his white blood cells. Other tests proved just as useless in diagnosing the cause of the fever. Yet all this time the patient felt horrible, and his whole face turned black.

Mr Yang's neighbour, a Mr Chen Han-ching, had a wife who attended our church, and she suspected that Mr Yang's problems could be the work of evil spirits. At that time Mr Chen had not yet believed in Jesus, and like many people in a technologically advanced society, he dismissed the idea of evil spirits as ridiculous. Still, he challenged his wife: 'Is it not true that Elder Wu Yung of your church has driven out demons? If you think our neighbour is possessed by demons, then ask Elder Wu to go see him. Then I'll know whether your Jesus Christ is alive and true or not.'

So Mrs Chen came to the church to tell me this news. As Mr Yang was then at the Adventist hospital in Chunglun, I said I would go to the hospital to see him.

On the day of my visit I asked Mrs Yang to wait outside with my wife, as I needed to talk privately with her troubled husband.

'Where do we find flies?' I asked the patient.

'Where there is garbage,' he responded.

'Where do we find mosquitoes?'

'Where there is dirty, stagnant water.'

'And where do we find demons?'

He said he didn't know; so I tried again. 'If you want to get rid of flies, what do you do?'

'Tidy up the garbage,' he answered.

'What is the best way to get rid of mosquitoes?'

'To clean out the dirty water.'

'Your answers are correct. Now as to where we can find demons, I will tell you: where there is sin. Because sin is filthy and demons are by nature filthy, sin provides opportunities for demons to come. What method can you think of to drive away this demon?'

'According to you – to drive away this demon, I need to get rid of my sins.'

'That's exactly right, Mr Yang. Do you have sins?'

'How can a man be without sins?' he said after a long pause. 'From childhood to adulthood, a person more or less must have had some sins.'

'Now if you want to drive away this demon,' I told him, 'the only way is to confess your sins. Only then can you make evil spirits absolutely powerless in your body.'

'Where do I start in confessing my sins?' he complained. 'From my youth until now I can't begin to know how many times I said things which I shouldn't have said, how many times I did things which I shouldn't have done, how many times I thought things that I shouldn't have thought, how many times I took what I shouldn't have taken, and how many times I went where I shouldn't have gone.'

'Let's do it this way,' I suggested. 'I'll mention a sin, and if you have committed it, you raise your hand and say, 'O Jesus, please use your precious blood to cleanse my sins!' If you have not committed this sin, you don't have to raise your hand or say anything.'

He agreed, and I began.

'Have you ever lied?' I asked. He raised his hand very co-operatively and said, 'Jesus' blood, cleanse my sins!'

'Have you ever stolen?' He raised his hand again and repeated his plea for cleansing.

I read one sin after another, and he confessed one sin after another. What he had committed he confessed to; what he had not committed, he did not confess. I cannot remember, but I must have faced him with a few dozen sins. Eventually he fell asleep, and after praying for him, I came out and let his wife go back in.

The next morning at about five o'clock, I suddenly heard someone knocking at the iron gate of the church property. Already awake, I called out, 'Who is it downstairs?'

'It is me!' came the answer.

'Who are you?' I asked.

'My surname is Yang.'

'There are many people in our church whose surname is Yang,' I said, just a bit impatient. 'Which one are you?'

'I am Mr Yang from the Adventist Hospital!'

Upon hearing his answer, I couldn't help but be a little nervous. Had the demon followed him to my house? So I asked him, 'What brings you here this early?'

'Ah, Mr Wu,' he said, smiling, 'yesterday after I confessed my sins, I fell asleep. When I woke up, that demon was no longer with me. Today I am going to leave the hospital, but before I check out, I want to thank God with you.'

Mr Yang became a fully healthy man. Today both he and his wife are godly Christians and faithful members of our church, serving the Lord with us.

Healing of a former college president

One day I visited a patient at Taiwan University Hospital whose name was Tsang Chi-fang – once the president of Northeast University and at that time the director of the Economics

Department of Tunghai University. He had come to Taiwan from China and was now over seventy years old.

In my years of ministry I've found that older people often appreciate a light-hearted approach, perhaps because age brings its own worries and troubles. At any rate, I took that approach with Mr Tsang. I told him that before I preach to people I needed an understanding of their educational level. 'If you are highly educated,' I told him with a half smile, 'I will give my advanced preaching; if your level is lower, my preaching will be simpler.'

'You make a lot of sense,' he said, 'but how do you know whether my level is high or low?'

'Simple. I only have to ask you a few questions to know whether you are high or low.'

'Are you going to test me?' he asked, obviously playing along with me.

'Yes, I am,' I told him. 'I hope you will condescend to allow a kid like me to test a senior citizen like you.'

'Go ahead!' he said.

'Listen carefully,' I instructed. 'The first question is, hydrogen plus oxygen equals what?'

He grinned and said, 'Water.'

'You've answered this first question correctly. Now I want to test your mathematics. Two plus two equals what?'

'Two plus two equals four.'

'Good!' I said 'You understand both science and mathematics; therefore we don't have to talk about science and mathematics. We won't talk about what you already understand. I will ask you the third question: The salvation of Jesus Christ on the cross plus our faith equals what?'

'What?' he blurted.

'Oh? That shows that you don't understand. So I need to explain. I know you understand science and mathematics, but not theology. So let's talk theology! The salvation of Jesus Christ on the cross plus our faith equals being saved.'

'Can it be that simple?' he asked.

'Just that simple. Because God gives grace, and we have faith, God's grace plus our faith in Christ equals salvation.

Ephesians 2 in the Bible explains it very clearly.'

'Since it's that simple, I therefore believe,' he said without hesitation.

'Do you truly believe?' I had some suspicion.

'Of course I truly believe. Tomorrow I will go through with all the procedures.'

'What procedures do you have in mind?' I asked, puzzled.

'Did you not say that one who believes in Jesus must also receive baptism?'

'Yes.'

'Then I will be baptised tomorrow.'

Afterward the nurse took me aside and talked with me. 'Mr Wu, I know you, and I have been to your church,' she said. 'That gentleman just now said that he wanted to receive baptism. Perhaps you are not fully aware of his condition.'

'I'm not,' I said. 'But when I was young, my parents said that if a man has swollen feet, his illness is serious; if a woman has a swollen face, her condition is serious. I can see that this old man not only has swollen feet but a swollen face, so I suppose his condition is very serious.'

'You need to know that his condition is very serious indeed. His heart has already been greatly damaged. The doctor in charge has repeatedly cautioned us to be careful even when we change his clothing, doing it slowly so as not to get him tense or excited, so that his heart will not be affected. I know that your church practices baptism by immersion, but he is so sick – if you put him in the water, and his heart fails and you cannot bring him up, what will you do?'

I thought her warning very reasonable. If this man, who was considered a VIP, should die in the baptistery and the newspaper reported it the next day, my own reputation would be of little consequence, but the church's loss would be tremendous. So I thanked her very much and, upon hearing Mr Tsang call for me, went back inside.

'So let's plan on eight o'clock tomorrow morning,' he said. 'My children will help me get there. You prepare the water, and then let's do it. The sooner it is done the quicker the matter of faith is settled.' When I saw that he was so firm, how could I refuse? I was caught between a rock and a hard place. But things had developed so far that I gave him my consent.

The next morning, as Mr Tsang predicted, his children brought him by car to our church, and we used a rattan chair to carry him from the car into the church and then to the baptistery. My colleague and I held him while his children took the rattan chair away; then we prepared to baptise him. To be frank, I was very nervous, especially after the nurse's warning. I first prayed a long prayer, entrusting this matter to the hands of the Lord, for he would have to bear all responsibility. Then my colleague and I helped the patient stand in the water.

'Tsang Chi-fang,' I asked, 'do you believe Jesus is the Son of God?'

'Yes!' he answered.

'Do you believe that he died for your sins on the cross and that he rose again on the third day?'

'I do.'

'Since you believe, I baptise you in the name of Jesus Christ,' I said, and my colleague and I immersed him in the water and very quickly pulled him up. I saw that he was smiling, which meant he was all right. Only then was I relieved. My colleague immediately dried off his face. Though his children offered to carry him, he refused their offer and walked all by himself out of the pool. Afterward he returned toTunghai University, where he continued to teach for a number of years.

What a beautiful thing God did! He not only gave Tsang Chi-fang his precious salvation, but also physical healing, neither of which could be done by us. How touching also is this grace to us, that he should use us in what he is doing!

25

The Power of God

As God's power working in us magnifies God's glory, I want to share something more of how wonderfully he has worked in people's lives over the years of ministry the Lord has given my wife and me.

A close brush with death

On my way out to do visitation one day I saw a youth standing by the wall at the gate of the church. He was smoking. He inhaled deeply and exhaled slowly. By his manner I knew he had troubles. Leaving my car, I approached him and asked, 'Sir, is something wrong? Can I be of help?'

The stranger turned his head away. Taking hold of his shoulders, I said, 'Tell me! I might be able to help.' The youth almost cried. Grabbing his hand, I said, 'Please come inside. I'll make you a cup of coffee, and you can share what's on your heart.'

Together we went inside. Eventually, with his head bowed, he said, 'I just came out of jail.'

'Out of jail!' I exclaimed. 'You should be happy. You are now free to start your life anew!'

'I have no place to go,' my young guest said.

'What about relatives?' I asked.

'I have some.'

'And friends?'

'I have them too.'

'Then why don't you go find them?' I pursued.

'Friends dare not take me in, and relatives dare not keep me. I don't know where to turn. Today I sat at the church door and thought about many things.'

He must be a very serious criminal not to be accepted by friends or relatives, I thought. Seeing my worried look, the youth took out a piece of paper. It was his prison-release document. It indicated that he had been in prison for more than two years.

'What crime did you commit?' I asked him.

He pointed to his forehead. Only then did I understand that he had been a political prisoner – what we Chinese call a 'thought prisoner' – a victim of Taiwan's severe treatment of dissidents under martial law. No wonder he felt so alone! Most people would not come near those suspected of political crimes, for fear of being themselves dragged into trouble.

Judging that because this youth was imprisoned only two years, his crime couldn't have been all that severe, I talked gently with him and assured him that he could stay with us until he found another place. He thanked me over and over.

'You don't have to thank me,' I said. 'After all, we all have times of difficulty.' I thought of the time I was in prison for expressing dissent.

One day, after the lad had been living with us some time, he didn't show up for breakfast. I asked my wife whether he had said he had somewhere to go. She said no. When the young man was still absent at lunchtime, I became anxious.

Then in the afternoon I received an express letter from our missing guest. It said: 'Mr and Mrs Wu, I will never forget your gracious love to me. But a healthy young man like me should not burden you. However, I have no other place to go. When you see my letter, I will no longer be in this world. . .'

When I read to this point, I wondered if the lad had found out about some of our financial difficulties. Had he overheard some of our conversations about the straitness of our circumstances? Was that why he felt he couldn't add to our burden? Though I couldn't remember any such conversation, for some reason he was obviously planning suicide. How could I stop him? How would I even find him in a city the size of Taipei?

I turned to my wife and said, 'I see only one thing we can do. We'll call a few of our church staff to meet at the church to pray for this young man. In the days of King Hezekiah, when the Assyrian king came to attack Jerusalem, he sent Hezekiah a letter demanding surrender, and the besieged king took the letter and spread it before the Lord. Now we must do the same. Only God can stop our young friend from taking his own life.'

So we as a staff spread the young man's letter before the Lord and prayed fervently that God would save this youth and turn him from the road of death. After we prayed we felt a deep peace.

That night about 1 a.m. someone called my name from downstairs, waking me up. Looking down from the window, I could see a policeman with another man by his side. Because the light was dim, I could not see who the second man was. The policeman said, 'I am looking for Mr Wu.'

'I am he,' I said.

'Would you please come down? We have something to talk to you about.'

I went down and found that the man standing beside the policeman was the young man who had wanted to commit suicide. As the lad had been a political prisoner, I was a little nervous now that the policeman was confronting me.

'Do you know this man?' the policeman asked.

As the Bible teaches that yes is yes and no is no, I could not deny him just because he had been in prison for his political views. So I replied, 'Yes, I know him.'

'Since you know him, can you take responsibility for him?' he asked me.

'What do you mean?' I asked.

'If you take responsibility for him, I can leave him in your care. If you don't, I'll have to take him away. This young man tried to jump off Green Lake Bridge today, but one of our police found him in time and stopped him. So I brought him to you. If you can take him off our hands, we will have one less case to worry about.'

'Thank you, sir. Just leave him with me,' I said, relieved.

So we counselled the young man, encouraged him, comforted him, and taught him God's word. We hoped desperately that he would believe in Jesus, for we knew that in Jesus he could exchange hope for disappointment and comfort for his distress. And when he did accept the Lord, he did indeed find comfort and security and no longer sought death.

How wonderfully God answered our prayers in this young man's life! We prayed in the afternoon, and God saved him that afternoon. And by our giving shelter to a stranger and praying for him, we saw God bring the dead back to life. That young man later graduated from the Baptist Theological Seminary and eventually became the chairman of the Baptist Church Union. He has remained a servant of the Lord to this day.

Confession brings health

Sometimes the line between belief and a changed life is not a straight one. A colleague in the Railway Department that I led to faith in Jesus, for instance, seemed to grow thinner and paler after he believed. When others in our office noticed, I had no comeback for them; I had noticed too.

One day, however, after a very long time, this man suddenly turned up at our communion service. He had completely changed; his face was radiant and healthy. 'After I believed in the Lord,' he explained publicly, 'my heart had a continual struggle. I knew that to believe in the Lord means to forsake sin, to be separated from the world. Repentance should accompany belief in Christ – not only confession of sin, but also abstinence from sin. That is true repentance. But as much as I struggled with my sins, I could not overcome them. The problem was that my certificate of qualification for my work in the Railway Administration was false. This was not only dishonest, it was illegal. I worried that if I dealt with this sin, I would lose my job. But because I didn't deal with it, my heart continued to struggle.

'One day, though,' he went on, 'the Lord won out. I boldly

went to the personnel director of the Railway Department to tell him about the false certificate. Unexpectedly he responded with a smile. 'You are not the only person with this problem,' he said. 'Since you are bold enough to confess, I'll keep this a secret. Just write a letter of resignation, and I'll settle the matter.' On the day I wrote the letter of resignation, sin left me.'

The man did lose his job that day. But he was full of joy – he had obeyed the Lord.

That same night, after he gave his testimony, a factory owner hired him to be his accountant. So he was not without a job even a day. How gracious God was to him!

A robber turned preacher

One day Chen Hsiu-ling, a university student, brought to see me a man she had won to Christ through correspondence when he was in prison. Later the man, Lu Tai-hao, was to write a book called *Put Your Sword Back Into Its Sheath*. The book is aptly named. Lu would in the months ahead give me much joy and a lot of trouble.

Before Lu was imprisoned, he was an awful character. Once when he went to eat at a seafood restaurant, the waiter started to take his order, but abandoned him to greet and wait on a foreigner first. Angry at being slighted, he summoned the waiter, then hoisted a chair and split the man's head open with it.

As a youth he had been a poor student and was often expelled, even from a military academy. Practically no school would take him. Without sufficient education, he lived a parasitic life in the Taipei area, earning a living by collecting gambling debts for underground gambling establishments. His occupation earned him both a lot of money and a bad reputation. When he went to homes to collect debts, he always used violence. Eventually he was convicted and imprisoned, then escaped. When recaptured, he was sentenced to over ten years behind bars.

It was then that Chen Hsiu-ling took pity on him and set herself to witness to him while he was in prison. After she had written him over two hundred letters, Lu's heart was touched, and in 1982 he received Jesus Christ. From that time on Lu began to change. His deeds showed that he had really repented. Not long afterwards he was let out on parole.

Though Lu really wanted to study in a seminary, he had to earn a living. By buying a book and studying for a pre-employment exam, he got a job at the Prince Electronic Company as business administrator, even though he had only a high school education.

When Hsiu-ling (she was then a member of the Nanking East Road Church) brought him to see me, he said that he did not want to be a long-term worker in the world, but wished to do the Lord's work. As I listened to him talk, I could really see that God had worked in him. I suggested he come to the Discipleship Training Centre which I was in the process of establishing, and he agreed to come.

After I found a suitable building in Yungho for the new training centre, I recruited Lu and Hsiu-ling to help clean it up. As we were crossing Fuho Bridge by car on the way to Yungho, a motorcyclist raced past us and, narrowly avoiding running into us, fell off his motorcycle. Stopping my car and getting out to help him to his feet, I said to him, 'I'm very sorry. Though I didn't hit you, our near accident scared you.'

I drove away, not knowing that this man was following me all the way to the front door of the Yungho Church. Parking his motorcycle, he came up to me with both hands propped at his waist and asked for compensation. Seeing that I was being insulted, Lu Tai-hao became furious. When he could stand it no longer, he jumped out of the car and hit the motorcyclist so violently that the man fell to the ground bleeding and unconscious.

I was terribly alarmed since Lu was on parole. If he were convicted of another crime, he would be sent back to prison. I told him to leave quickly and that I would take responsibility. Lu got into a taxi and was gone when the man regained consciousness. But by this time a crowd had gathered, including members from the church who heard the commotion. Brother Chi Nan-chih of the church asked me what was the matter.

'Don't ask!' I said. 'Take him to the hospital. We'll talk later.'

It took several stitches to close the motorcyclist's chin. Because Lu was strong and knew karate, his few hits had done a good bit of damage. When the doctor was finished, the young man insisted on going to the police station. Grabbing my tie, he dragged me with him.

After I related to the policeman the sequence of events, he told me that since I had not hit the man, if I could find the man who did, no trouble would come to me. After taking our identity cards, the policeman released both me and the motorcyclist.

Can I bring Lu Tai-hao to them? I wondered. If I gave them Lu, wouldn't that be sending him back to prison? I knew that he was a repentant prodigal son and that Satan was trying to prevent him from serving the Lord. Thus, after much consideration, I decided only to pray for him, not to look for him. However, the police had me report to them every day. After five or six days I became impatient with the time this daily ritual was stealing from my ministry and prayed for God's solution.

That day Lu came. He was straightforward with me. 'Since I caused this problem,' he said, 'I should take the responsibility and not burden you, Elder Wu. Take me to the police station; if I have to go to prison, then I will go to prison.'

I thought for a moment, then said, 'Well, if you want to go to the police station with me, there is one condition: if that man wants to hit you, you let him hit you; if he wants to kick you, you let him kick you.' He agreed, and we went to the police station together. I had him wait outside while I went in first to see the motorcyclist, who had been advised of our coming, and the policeman.

Amazingly, when I went in that day, the injured man said to me, 'Mr Wu, I can tell that you are an honest man. Originally I wanted to blackmail you, but my conscience has been uneasy. So I want to make a compromise with you: if you give me just a small sum of money for my medical bills, I'll drop my complaint. Then you will be free.'

Overjoyed, I thanked him profusely and quickly settled with him. Once he had written me a receipt for the money, I said to the man, 'I brought Lu Tai-hao to apologise to you.'

Lu stepped up to the bandaged man and said to him, 'Sir, I was very rude to hit you. Now if you wish, you can hit me back!' Having said that, he closed his eyes, waiting to be hit.

'No need!' said the injured man. 'Just take the incident as my bad luck!'

How we thanked God for a peaceful end to what seemed to be an unending and potentially serious problem!

Eventually Lu came to study at the Discipleship Training Centre. Sometimes he was still like a leopard who could not change his spots. He would pound the table and threaten people who disagreed with him. 'I'll fix you!' he would say. Other students feared him.

One day he came to me very agitated, telling me that Taipei gangsters wanted him to go to Taichung to resolve a problem between two gangs. It put him in a very difficult position. After pondering the pros and cons for a while, he consulted me.

'You can't go because now you belong to God and have to do his work,' I advised.

'I know. But if I don't go, they would take me as disloyal. This time I am not going to fight, but will try to bring the two parties to a peaceful resolution.'

Because he would offend both parties if he didn't go, in the end I had to let him go, as I could see no other way. But I was afraid that he would again run into difficulties and lose his temper. 'Please be gentle!' I told him.

When Lu had first come to the Discipleship Training Centre, most of the brothers of the church were not happy to have him because they found his spiritual life shallow and his behaviour unstable. They were afraid he would hurt the church's reputation. But since I had accepted him for training, I had to take the responsibility for him. After he left that day on his mission, I prayed for him earnestly.

Obeying my advice, Lu was gentle and humble in working to bring the two sides together. Without weapons, he was able to bring an end to the conflict between rival gangs.

Understandably trying to find a church for Lu's pastoral

internship was a problem. Normally he would have returned to Linsen South Road Church, but the congregation there did not invite him because they felt hesitant about him. What should we do?

I went to Jonathan Chiu of the Campus Crusade to see if the ministry he was involved with was willing to accept a questionable intern. After I introduced Lu Tai-hao to the group, the leader thought it over for a while, then consented to accept the former prison inmate. Thus Lu joined the ministry of the Tabernacle Church at Chungshan North Road, where his service reaped much fruit. Not only did the people in that church come to like him very much, many were helped by his testimony.

Lu wanted very much to witness to his father, who was a military man. However, the generation gap between them was very wide. After a time his father tried to avoid him, even going so far as to eat his meals in his bedroom.

One day while his father was watching television in the parlour, Lu, after fervent prayer, mustered his courage and strode in and turned off the television. With tears in his eyes, he pleaded with his father. 'Dad,' he said, 'I can give you many things, but one thing I can't give, and it concerns the issue of life and death. As your son, how can I not care about your eternal salvation? What's more, the difference between salvation and perdition can be made in a moment.'

The father was stunned. Although what Lu did seemed rude, the two words 'salvation' and 'perdition' penetrated his father's heart, and some time later the senior Mr Lu attended a service at Linsen South Road Church and received Jesus as his Saviour.

When Lu Tai-hao and Chen Hsiu-ling began thinking of marriage, they asked me to approach Hsiu-ling's family for them. Being matchmaker in the circumstances was difficult because the Chen family knew that Lu had been a ruffian. To ask them to let their daughter Hsiu-ling, who was a graduate of the law school of Chung Hsing University, marry a vagabond who had only a high school education and a criminal record was a bit of a stretch. Though somewhat fearful of failing, I accepted the task because the couple had been dating a long time and were deeply in love, and I felt spiritually responsible for Lu.

When, after prayer, I went to the Chen home to approach the father about the marriage, he caught me off guard with an unexpected question: 'Mr Wu, if my daughter were your daughter, what would you think of this proposed marriage?'

I could not answer at first. When I had thought a bit, I said, 'Lu Tai-hao is someone whom God has completely changed into a new person. He truly belongs to the Lord. In the future he will be the Lord's servant.' Then I listed some of the evidences of Lu's change of heart. I suggested that since these two young people were deeply in love, we elders could only agree to their marriage.

'Mr Wu,' Hsiu-ling's father said deliberately, 'I can consent to this marriage because I trust you.'

After the wedding in Nanking East Road Church was over, the newlyweds came upstairs and placed two cushions on the floor in front of me. 'What are you doing?' I asked them.

They said, 'Today we come to thank you for your kindness to us.' They obviously wished to kneel to thank me.

I stopped them. 'You know,' I told them, 'after Paul performed miracles, the people presented him with wreaths of flowers, and he was afraid to accept their praise because only God deserves our praise.'

After graduating from the Discipleship Training Centre, Lu, like the blind man in the Bible, went back to his own village and relatives to witness to what a mighty work God had done in him. I said to him before he left, 'You will work in Wuku.'

'How can I work in Wuku?' he asked. 'In the past the villagers let off firecrackers to celebrate my capture because I would stop at nothing in terrorising people. Now you ask me to go evangelise those villages. Who's going to listen to me?'

'You show them what the new Lu Tai-hao is like,' I encouraged.

Lu ultimately agreed and went to Wuku to do pioneer Christian work, renting a small shop and equipping it with forty seats to serve as his evangelistic centre.

But before he could win the people's hearts, Lu felt he had to visit a lady who would surely be holding the deepest hatred toward him because he had led her children astray at a young age. Sure enough, as soon as the lady saw him, she fumed in anger and threw a broom at him. He had to leave without giving her the gifts he had brought or uttering a word. The next day, because he heard that she had heart problems, the result of stress over her sons' problems, Lu took a cardiologist with him to visit her. This time she received her guests, and eventually Lu regained her friendship.

God greatly blessed Lu, and the work began to grow. The little shop-front chapel was soon too cramped, and the group moved to a new, larger site. That too was packed with people. After the Wuku church had grown so large that the congregation was able to buy its own building, Lu left the work and let a classmate continue it.

Lu moved to a busy and flourishing Chunghsiao East Road in eastern Taipei, again to do pioneer work. Through street preaching and other means of witness Lu and a group of zealous young Christians have quickly filled their rented meeting place in the basement of Elim Bookstore. God is mightily using this bandit-turned-preacher. I praise God for having had a small part in what God was doing in his life.

Light in the prison

For twenty-eight years my wife carried on an evangelistic ministry in the female section of the Taipei prison. She began this ministry as an expression of her gratefulness for God's healing of my cancer in 1951. At that time the prison was at Aikuo East Road, a little over ten minutes' walk from our house. I wanted her to give up the prison ministry when the government moved it to Taoyuan, much further away. But the prisoners' tears would not let her give in to my wishes.

Many women prisoners, including a woman on death row, have become new creations in Christ over the years. But also one man came to Christ through my wife's ministry in the prison's female section. Sent by his department to interview us and to make records of our work in prison, Officer Sun sat in on my wife's weekly meetings. Even after he obtained permission to stop keeping records, he continued attending Friday after Friday. Not only did he eventually believe in Jesus, but his whole family believed and became members of our church, serving the Lord with us together.

After Officer Sun believed in the Lord, our work in the female prison became easier because we could come and go without hindrance.

But the greatest change came in the months after God saved a female hooligan by the name of Chen Chin-chih, a narcotics dealer and a member of a sinister organisation. With her 'credentials', she had become a 'chief' in the prison. To fill that role she had to be truly cruel and capable of bullying others. All of the prisoners were afraid of this woman and treated her with careful respect.

Every time we went to evangelise the prisoners, Chen sat on the last row. Since she had absolutely no interest in religion of any sort, she was antagonistic, though she really didn't know why.

One day the Holy Spirit worked a miracle in Chen Chin-chih. Suddenly moved by the word of God, she ran to the front. All the female prisoners, knowing that Chen was a hard one to rattle, became very tense, fearing for my wife's life. But contrary to their expectations, Chen didn't go to the pulpit to attack, but to kneel and to cry. She sobbed so loudly that her cries resounded throughout the prison. Weeping over her sins and confessing them before God, she asked him to forgive her and manifest his glory through her.

As she quieted, my wife prayed for her, and when the broken woman got up from the floor, she had changed from a wolf to a lamb because the Holy Spirit had entered her heart. Not only had her heart changed, but her appearance as well.

As the weeks passed, the change was more and more obvious. Chen's dirty language disappeared. Instead of demanding others to serve her, the new Christian started serving others. Previously she had demanded that others respect her; now she respected others. Seeing Chen Chin-chih's dramatic change, other prisoners became convinced that Jesus Christ is the living and matchless God of heaven and earth.

Suddenly everyone in the prison became enthusiastic about the word of God. Before, prisoners came rather reluctantly to the one meeting on Fridays. Many, in fact, refused to come. But after Chen trusted the Lord, many began meeting almost every day. Little knots of prisoners gathered often to pray or to talk of God's grace. On Fridays, when my wife reached the prison, she could hear the prisoners already singing hymns inside.

Previously anyone who got sick would at once seek the doctor. Now prisoners first sought Jesus. They prayed for each other, and diseases were healed. Quarrelling stopped. In love women helped and sustained each other. Although the prison housed both young and old, Taiwanese and foreigners, and all from a variety of backgrounds, they seemed now to become a big family living peacefully together. This news even reached the government disciplinary department.

I thank God for my wife's faithfulness in the prison ministry over the years. And together we thank him for his power to change lives.

26

Death of a Daughter

Not long after our eldest daughter went to America, she met the man of her heart's desire. I travelled to the States to give her away at her wedding. I have to admit that giving our daughter's hand to the man who would become our son-in-law mingled some sorrow with the joy at seeing her happiness. When, in fact, I took her hand to walk her down the aisle, I wished for a very long aisle and the very slow pace normal in Taiwan instead of the quick pace customary in America. With normal parental sadness, I was reluctant to give up the little girl who had for so many years brightened our home.

Apparently the bride had mixed emotions as well. When she and my son-in-law were leaving for their honeymoon, I was all alone inside, watching, when suddenly, before the car could pull away, the door flew open, and my daughter rushed out and ran upstairs and into my arms, crying, 'Dad, I'm not going! I'm not going!'

What could I do, with a daughter holding me tightly and her husband waiting downstairs? Since an inexpressibly deep love had built up between us, the separation was heartbreaking. I could only persuade her to go and to try to comfort her, taking her down to the first floor and then to the car. When she continued to hold my hand tightly, I could do nothing except to force my hand away from hers.

After her marriage, our daughter never forgot her duty to help her parents. To lessen our load and to free us to serve the Lord wholeheartedly and without distraction, she determined to look after our other six children as they came to America, one after another. In fact, she practically became their parents.

During her third pregnancy, this married daughter noticed a lump in her breast. The doctor she consulted said it was only a milk cyst; unfortunately he was wrong – she had breast cancer. By the time the cancer was diagnosed, it had spread to her lymph glands and bones. Though she had surgery, chemotherapy, and radiation and even laser treatment, nothing was successful in destroying the cancer cells. Cancer spread to her brain and then her spinal cord, eventually paralysing her neck. My wife and I looked after her as her condition worsened each day.

Near the end our dying daughter found it increasingly difficult to talk. In all, she spoke to us only three times. The first time she told us how sad and lonely it made her feel to think of being alone up in the hillside, in the grave. 'I feel very afraid,' she admitted. These words pierced my heart, but we dared not cry in front of her. We could only comfort her and say, 'Don't be afraid. The Lord will be with you. He is our companion. The Bible promised that he will be with us unto the end of the world.'

The second time our daughter spoke to us was very near the end, when her speech was almost gone. 'Dad, Mom,' she said, 'after I go, what will you do? I can no longer look after you.' Even on her deathbed her love and concern for us never wavered. 'You must take care of yourselves somehow!' This made me think of Jesus Christ who had done the same when he was hanging on the cross. He saw his mother and said to her, 'Mother, see your son.' And then he said to his beloved disciple, 'See your mother', and in so doing gave his mother over to the disciple John. Here our daughter, at this time of great pain, was expressing concern for us! Her heart mirrored her Lord's.

The last words our daughter spoke were, 'Dad, I love you so much!' Those words were like a sharp knife piercing my heart.

But before those last words our daughter had made us promise that on the day of her funeral we would not escort her body to the tomb on the hill because she felt we would not be able to stand it. Though we felt hard-hearted in agreeing to her request, she insisted. It was what she wanted.

After our dear eldest died one sad day in 1982, we held to our promise and did not walk to her grave with the burial party. But we wrote two epitaphs for the gravestone as a memorial to her: 'From the time we bought her cradle to the time we found her tomb, our love for her stretched our hearts almost to the breaking' and 'We wish for the Lord's quick return, so that we can see our kind daughter and have our sorrow removed.'

27

A Son Like Me

Though my wife and I have had seven children, one especially, our eldest son, obviously carries my genes.

When we first sent this eldest son abroad, he was only sixteen years old. You can imagine how my wife felt when I took him with me to North America. She cried every day. He also was sad to be separated from his mother.

In Canada we met a servant of the Lord, Rev Stephen Knights of the China Inland Mission, now known as Overseas Missionary Fellowship. This aged pastor received us into his home and asked his daughter to entertain my son. But my son was thinking too much about his mother to want to play. Wanting to relieve my son's homesickness, Rev Knights took us to the Toronto Museum to see some ancient Chinese artefacts. He thought the trip would cheer the boy up.

I was amazed at how many Chinese antiques lined the walls of that museum. They were simply uncountable. *How could all these artifacts be in Canada?* I wondered, deciding that they must have been smuggled out by thieves. My son must have had the same thoughts because he suddenly turned to Rev Knights and said, 'How can you bring us to such a place as this? These objects were obviously robbed from China. You bring us to see these stolen treasures. Why have you done this?'

When I heard my son talking so rudely to God's servant, I felt embarrassed and apologised. But he replied, 'Don't worry, your son is in a bad mood. This is only his patriotism coming out. You don't have to worry because I don't blame him a bit.'

Just the same, I felt sorry for the insult.

My son and I then left Canada for America for him to enrol in school. He lived in a friend's house. The arrangement was fine until another student came to share his room, a student from a rich family. When both my son and I felt that the other student's lifestyle was too different for them to share the room, I asked my friend whether the old house trailer in his garden was still usable and if my son could live in it. My friend did not think this a good idea. He was afraid that it would seem as if the rich boy was given favourable treatment while my son was 'banished' from the house to live in an old trailer. When I insisted that this was our choice and that he should not worry about it, he finally agreed. So my son tidied up the trailer and moved in.

One day, right before my son faced examinations, it was very cold. Because the house trailer was not equipped with proper heating, my son hooked a pipe he found at the back of the trailer into a gas line and rigged up a makeshift heater. That very day my friend's grandson came to see my son, wanting to play with him. Since my son had an exam the next day, he was in no mood to play. So he rustled up some toys for the boy to play with and said, 'You play with these things by yourself.'

While the boy played, my son continued to review his notes and hardly noticed when the boy, tiring of his play, got up to go home. As the youngster left the house, he accidentally bumped the gas pipe and opened it. The door closed with a thud and the click of the latch.

My son felt himself getting tired. Had he yielded and gone to sleep, the gas fumes escaping from the pipe would have asphyxiated him. But, marvellously, while he was yet conscious, he heard someone calling him. He tried to stand up, but was unable. The calling continued without stopping. My boy tried his best, but was unable to stand up. As the calling became more and more intense, he turned his body and fell to the floor. He continued to struggle but at this point was unable to see clearly. Finally he managed to get to his feet, but was groggy and confused. Staggering, he fell toward the window, his head crashing through the glass. With his head dangling out of the window, he began drawing fresh air into his lungs, thus avoiding death.

Hearing the noise of breaking glass, my friend's family ran to open the door. When they smelled gas, they dragged my son outside and immediately sent him to the hospital. Since he had inhaled so much gas, my son should have died or at least been brain-damaged. He not only survived, but survived with his mind undiminished.

Certainly God had intervened. My wife had prayed each day for our son since the day he went abroad, entrusting him to the Lord. In mercy and grace our heavenly Father responded by helping our boy escape death without harm.

Later, when this eldest son was visiting Taiwan, my mother-in-law was preparing to go to America to visit my brother. My son escorted her to the American consulate to get her visa. As Chinese people usually care little about order, a big crowd was milling about the door. To clear the area, the officer at the consulate said to them, 'Leave your passports here. We will call your names according to the passports.' Though the people gave him their passports, they would not leave the area. As a result the officer got angry and threw the passports and application papers all over the floor, leaving the people to scramble for them.

My son was furious. He rushed inside and said to the officer, 'Don't you know that these passports represent our country? Today by throwing them onto the floor, you are openly insulting our nation!' He went on to scold the officer severely. Although cheering silently my son's actions, the other people applying to go abroad were afraid that the American consul would become angry and refuse to grant anyone's visa.

Not satisfied, my son ran to the police station to report this incident. The police advised him not to create a scene. Upon finding that the police would not intervene, my son went to the Ministry of Foreign Affairs, requesting them to take action. Apparently both my son and I tend to have a strong patriotic sense of justice and love for country and tend to react rashly when that sense is violated. My son, who has long finished his education and is doing business in America, is still indignant and disturbed about this matter. I cannot forget the actions of my grandfather years ago in China. My son comes by his temper honestly.

28

The Witness of our Lives

Loving one another

The chief mark of a Christian is not holding a Bible, nor giving a long prayer with uplifted head at church, nor always being at church. No, 'if you have love for one another,' Jesus said, 'all men will know that you are my disciples' (John 13:35).

But love is something which is not expressed in writing or speech alone. If you love someone, you want to spend time with them. You care about how they are feeling. You want to give them something they like.

Christian love thinks of the other person first. As many wives would do for their husbands, when my wife goes to the market, she buys what I want to eat, not what she wants. Love is forgetting oneself and thinking of others. If we as members of the body of Christ truly love and care for one another like this, others will indeed know that we are Jesus' disciples, even if we don't give any powerful sermons.

God's management of my health a testimony

Sometime in the 1970s I entered the Veterans General Hospital for a three-day check-up. The doctor there asked me what diseases I had had in the past. I told him that I had had surgery for a sinus infection. Second, I had an enlarged heart, the result of holding stressful matters inside me. Third, X-rays had revealed a shadow in my right lung – a condition, though at one time worsening, was then stabilised. Fourth, I had had a malignant tumour.

'Where was the malignancy?' the doctor wanted to know.

'In my upper colon,' I said.

'Have you had surgery?' he asked me.

'I have had,' I said, loosening my clothing to show him the ten centimetre scar on my left abdomen and the six or seven centimetre scar in the middle of my chest.

'When did have you have this surgery?' the doctor asked. I told him 1951. 'Congratulations!' he said. 'You are still well. Your operation was very successful.'

'Doctor, my health is not because of the success of the operation,' I told him. 'After the surgeons opened me up, they saw that the cancer had spread too extensively to be remedied surgically, so they just sewed me back up. Yet I am living today.' He was dumbfounded. 'This is impossible,' he said, 'save for a wrong diagnosis. You must not have had cancer.'

'Doctor,' I said, 'I don't know how many times I have heard this. People just don't believe I had malignant cancer.'

'If you really had a malignant tumour, how can you still be alive today without having it removed?' He paused, then said, 'Enough! Let's not argue. What other problems have you had?'

'I also have high blood pressure. I have had it for years.'

'What is your blood pressure reading?'

'The high number always stays around one hundred and ten, and the low number is around one hundred and six.'

'What?' he reacted. 'The high and the low are only a few degrees apart.'

'I regularly take my blood pressure, and it is always the same. It's been that way for over ten years.'

'Mr Wu,' he explained, 'the high reading is for the contraction of the heart; the low number is for the expansion of the heart. One measures the heart's pumping and the other the heart's resting. If the difference is only a few degrees, the rate of your heart's activity is too minimal. Your heart will fail in half to one year's time. But you said that you have had this blood pressure reading for over ten years. Looking the way you do, this is simply impossible.'

'If you don't believe me, take my blood pressure and see,' I suggested.

The doctor called a nurse to take my blood pressure. When he saw the reading, his eyebrows wrinkled, and he ordered the nurse to use another meter. The result was the same. 'Strange!' he said solemnly. 'How can you survive with such blood pressure for so long? When I see your blood pressure, I can no longer doubt your story about that malignant tumour. I can't understand how you can still be alive.'

'Neither can I. But I live very nicely and happily. I continue working, travelling everywhere, in Taiwan and abroad.' He shook his head and left.

When I arrived at the examination room, I heard the doctor reporting my condition to the other doctors and the nurses. The husband of a woman in our church, General Chou Po-tao, was also in the room having a check-up. Overhearing the doctors discussing my medical history, he was curious and asked who they were talking about. My doctor pointed me out. When he saw me, he said, 'Him? He sometimes comes to our house to visit my wife. His name is Wu, and he is the minister of the Nanking East Road Church.'

Later that afternoon the sisters were meeting at our church. Right in the middle of their session General Chou hurried up to the door of the church and called loudly for his wife to come outside. 'The speaker is delivering a message,' she scolded when she came out, 'How can you be so impolite as to shout during the meeting?'

'But I have to tell you some good news,' he said. 'I want to believe in Jesus.' He then recounted the day's events at the hospital. Miracles that God had wrought in my body had been powerful witnesses to God's grace. Even though many years had elapsed since God had healed me of cancer, the Holy Spirit had used the testimony to work in him and to save his soul.

'Even eight winds cannot move my heart'

An ancient Chinese scholar, Su Dong Po, once wrote a poem called 'Even eight winds cannot move my heart'. The winds he identified as being such things as success or failure, damage to one's honour, poverty or wealth. The poem was about not letting life's winds control his inner reactions.

From the time they were small, I have admonished my children not to let other people control their emotions i.e. when other people make me feel comfortable, then I am happy; or when other people make me feel uncomfortable, then I am distressed. If our hearts rise and fall with the ebb and flow of this changeable and tumultuous world, we will surely lack peace and stability in our lives.

But there is an amusing story attached to Su Dong Po and his poem. After writing these self-confident lines, Su sent a copy to a fellow poet for evaluation. After reading the poem, the friend wrote one nasty word on it in red ink and sent it back to the author. Insulted, Su strode in a cold fury to his friend's house. It was exactly the reaction the friend expected. So much for being unmoved by adverse winds! One word was all it took to enrage him.

Sometimes we believe our spiritual condition to be very healthy, when, in fact, it is not. We have the knowledge, but we don't have the life. You say you are humble. In your mind you are humble, but in reality you are not humble. You say that you are gentle, but you are not gentle. You say that you have died and risen with Jesus, and intellectually you know what it is to have died and have risen with Christ, but your life lacks evidence of it. Our problem is the same as Su Dong Po's. We cannot be spiritual only in our minds; we must experience Christ in our lives. As James 1:19–25 instructs, we must 'do' the word of God, not just listen to it.

A Christian's behaviour is very important. I am reminded of the time my wife sent me to the market to buy some carrots for the children. Trouble was that I couldn't tell good carrots from ones that were soft and pithy on the inside; both looked the same on the surface. Because I knew that if I bought inferior carrots, my wife would scold me, I paced back and forth uncertainly. Then I saw a lady buying carrots. As I watched, she picked one up, thumped it, and set it aside. She picked up another, thumped it twice, and placed it in her basket. As I listened to the thumps with her, I discovered that if the inside of a carrot is solid, the thump is loud and resonant, if not, the sound is soft and dead. I went home with good carrots!

Our spiritual lives are the same. Are you strong or weak on the inside? You can't prove one way or the other with your mouth. You must have other people give you a 'thump' to tell. Hence, when we grow spiritually, God allows others to give us 'thumps' so as to make our true condition evident.

Peter provides us with an example of this. 'Others will fall, but I will not,' he bragged. When he said this, he sincerely believed it. But while Jesus was being abused inside and Peter was warming himself at a fire in the courtyard, a maid recognised Peter and accused him of being one of Jesus' men. Peter said, 'What are you talking about? I am not!' Later Peter even swore that he didn't know Jesus. What happened to the Peter who declared that he was willing to die with the Lord Jesus? He thought that he was really that strong, but in fact he was far from it. A young woman's accusation showed him weak and timid like the others. It was a lesson he needed to learn. We do too – over and over.

29

Lessons for Life

Is making friends with the opposite sex unspiritual?

One day I gave a young girl a lift in my car as we were going to the same place. The girl seemed to want to talk to me about something, but her hesitant manner and inability to find the right words suggested that it was a difficult subject for her. Dawning on me that young girls are inevitably shy about discussing the subject of marriage, I gave her a gentle verbal push: 'What is it?' I asked. 'Is it about marriage? This is okay to talk about, because young men and women should get married when they reach a certain age.'

'Oh, Elder Wu,' she said, 'the people in our church say that making friends with people of the opposite sex is unspiritual. If making friends with those from other segments of society is even more unspiritual, then what are Christians supposed to do?' I could hear her frustration. 'What's more,' she continued, 'I am getting older. Parents generally feel that a twenty-five-year-old is already too old. They inevitably become worried and push their daughter to find a boyfriend. I really don't know what to do.'

I laughed heartily, and said, 'If you are afraid of what people in the church say, you might well become an old maid. Sister, God allows making friends with the opposite sex. In the beginning when God created Adam, God declared that it was not good for him to be alone; so God created a mate to help him. Marriage is set up by God, and he allows a man to took for a woman and a woman to look for a man. One caution: we must proceed according to the Biblical principle that only a believer is fit for another believer. Within this principle we can freely take action and make friends. Whether in church or in society at large, acting according to this principle is always spiritual.'

The girl was relieved. I admired her. Having a heart which honours the church is an admirable attitude and not to be despised.

Should people of differing faiths marry?

I was preaching at a summer camp held by Ambassadors for Christ at Pine Brook in Pennsylvania, USA. One day a young girl came up to me and asked, 'Elder Wu, can I talk with you?'

'Of course you can!' I said. As we walked together, she told me that she had had a boyfriend for a long time and that they had a fairly deep mutual understanding. They had known each other in their home town, later entered the same college, and then both came to study in America. She had considered the matter of marriage with him over a long period, but was not sure what to do.

'What is left to be considered?' I asked her.

'There is a difficult problem between us,' she answered. When I asked her what, she said, 'I am a Protestant, and he is a Catholic.'

'Oh, that's the problem!' I exclaimed. It truly is a big problem. People of different faiths who marry are letting themselves in for a lot of difficulties. I paused, then asked her, 'Has your boyfriend come to attend this summer camp?'

'No, but tomorrow he will come to camp to see me.'

I wanted to help them, so I said, 'Can you bring your friend to see me tomorrow? I want to talk to him.' She consented and the next afternoon brought her boyfriend to see me. Well-mannered, tall and fair-skinned, the young man looked to be very attractive husband material.

I asked both young people to sit down, and I talked to them directly about this matter. 'You have been seeing each other for

many years?' I asked. They nodded. 'And you have already arrived
at a stage in which you understand each other very well?' They
nodded again. 'If so, do most people think you two can talk about
marriage?' They both lowered their heads. Then I said to the boy,
'I hear that you are a Catholic and your girlfriend is a Protestant.
One day if the two of you get married and establish a family, then
the two of you will become one. The Bible says that what God has
put together man should not put asunder. But you are a Catholic,
and she is a Protestant. That could cause some trouble. If she
attends a Protestant worship service, what would you do?'

'I will accompany her,' he said.

'What if you go to mass?' I asked him, but glancing at the girl.

'I won't go with him,' she said.

'Does this mean that every Sunday you will accompany her to
worship and will not go to mass?' The boy would not answer.
'Let me give you a suggestion,' I went on. 'Either you give up the
Protestant faith, which you believe in,' I said looking at the girl,
'or you give up the Catholic faith, which you believe in,' I said,
nodding to the boy. 'You need to be one in faith. Now how can I
assist one of you to give up your faith?

'Perhaps I should start by listing some of the weak points of
Protestants,' I said with purpose, 'so that you yourself can decide
whether you should forsake the Protestant faith.' Then I proceeded to talk about the interpersonal difficulties which
Protestants have, the many denominations such as Baptist,
Presbyterian, Methodist, Anglican, etc., with their many differences and conflicts. 'Protestants really do have these weaknesses,' I said earnestly to the young man.

I then turned to the girl. 'Sister, you are a Protestant. Since I
listed the weak points of Protestantism, would you like to give
up your faith?'

'Oh, Elder Wu,' she cried, 'these are but man's weaknesses,
not the error of Protestantism itself. These faults are man's
faults, not the Bible's faults. Therefore I cannot give up my faith.
There are people inside the church who look like Christians but
actually are not Christians. Even among the twelve disciples of
Jesus, there was a Judas!'

'Now it's up to you to decide what you'll do,' I said to the boy. 'I'll be fair. Although I myself am a Protestant minister, I won't talk about the good aspects of Protestantism. Now that I have laid out the weak points of Protestantism, I must likewise explain the weak points of Catholicism.' I could have counted many, but I mentioned only a few.

'First,' I said, 'though the Bible says there is only one mediator between God and man, and that is Jesus Christ, Catholics advocate another mediator, the Virgin Mary. If you want to pray to Jesus, you must first pray to Mary, pleading with the mother to give command to her son. Second, there are two things the Bible says most disgust God. One is idolatry. I have been in Catholic churches in Israel and France. Inside are many statues of the apostles, Mary, and Jesus. Though the Bible says that you are not to worship any images of anything in heaven or earth, I saw many people worshipping these images, and this is abominable to God. You can see that there are great discrepancies between Catholicism and the Biblical faith. Do you, young man, want to forsake Catholicism and accept Protestantism so that your future family will be unified and not go separate ways?'

'Elder Wu,' he replied. 'I have nothing to say concerning what you just said, but I cannot forsake my Catholic faith. I was able to study in America because a priest sponsored me. I cannot be so ungrateful as to leave Catholicism.'

'Then I'm sorry,' I said. 'Today I wanted to help resolve your problems. But neither of you will forsake your own faith. Your future together is certain to have difficulties.'

After a moment the girl stood up and said to me, 'Elder Wu, thank you. I thank you very much for your help today. Since we have come to such a decision point, I have already made up my mind.' Then she turned to the boy and said, 'Tomorrow I will buy a plane ticket to go back to Taiwan. Our friendship stops at this point. Good-bye.'

As she turned and left, the boy stood there looking at her. I saw his eyes reddening and could see his tears. Why did she have to walk away? Because she wanted to respect the Bible and her faith. She had a heart to keep her faith, even if it meant suffering a break-up with her boyfriend. I deeply believe God will bless her as she firmly holds to what she believes. God will arrange a good future for her. Had she compromised, her suffering and troubles would have multiplied. We have seen many practical examples of these truths among the brothers and sisters of the church. Indeed, marriage is not to be entered into lightly.

Worldliness

Hebrews 12 talks about laying aside the weights which so easily entangle us. What are these weights? Because the following chapter talks about sins, I don't think the weights are sins so much as worldliness or that which represents the love of the world.

I don't think the Bible tells us not to pay attention to the world with all its affairs and physical things. When God created Adam, he put him inside the Garden of Eden and said to him, 'You can eat all the fruit of this garden.' Fruit is a physical thing of the world. God also told Adam to rule over the creatures and to care for the Garden of Eden. This represents the affairs of life. Then physical things and the affairs of life cannot in themselves be classified as 'the world'.

What then is 'the world' that we should not love? To give an example, our bodies need exercise. The more we just sit without exercise, the fatter we get, and the fatter we get, the more we are set up for heart disease, high blood pressure, and diabetes. We must have a suitable amount of exercise. We sit in our offices for five days a week and do housework on Saturdays. That leaves only Sundays. But Sundays are for worshiping God. Yet because of the body's need, people use Sundays to do exercise. Thus exercise becomes 'the world' to those people, because it blocks their relationship with God.

President Franklin Roosevelt was so stressed by national affairs that he struggled to sleep at night. His solution was to get absorbed in detective stories to help him relax. That's okay. We can read fiction, but if we become too absorbed, letting it occupy so much time that we have no time for reading the Bible and for prayer, then story-reading becomes for us 'the world'.

Whatever becomes a spiritual block is worldliness. If we are conscientious about our business and earn money honestly, we line up with Biblical principles. But if we are enticed and bound by money and grasp for it in a way that creates a barrier to our relationship with God, money becomes 'the world' for us.

We need to be clear about the difference between what is good and what is of the Devil so that we are not bound, either by being entangled by the love of the world or by a wrong idea of how we are to relate to what God provides for our living.

When Satan intruded in a testimony meeting

At one of our weekly Sunday evening testimony meetings a sister who lacked the ability to express herself got up and droned on for ten minutes. As there were over two hundred people attending the meeting, Brother Yao Tung-yueh became impatient. He stood up and said, 'Sister, you have already talked for more than ten minutes, and we still can't figure out what you are talking about. What are you trying to say? Please sit down. Sit down!'

This sister's face turned red and then turned pale. I felt rather anxious, not knowing what to do. She was crying, at the same time asking the Lord to vindicate her, because she felt despised and criticised. As the meeting became increasingly tense, I called all the brothers and sisters to kneel down and pray aloud. I hoped that our prayers could drown out the sound of the offended lady's weeping.

Trouble was the louder the congregation prayed, the louder the sister shouted out her grievances. Eventually we had pandemonium.

In the middle of the tumult, suddenly, I heard the sounds of slapping. Afraid that the sister was hitting people, I opened my eyes and saw that she was slapping her own mouth and praying to God: 'O Lord, how can I be like this?' she wept. 'How can I let Satan use me to disturb the meeting? I beg you to have mercy on me. How can I be like this? How can I be like this?'

Brother Yao went and knelt beside her. 'Oh, sister, please forgive me,' he said, 'for it was I who lit the fire tonight. If you want to scold or deal with anyone, it should be me.'

'Brother Yao, that's not it,' the sister told him. 'I originally thought that my spiritual condition was quite good. If you hadn't stopped me tonight, I wouldn't have known what my inward condition was. Your comment brought out pride, a bad temper, and all the undesirable things inside me. As a result, I came to know what kind of a person I am and now come before God to ask for his forgiveness.'

The sister's confession started an avalanche. All the people began confessing their sins to each other. Husbands confessed sins to their wives, and wives confessed sins to their husbands, and brothers and sisters all confessed their sins to one another. What started out to be a most awful meeting turned out to be a most beautiful meeting. Getting the congregation down on their knees to pray turned the tide. Prayer blocked any further success of Satan to bring destruction. God turned disgraceful behaviour into behaviour which honours God. I cannot remember a more glorious triumph of God over the evil one.

30

The Founding of China Evangelical Seminary

In the late 1960s Professor Chang Ming-che and James H. Taylor III had a similar vision. Although the Baptists, Presbyterians, and Lutherans all had seminaries in Taiwan, these two men saw the need for a seminary that was both interdenominational and evangelical, whose graduates could help meet the great shortfall of workers for this relatively small, but largely unharvested field. Both felt that, since Taiwan's educational standards were increasingly high, such a seminary should accept only college graduates.

After discussion, Brothers Chang and Taylor set up a planning committee and invited me to be a member. Judging the endeavour very important, I accepted the invitation to help in the preparatory work. The committee later voted me chairman. Now, though I no longer carry any actual administrative responsibilities, I still have a title at the China Evangelical Seminary.

When we started developing CES, we had empty hands. We did not have money, teachers, a campus or students. All we had was a burden and a vision.

The vision began to take on substance when the Rev Stanley Yu came to see me to tell me that he planned to discontinue his Bible study class. He said that if there was anyone willing to carry on a ministry of teaching the word of God, he was willing to offer the use the house, tables, chairs, and other materials, even the land, for a token sum of money. For CES, surely the opportunity was God's answer to our much praying!

But where would the money come from? In the end, the China Overseas Missionary Association paid for all of Brother Yu's supplies. After acquiring the property and the furniture, we formally inaugurated the China Evangelical Seminary, with James H. Taylor III as its first president.

Because at the beginning the workload was extremely heavy, Dr Taylor needed someone to take care of business administration so that he could concentrate on development. Dr Taylor recommended to Professor Chang and me a graduate of National Taiwan University, Wilfred Su, who loved the Lord very much and was active among young people. He felt that if we were to challenge Wilfred, he might well become a staff member of the new seminary. So Professor Chang and I went together to Kaohsiung to tell Brother Su about our thoughts.

Su accepted our offer and resigned from his job at Philips Electronic Corporation to join the development team at CES. Trouble was, very few people knew of the seminary-in-the-making, and financial contributions were few. Where would we find the money for Su's living expenses? God revealed his answer when Elder Henry Co from Manila came to my house to see me and discovered a brochure on the proposed China Evangelical Seminary on my table. 'Are you founding a seminary?' he asked.

'Yes,' I said, and explained why.

Immediately excited about our plan, Elder Co responded, 'As this work is invaluable because workers must come before there is work . . . I am willing to supply the funds for one worker's wages.'

Surely this was God's doing! Though his financial needs were yet unmet, Brother Wilfred Su had already begun working in CES development.

Later, impressed with young graduates of American seminaries who were open to returning to Taiwan, including Brother Jonathan Chao and Brother Tan Che Bin, we decided to invite several to come to CES as faculty. Although having just graduated from seminary and comparatively inexperienced, they had every potential to develop with training and experience.

Now with the place, the facilities and faculty, we started

advertising for students. The first advertisement brought seven people. One of those seven, Brother Caleb Huang, would, twenty years later, become president of CES, following Dr Timothy Lin.

From these beginnings CES has continued to use the strategy of training future faculty. Because we believe the quality of faculty is more significant than almost anything else, we have continually sought suitable students to send abroad for advanced studies with a view to their returning as staff. The practice has proved invaluable in building a strong base.

Eventually Brothers Jonathan Chao and Tan Che Bin moved to Hong Kong to found the China Graduate School of Theology. During North America's first Chinese Christians Winter Conference, participants made the two new seminaries chief prayer items. When President Taylor discovered during a visit to the US that participants left the conference feeling strongly that the two schools should merge, he called me.

'Since all have this opinion,' I responded, 'this may be the Lord's good will. However, due to practical needs, I think I ought to pay a visit to America to see what the actual situation is before I decide.' And that's what I did.

I found that Chinese Christian students did indeed feel that combining the China Evangelical Seminary and the China Graduate School of Theology into one would translate into a stronger teaching staff and greater overall strength. In the end, though, because of the distance and differences between Taiwan and Hong Kong, we decided that for practical purposes the two schools should remain separate. They have run parallel to this day, with CES training young people in Taiwan, CGST training people in Hong Kong.

During this early period a business tycoon in Singapore, whose daughter-in-law was a Christian, died, leaving money in a foundation to be used for education and social work. As theological education would qualify for funding, the daughter-in-law wrote me a letter upon learning that we in Taiwan had founded a seminary. She said that if we applied to the foundation, she could influence her husband, who was chairman, to make a grant that could establish a financial base for CES. We, of course, were excited at the prospect.

President Taylor and I went to Singapore to see this sister. Investigating the foundation before we met with her, however, we discovered that the founder was a zealous Buddhist and had to turn down the daughter-in-law's generous offer. Expressing our gratitude, we told her kindly that we Christians were unwilling to receive financial aid from a non-believer, even less willing from a donor of a different faith. We felt we had to display the kind of principles our students could be proud of and follow.

China Evangelical Seminary began in Shihlin, on a hillside spot which belonged to the Bible Baptist Mission. Later it moved to a comparatively larger site in the town below. Use of this property was offered without charge by the Evangelical Covenant Mission. But as the number of students kept increasing, the new location also became too crowded.

At the time our Hsuchang Street Church was helping TEAM, formerly known as the Evangelist Alliance Mission, run an orphanage on Tingchou Road. After three years TEAM, pleased with our handling of the orphanage, suggested that we keep on with the ministry there, but that we divide the site between the orphanage and Morrison Academy, even possibly selling half to move the orphanage to the suburbs. Aware of the seminary's need for a larger site, we proposed instead that we give up the orphanage to make the site available to CES. TEAM agreed, and CES was glad to accept the land as God's provision for the school. CES's initial building project on Tingchou Road was completed during James Taylor's presidency.

When Dr Taylor accepted the invitation to become general director of Overseas Missionary Fellowship, CES invited Dr Timothy Lin to be its president. Dr Lin was chosen because of his virtue and good reputation, and because he was an authority in theology. His leadership at CES brought new development at the school. Each year, the student enrolment rose, and eventually the seminary added a second building close to the original one.

God has continued to bless in the more than twenty-five years the school has been training Christian workers for Taiwan and beyond.

31

The Founding of Discipleship Training Centre (DTC)

China Evangelical Seminary's President Lin, convinced that all together the seminaries in Taiwan trained only one-fifth the needed number of Christian workers, advocated the founding of a school which required no educational prerequisites. Thus the idea of founding Discipleship Training Centre was born.

When I suggested that the new school be organisationally linked to CES at the trustees' meeting, Dr Paul Han said that it could not be so. He explained that when CES started, it had made an agreement with other Taiwan seminaries not to offer educational programmes other than those on a college level.

While we were still praying for money to purchase a meeting place for our proposed training centre, I met a brother who expressed his conviction that non-college graduates ought to be trained for the ministry every bit as much as college graduates. When I told him that we were planning a centre for discipleship training for the less educated, he said, 'Since you have planned it, you should carry it out!'

I said, 'Yes, but we need a place and money before we can do it.'

'If a suitable place is found,' he said matter-of-factly, 'I will take care of the money.'

Actually we had found a place that would work very well for our purposes. The lower part was set up as church premises; the rest was quite adaptable for our other needs. The price was eleven million Taiwan dollars. The man's company bought it for us.

Our first advertisement for students drew a total of nine applicants. Some of these are now part of the school staff. We learned from CES!

Many difficulties beset us at the beginning. After both I and Elder Wang Hung-fan had served as temporary heads of the school, we knew we needed a full-time leader who would wholeheartedly take up the responsibilities of this work. When I discovered another brother who was preparing to start a discipleship training scheme of his own, I said to him, 'DTC has already had some success. Why do you waste your effort in reinventing the wheel? Why don't I give you this work so that you can run it?'

This brother agreed and became DTC's director.

Soon the rumblings of interpersonal conflict began under-mining the effectiveness of Discipleship Training Centre. When the board of trustees voted to end the employment of the director as a result, I disagreed. I thought errors and weaknesses were inevitable. I believed we should tolerate and forgive one another, for who, after all, is perfect?

Not wanting the conflicts to erupt into a major storm, I hid the votes and did not announce the board of trustees' decision. *DTC really needs this man to run it, I thought. Without this man, how can this work continue?*

Half a year passed, and this brother continued serving as director. More months went by, and though students had fre-quent disputes with him, I held my peace. Then one day, in a sharing meeting, a group of students said, 'If we walk out of the Centre, we will never return.'

My heart felt very sad. The students should have more positive feelings toward their school. I had no choice but to announce the decision of the board of trustees of more than a year earlier and let this brother go.

Without a director, the situation at the school progressively worsened, becoming more and more disorganised. The board of trustees had to move to find a new director. As we met, we thought of Brother Wang Chuan-sheng as a possibility. He was a man who already had the students' respect, both spiritually and academically.

When Brother Chang and I went to Brother Wang's house and asked him if he would consider taking up the leadership of DTC, he said that he would have to pray to find out God's leading before he could give us a reply. Six months later he took over the post, sure that God had indeed chosen him for this ministry of training workers for the harvest.

In the years since then God has blessed Discipleship Training Centre. Already graduates are immersed in his work, living testimonies of the value of the training they received. Brother Sung Hsien-wei, for example, took over the work of the Yungho Church after the former pastor retired and is doing a beautiful work there. Sister Wang Liang-yu is serving as academic dean at DTC. Brother Lu Tai-hao, whose story I told earlier, not only established a church in Wuku, but is now the director of China Missionary Fellowship. When I see the students trained at DTC gradually finding their places in different fields for the Lord, my heart is truly warmed. By God's grace I have been able to participate in two extremely meaningful ministries of training.

32

The Chinese and Missions

Are Chinese Christians exempt from obeying Jesus' last command? Most of us act as if we are.

After his resurrection and just before he ascended into Heaven, Jesus ordered his disciples to be his witnesses in Jerusalem and in all Judea and Samaria, even unto the remotest parts of the earth (Acts 1:8). Jerusalem and all Judea shared the same culture. Samaria had a similar culture, but not the same. The remotest parts of the earth, of course, would have had very different cultures. Jesus meant that the propagation of the Gospel should move from within the same culture to similar cultures and then to foreign cultures. Mainland China, Taiwan, and at least first-generation Chinese abroad share the same culture. Korea and Japan have similar cultures to that of China. Malaysia, India, Europe, and America have different cultures from the Chinese. Evangelism beginning within a people's own culture group and moving out cross-culturally is a divinely ordered pattern.

Early in modern history Westerners began taking this command of Jesus seriously. But though Chinese church history goes back over two hundred years, obedience to the command among Chinese Christians has been the exception rather than the rule. If Jesus spoke the command in Acts 1 to near-Easterners, is it not also meant for his followers who are far-Easterners? If so, why then do Westerners take up the responsibility of mission while Easterners don't?

Why the gospel didn't spread eastwards

In Acts 16 we read that the Spirit of Jesus forbade Paul to continue preaching in Asia. Later, when Paul wanted to go to Bithynia from Mysia, the Spirit of Jesus again would not allow him to go. Going to Troas instead, Paul there saw the vision that included the call, 'Come over to Macedonia and help us.' So Paul went to Macedonia.

Why did the Spirit not allow Paul to go eastward? Why did the vision send Paul westward? If God had allowed Paul to continue going east, then we Chinese would have been among the first ones to hear the Gospel. As it was, Paul's response to the Macedonian call took the Gospel west, and the West took the Gospel to the East. Why didn't God first give the good news to the East and let the Easterners take it to the West? The Bible does not give a clear answer. We will have to ask God when we get to Heaven.

But let me suggest a possible answer, using a story to explain my speculation. During the time in which China was split into three kingdoms, a doctor by the name of Hua Tuo had reached the summit of medical achievement. When a man named Tsao Tsao sought relief for a searing headache, Hua told him that no medicine could cure him, but that a cure was possible if Tsao Tsao would allow Hua to open his skull.

Tsao Tsao thought the doctor's suggestion totally unreasonable. As it seemed like a tricky plot to murder him, the headache sufferer captured Hua and imprisoned him.

Hua, afraid for his life, felt desperate to pass his medical discoveries on to someone before they were lost forever. As the prison guard treated him kindly, the doctor began sharing the intricacies of brain surgery and other therapies with the guard. One day he sent the guard to his house to retrieve his medical books and notebooks. When the guard arrived at the doctor's home, Hua's wife was burning the books. 'My husband was harmed by these medical books,' she explained. 'That's why he fell into such a hopeless situation. What's the use of keeping them?'

Quickly the guard rescued what books were not yet destroyed. One of the salvaged books described how to castrate chickens and pigs; thus this medical skill was passed on to succeeding generations. Unfortunately the how of doing brain surgery was lost. Though brain surgery is a recent development in the West, Hua Tuo developed it centuries earlier.

Then why did Chinese medical technology fall behind? Because Chinese desire to keep prescriptions secret. Discovered medicines and medical practices are passed only from father to son and from son to grandson, rarely to outsiders. Given this propensity among the Chinese, my theory is that if God had permitted Paul to bring the Gospel first to the East, the Chinese, upon finding that it was precious, might have treated it as a secret prescription and hidden it!

Misconception has also hindered the Chinese from obeying Jesus' last command. When we talk of messengers to take the Gospel to people of another culture, Chinese tend to think of Westerners with big noses and blue eyes. We Chinese received God's word from Westerners, and we think that only Westerners can do missionary work. We think we can look on with folded arms and sit down to enjoy the fruits of their work.

Prejudice is another factor in the slowness of the Chinese church to obey the Great Commission. I can't help but think of Jonah here. When God called him to preach to Nineveh, he refused to go. Instead he got onto a ship headed for Tarshish to escape Jehovah. When God raised a storm at sea, Jonah said, 'I think this storm is because of me. Throw me into the sea, and then the sea will become calm for you.' And as he predicted, when the ship's hands did throw Jonah overboard, the sea stopped its raging.

But why did Jonah not obey God? Many people think that he was afraid of suffering. Some say that he lacked faith. I think neither of these assumptions is true. No, Jonah was a brave man, and he knew God. When the ship was sinking, he told the crew that the storm was the result of his disobedience. He voluntarily suggested that they throw him into the sea so that it would be calm for the rest. Since he didn't seem to be afraid to die by drowning, how can we judge him afraid of suffering?

Then why wouldn't Jonah go to Nineveh? Obviously he wasn't without love and concern for the ship's crew and passengers. Why, then, couldn't he love the people of Nineveh? Why? Because he was prejudiced. The people of Nineveh had once occupied his country and had killed and captured many, many Israelites. Jonah couldn't forget, and that prejudice against former enemies kept him from going to Nineveh.

Today the Chinese church has a similar prejudice against taking the gospel to people of other cultures. The problem of missionary debt has become one of the most significant and urgent matters among Chinese who are part of the Body of Christ.

Prerequisites for mission work

Reading about the wise men from the East who offered gold, frankincense, and myrrh to Jesus in Matthew 2, I realised one day that these offerings could easily represent important elements in foreign missionary work. The first is faith, represented by gold. Peter makes this comparison in his first epistle. But the gold also represents money, as it was the gold that the wise man gave which Joseph used for travel expenses in fleeing to Egypt with Mary and the infant Jesus. Without faith and funds, missions will go nowhere. Faith cashes in on God's promises, and money pays the expenses of obedience.

When God called Abraham to go to Canaan and leave behind his own family, land, and tribe, Abraham obeyed without hesitation. He did not ask if the Canaanites were fierce, if the weather was good or bad, or if the soil was fertile or infertile. God called him; so he went. He simply believed that after he arrived in Canaan, God would take care of all the obstacles. This was faith. Today, when we go to distant places to spread the gospel, we tend to take with us our apprehensions about life, our work, the new place, and all kinds of unknowns. Faith, solidly placed in the God who calls us, puts those apprehensions to rest. We *can* trust him to take care of us.

Frankincense represents prayer, a very important prerequisite for mission work. Our prayers are God's means to fulfil what he has promised to do. For example, God said through Jeremiah that after seventy years the Israelites would return from Babylon to Israel. This was his promise. Daniel, wanting to claim Jeremiah's words because Jerusalem was still controlled by the Gentiles, opened his window facing Jerusalem and prayed three times a day. In the book of Ezra we see the fulfilment of God's promise when he moved the heart of the Persian king to permit the Israelites to return to Jerusalem. Still today fulfilment of God's promises come through prayer.

Prayer is a lifeline to the person who goes to a distant land with the gospel. He can enjoy peace and stand strong in hardships when there are people standing behind him in prayer, encouragement, and financial supply. The missionary is like a deep-sea diver going to the depths to search for treasures, depending on a hose for oxygen and a cable for communication. Because people in the boat are supporting him, the diver does not feel alone when he is under water. So the well-supported missionary hunting treasure does not have to feel alone amid the hardships and dangers of a far-off land and can work effectively to bring glory to God.

The last prerequisite for mission work is represented by myrrh, which needs to go through grinding and pounding in the process of being refined. Myrrh symbolises a willingness to suffer. Today many people are moved by the call to missions. But they don't take action. Why? Often because they are not willing to suffer. They don't want to serve God outside the comfort zone of the familiar. Preaching in a distant land requires more energy, more commitment, and more selflessness. Long ago, when the Antioch church sent out their first missionaries, did they send ordinary men? No. Because of the demands of missionary work, the Holy Spirit instructed them to send Barnabas and Saul, among the church's best and most talented leaders.

Centuries ago Columbus discovered the New World. If he had not been willing to take risks and to suffer hardship, he could not have crossed so many seas in his search for new lands. Missionary work inevitably requires many sacrifices. When Hudson Taylor came to Shanghai, the Chinese, like other peoples, felt racially superior and discriminated against him when they saw his blond hair, blue eyes and white skin. Some said he was a ghost. When he couldn't find anyone willing to rent to him, he sometimes had to live in a temple. Letters from home took six or seven months to arrive. Few people would listen to his message, for in matters of religion, the Chinese at that time adopted the concept 'first come, first rule', and since Buddhism, not Christianity, was the first to come to China, Buddhism should 'rule'. Hudson Taylor suffered much to bring the gospel to China.

In Brazil I met a Brother Tsai, a tea merchant, who had a book called *Monotheism*. Mr Tsai told me that the book described the Mar Toma church, the fruit of the Apostle Thomas's testimony in India, and the Nestorians, a sect of early Christianity that brought Christianity to China long before Robert Morrison did. Why did Nestorianism fail to take root in China, leaving behind only a stone monument? Because the Nestorian faith was quietly destroyed by culture and devoured by the local religions of the time.

Culture and religion remain strong opponents to Christianity in Chinese society today. One day, for example, a student at National Taiwan University came to see me and told me that his father and mother were going to get a divorce.

After more than twenty years, why, I wondered.

'It's because my mother believed the Lord and would not kowtow to our ancestors,' he explained. 'My father said that because of my mother he has not received his ancestors' help for many years, and that is why he hasn't gotten rich and why he has ended up in various sad situations.'

Such belief is a religious/cultural obstacle. Because Christians must worship only God, Christianity in China unavoidably produces conflict with this and other customs rooted in Buddhism. Chinese still believe, too, that since they already have a religion, they have no need for another. 'Why do we need to believe in a foreign god?' some say. As in the past, missionaries to the Chinese today must pick their way through all kinds of obstacles to the Gospel's taking root in China.

In short, willingness to endure hardship is part and parcel of doing evangelism in a distant place. The Chinese are not without this willingness. No matter where you look – in Europe, in South and North America, in Australia and Africa – the Chinese do not mind suffering great hardship as they work to make their fortunes, often having started with nothing. In fact, our pioneer spirit in setting out and 'making it' abroad is not second to Westerners; indeed, it even exceeds theirs. Yet, sadly enough, though we suffer willingly if what we do benefits us personally, it seems that suffering for the sake of others is out of the question. For this reason Chinese missionaries are as rare as the feathers of a phoenix and the hooves of a unicorn. If you read Chinese church history, records of sacrificial missionary work are few. To preach the gospel cross-culturally, in fact, is one of the almost untouched responsibilities of the Chinese church today. On the day that we stand before God, let us not be empty-handed, unable to give an account of this matter. The command was given to us long ago. We must get beyond prejudice, selfishness, fear of suffering, and our lack of faith, and do the work of missions, whether in our own Jerusalem or in the remotest parts of the world or somewhere in between.

Sometimes God assigns us a role in taking the gospel cross-culturally that is right at home. A Mrs Chi in Thailand, for instance, has opened her home to missionaries sent by the Overseas China Missionary Alliance. Unfamiliar with the people, the place, and the culture, new missionaries need someone to care for them. Mrs Chi has tried her very best to create for new workers a warm atmosphere in her home so that they would have someone to depend on and someone to discuss things with. Being hostess is demanding, and sometimes problems arise. Yet Mrs Chi hasn't complained, but has instead carried on consistently in this ministry to missionaries. She has found her role in what God is beginning to do through the Chinese church 'in the uttermost parts of the earth'.

33

Travels in Asia

The 'me-too' incident in Japan

In one of my visits to Japan, an elderly brother arranged to pick me up. Concerned for me because I couldn't speak Japanese and didn't know where I was supposed to go, he asked an overseas Chinese travel agent to wait for me inside the arrival area. But as the travel agent did not see me, he told the elderly brother that I had not come.

Meanwhile I had reached my hotel, where I met Rev Wang Chih. We had known each other in Taipei, for he often was invited to speak in our church services. He asked me why I was in Japan, and I said I had a speaking engagement. When I asked him the same question in return, he said, 'Me too.'

Wang then asked me who had invited me, and I said, 'The Tokyo Overseas Chinese Church.'

'Me too,' he said, puzzled at how a small Chinese church in Tokyo could invite two speakers at the same time.

The truth was that one group of church members had contacted him, and another group had contacted me. I wondered if there might be some problems within the congregation. At least the two groups had obviously not communicated with each other in inviting two speakers at the very same time. Much older than I, Rev Wang said gently and wisely, 'Mr Wu, the problem lies with them and not between the two of us.'

When the church discovered that we both had come, they sent Rev Wang to another place to preach while I stayed to preach at the prearranged meeting. Later I went to the other location while Rev Wang held a meeting in Guan Dong.

I learned much from Rev Wang. He is the one who gave way to me and was therefore blessed. If churches would follow his example and work together without contention, how much God would bless! Psalm 133 says: 'See! How good and pleasant it is when brothers live together in unity! It is like precious oil poured on the head, running down on the beard, running down on Aaron's beard, down upon the hem of his robes. It is as if the dew of Hermon were falling on Mount Zion. For there the Lord bestows his blessing, even life forever.' 'Look!' or 'See!' is an exclamation. If we are able to live together with our brothers in harmony, God will shout with joy. He will be satisfied and happy about it. The 'precious oil' is the blessing of the Holy Spirit; the 'dew of Hermon', the blessing of grace. How much I would like to see churches everywhere making God happy by living in harmony, thus enjoying the twin blessings of the presence of the Holy Spirit and God's abundant grace!

Discussion of Bible study groups in Tokyo

While I was in Tokyo, Dr John Chang, son of Litsen Chang, visited me at my hotel. He asked me if I had been to the United States, and when I said I had, he went on to ask if I had any insights from my visits there.

'Nothing in particular,' I said. 'But I saw Chinese having Bible studies everywhere I went – even in Phoenix and Tucson, two Arizona cities with small Chinese populations.'

I told Dr Chang that I had been invited to a group that met Friday nights in London, Ontario, half way between Toronto and Detroit. This study did not have designated leaders. They simply read the Bible and then shared their insights. Despite the tendency for these groups to be either boring or to degenerate into heated arguments, I confessed to him, many had come to Christ through these unstructured meetings around the word of God.

'Elder Wu, do you know the reason behind such Bible study groups here in Tokyo among the Chinese?' Dr Chang asked.

I said, 'I'm quite curious about their motives. Is it because they love the Lord? Compared to the Koreans, the Chinese lag far behind. A Korean Christian will wake up before the sun rises to go to church to pray, even in winter. This is why the Korean church is so vigorous. An open-air evangelistic crusade in Korea will be fully packed, even when it's raining hard.'

I wondered if unity were behind it. 'Compared to the Japanese, the Chinese are again far behind,' I observed. 'When two Japanese put their strength together, they double their strength, whereas two Chinese will decrease their strength. Japanese, even if they have not known each other before, can work together as a group. The Chinese can't,' I complained.

'So how come there are so many Bible study groups in the colleges and universities in the United States?' Chang challenged. 'The groups exist no matter how many come.'

Why? Our only explanation was God's mercy and his glorious working.

Mediating a dispute about hymnals

In the early years the Tokyo Overseas Chinese Church was made up of small groups and individuals from different backgrounds. So something as simple as the choice of hymnals could cause problems. When the church bought Chinese hymnals that are widely used in Taiwan, some of the members thought the hymns it contained were not spiritual enough. The objectors, members of the local church back in Taiwan, wanted to use hymnals they had compiled themselves. But, having just bought hymnals two months earlier, members from denominational backgrounds didn't want to change hymnals. Because I happened to be in Japan at the time, they asked me to solve this problem.

Both sides presented their views. One group said: 'Our membership is made up of people of different backgrounds. Some complain that they are not accustomed to singing hymns from the

Praise Hymnal. But since we have people from Presbyterian, Baptist, Anglican, and Wesleyan churches, how can we ever settle this problem if one segment can demand change? So we insist on not changing, but continuing to use the *Praise Hymnal*, which doesn't belong to any one denomination.'

The other side said: 'We should not place too much importance on money, but rather on the content of the hymnal, whether or not it will help us spiritually. Whether or not our spirits can sing in harmony is essential. So we demand a change of the hymnals.'

Both sides having given their arguments, they waited for me to give the verdict. 'Being but a visitor among you . . . I'd like to talk to each group separately before making any decision,' I said.

So both groups dispersed to wait for my call. But before calling either group in, I pondered the solution to the problem. Within a family with many children, I thought, if brothers quarrel, the parents usually would reason with the older one, not the younger. But in the case of the Tokyo church, which side should I consider the more mature?

Figuring that the members from the independent churches were the more mature because they put more importance on spirituality than money, I went to them first and related this parable: When two brothers cross a street, the older would cross the street in such a way as to protect his younger brother. A thoughtful brother would not self-centredly cross the street in big steps, dragging his younger brother along after him. Understanding that the younger one needs to walk more slowly, the older would have to be patient, slow down, and walk in such a way that both of them could cross to the other side safely.

'I consider you to be the older brother because you put more importance on spirituality,' I began. 'What, then, is spirituality?' I went on. 'I think you would agree that it has nothing to do with position or knowledge. It is rather not being governed by self or the body. So how do we distinguish someone who is spiritual? Certainly a spiritual man will have a good relationship with God; yet one's relationship with God is also based upon the relationship one has with others here on earth. In the Bible narrative, when Lot's people argued with Abraham over water and pasture, Abraham said, "Let's not have any quarrelling between you and me . . . for we are brothers. . . If you go to the left, I'll go to the right; if you go to the right, I'll go to the left." Abraham gave way to Lot, a sign of his true spirituality. Likewise, how did David treat King Saul? Though Saul was trying to kill him, David refused to dishonour the Lord's anointed. Though he had chances to take vengeance into his own hand, he did not. He endured.

'So our spirituality depends upon our relationship to others,' I went on. 'It depends on our giving and enduring. What do you think Abraham would have done in regard to this argument over hymnals? He would say, "Let's not quarrel." Arguments are appropriate when our central beliefs are at issue. If the issue, for instance, is denying the incarnation of Jesus, then go ahead and argue with your brother. . . as the difference in spirituality between the hymnals is minimal, I think we should not argue about such a trivial matter. Putting importance on spirituality by the local church is right. Yet we can wait for our brothers to grow spiritually, to be like us. Until then they won't know what is meant by spirituality.

'I came to talk to you first today because I hope you will stop quarrelling, as an older brother giving way to the younger,' I concluded, 'because this issue has nothing to do with basic doctrine.'

Though they agreed that this approach was quite reasonable, they insisted on asking permission from the local church office in Taipei.

'I'll help you ask their permission,' I encouraged, 'because I'm acquainted with your brothers in Taipei.'

With the Tokyo group's permission, when I returned to Taipei, I went to talk with leaders of the local church in Taipei. Quoting their founder, Watchman Nee, who said, 'Churches are not to compare big size or small size,' I said, 'This means a Taipei church cannot control a Taichung church. If it does, it is using its size to compare.' I told them that I agreed with this teaching and hoped the church I go to adopts such a principle. 'I see that practising this principle is harder than teaching it,' I told them.

'What are you referring to?' they asked.

I told them that their hands of control were extended not only to Taichung, but also across the Pacific. Explaining about the arguments over the hymnbooks in Tokyo, I told them that their former members requested me to ask permission for them to use the hymnbooks already bought.

The local church brethren protested that they were not insisting on control, but that this situation was of the Tokyo group's own doing.

Whatever the truth in this case may have been, control of others is often written in the hearts and minds of the people involved, whether written regulations exist or not. In churches we must not only preach the truth, but practise it. If we don't, we will hurt people. And we must avoid dividing ourselves over trivial matters, or we shall lose the Lord's presence. Nothing is worth that result.

The Tokyo church, by the way, continued to use the *Praise Hymnals*. The Taipei office did not give an opinion.

Passport debacle

Once when I had a speaking engagement in Japan and my wife was planning a visit to America, Bao Lian suggested that she travel with me as far as Japan and stay with me for a night before going on with her flight to the US. I agreed, and we flew to Japan together.

The next morning I took my wife to the airport and checked her in so that she would have nothing to worry about before departure. As her flight wasn't to depart until late at night, she urged me not to wait, but to go back to the hotel and get to bed early. She knew I had to get up early to go to the campsite where I was speaking. Agreeing, I gave her the passport from my bag, saw her to a line at immigration, and headed for the Tokyo Railway Station. I bought a ticket and boarded the train.

Meanwhile, when my wife handed the immigration officer the passport she had, he asked, 'Lady, is this passport yours?'

'Yes,' she replied.

But it wasn't. It was mine.

What was she to do? She was terrified. In a city the size of Tokyo how would she ever find me? And if she could not find me, she couldn't go to the US nor back to Taiwan. In any case, she had no choice but to leave the immigration area.

Back at the station my train had not yet departed. Suddenly instead of peace, I felt an inexplicable sense of uneasiness. When I heard the whistle blow to alert passengers that the train was about to depart, I jumped off the train and walked back to where I had left my wife. When I caught up with her and asked why she had not gone in yet, she could not answer me since she was so nearly in shock. I asked her again. This time she showed me the passport. 'Oh, no!' I exclaimed. 'I am so careless. Why did I give you my passport and keep yours?!'

How I thanked God then and still do that he gave me that feeling of uneasiness so that I could correct the matter in time to avoid a disaster! Even if we make mistakes, his grace is sufficient. If my wife hadn't retrieved her passport that day, she couldn't have moved. I was in the same boat – without my passport, I couldn't have moved either. How would I ever have got back to Taiwan after the camp?

As it was, we exchanged documents, and my wife was able to continue on her flight to the US, frightened, but not really hurt.

Lifestyle evangelism

I got to know a certain Sister Liu in Japan whose husband was Japanese, whom she had met in north-west China. Kao Chiao was a manager in one of Tokyo's banks. While the wife came to believe in Jesus after they were married, he did not. Although he did not want her to believe in Christ, he respected her decision.

One time, as the Christmas celebration went late into the evening, Sister Liu went home later than usual. She knocked expectantly at the door, but no one opened the gate. Unhappy about her being late, her husband had decided not to open the door to give her a warning not to go to the church again. Not knowing what her husband was thinking, she chose to squat by the doorway in the cold and not go to another house to stay. In the morning, when Kao Chiao came out of the gate to go to work, he saw his wife crouched into a ball, with her mouth and face turned black from frostbite. She was almost frozen to death. He carried her inside and warmed her until she regained consciousness.

It would have been reasonable for Sister Liu to hold this incident against her husband. But she did not do so. Instead, when Kao Chiao came home from work, she prepared a hot towel and hot water for him to refresh himself.

Comparing his behaviour to his wife's, Kao Chiao was ashamed of himself. He expected that his wife would be cold to him and hate him from then on. Instead she was more loving and warm toward him than ever, not saying one hurtful word about the whole incident. So touched was he by her witness that he went to church with her. When we met, he had already accepted Jesus Christ as his personal Saviour and had been baptized. He could have argued with a lecture on theology; he could not refute the testimony of his wife's loving forgiveness.

Kao Chiao became a brother through lifestyle evangelism.

Peace in a 'haunted' hotel

When a brother in Christ heard that I had a cardiac problem and that I didn't get enough rest while in Taiwan, he invited my wife and me to come to Hong Kong for a vacation at his expense. He said he wouldn't let anyone know where we were so that we could have absolute rest. He had already booked me and my wife in a hotel that was built on a causeway jutting out into the sea, where the air was fresh and clean. Not reachable by public transportation, the hotel, he added, was a good place to take a rest. He wanted my wife to come to ensure that I would get well as soon as possible. Grateful for his love and thoughtful arrangements, we accepted his offer and flew to Hong Kong.

The hotel was a paradise. In our two-week stay everything we needed was provided. We really had no need to go into the city.

My heart enjoyed complete rest in the quiet luxury of the place. But I was curious as to why almost nobody was staying at this beautiful tourist spot. During our stay we saw only two Westerners, and within two days, they had left.

In the middle of our stay we went to Hong Kong Island to visit a brother in Christ. When we told him where we were staying, he looked at us strangely and became silent. His expression made me wonder if something was wrong. Yet the hotel in which we were staying was very beautiful and quiet, almost ideal for someone as sick as I. I wondered if I were reading too much into his expression. But his reaction made me curious.

After our half-month rest, I had regained my strength and felt ready to go home. Besides, we didn't want to continue living in such a luxurious hotel, spending so much of our brother's money.

When we were about to go back to Taipei, the brother who had had the questioning expression came and asked us whether we had had *peace* during our stay at that hotel? His question seemed as strange as his earlier reaction. Why did he ask if we had peace? People usually ask if someone is comfortable or not.

At first he didn't want to explain his reason. But with my insistence, he said finally: 'Now that you are moving out, my telling you the story won't make any difference.' He hesitated. 'Didn't you notice,' he asked, 'that no other tourists were at such a beautiful hotel?'

'Yes,' I said, 'but I assumed the hotel was too far from the city and not convenient for shopping purposes.'

'That's not the reason,' he said. 'If one can afford to live in that hotel, he can afford the taxi rides to and from the city.'

'Then what is the reason?' I probed. 'Is it that the service is not good?'

'No.'

'Then why?' My curiosity was now fully aroused.

'Because people who check in there have often had problems with ghosts. When such rumours spread around, people stopped staying at that hotel,' he explained. 'During your stay, did you see any ghosts?' he asked.

'No. None.'

Amazingly during our stay at that hotel we had absolute peace. God had shielded us. Praise him that we didn't even hear about the spirits until after we left! Knowing of the rumours might have disturbed our tranquillity and interfered with the rest I so needed. I praise the Lord every time I remember God's grace in those precious two weeks.

Rare commitment

When I went to preach the word of God in Swatow Life Church at Tsimshatsui, Hong Kong, one of the brothers who attended one of the first services was a man I knew from Singapore, a man who had only recently earned a large sum of money. During a meal with him the following day he told me that he had sent a telegram to his wife and kids in Singapore, asking them to come to Hong Kong immediately.

'Is it because of your business here in Hong Kong?' I asked.

'No, I asked them to come to listen to the word of God,' he said. 'I'll bring them to your service tonight.'

What commitment! Sometimes when I hold a series of evangelistic meetings, people aren't even willing to take a one-hour trip, even a half-hour trip, to join us, much less fly from Singapore to Hong Kong, spending money for hotel accommodation just to listen to a few sermons. Yet this man did so. And he and his family were greatly blessed because of the value he placed on the preaching of the word of God.

True love

One of the times I was in Hong Kong, a sister invited me to her home for a meal. Her husband, the boss of a company, was quite fat. Being a hospitable lady, the wife focused her full attention on me, making sure I ate some of every dish that she had prepared. She feared that as a minister, I might be too shy to eat to my full.

The woman's husband, seeing that she was busy entertaining me and not paying attention to him, quietly served himself to a second helping. His wife immediately ordered him to put the meat back. I was curious as to why this wife was disciplining her husband, and more why she was getting away with doing so.

A little later, when the wife wasn't looking, the husband got another piece of meat and put it into his mouth. But turning her head and catching him cheating, the woman pinched his cheek and patted his mouth, saying, 'Spit that meat out.' He did so.

I found out later that my hostess was acting out her concern for her husband's weight, with the probability of its causing him physical problems. She was acting out of love, and because her husband knew it, he did not get angry. Love shows concern, and love is not mindful of being disciplined. This couple modelled this reciprocal love and its outworking beautifully.

Stress and sleeplessness cause a mild stroke

On the second to last day of another series of revival meetings in Hong Kong, I suddenly suffered a mild stroke. I felt weak, my heart and tongue felt numb, and my arms became spastic. No longer able to stand, I collapsed onto the stage.

When I had stabilised, someone put the microphone near my mouth so that I could continue to preach. I was able to finish the message, but with a much weaker voice. The few thousand listeners were nervous for me, and the organisers sent me back to the hotel immediately. Everyone wondered how I could make it through the final session the next day, which was to be the climax of the series.

A representative of the congress, Mr Yang Chih-hsiung, called a doctor to come to where I was staying. When the physician asked me what happened, I told him that because the revival meetings had been going for two weeks, some of them in Hong Kong and some in Kowloon, I had became so emotionally keyed up that I was not able to sleep. I had not really slept, in fact, for more than seventy hours.

'So that's the reason!' said Mr Yang.

After the doctor had given me some sleeping pills, Mr Yang asked him how long it would take before the medicine took effect. About ten or twenty minutes, the physician said.

Telling me that they were going home, the doctor and Mr Yang left the room, but I could hear them talking outside my room. Although I lay down on the bed, I still couldn't sleep. When they peeked in half an hour later, my eyes were still wide open. 'You haven't gone to sleep yet!' exclaimed Mr Yang.

I said, 'You're right. I don't know why I can't sleep.'

Mr Yang then urged the doctor to find a solution because the meeting the next day, being the finale, was the most important. If I were not able to preach, the congregation would miss a lot.

When the doctor had increased the dosage of the medication, Mr Yang again asked when it would begin to take effect.

The answer was the same: ten or twenty minutes.

The two went out again. It was already two in the morning. As I could not bear the sight of an eighty-year-old man standing outside my door worrying about me, I decided to close my eyes and snore when he opened the door again. The plan worked, and he stopped worrying and went right home.

In actuality I was still unable to sleep. Yet, because of the love of that brother, I got up the next morning refreshed and strengthened. That evening I completed my fifteenth day of revival meetings without further incident.

Plan to experience missionary life first-hand

We Chinese are greatly indebted to missionary effort. Yet, despite two hundred years of Chinese church history, we are yet at the starting point of our own missionary effort. For this reason some of us established the Overseas Missionary Association, hoping to perpetuate a vision for the world and arouse the Chinese church to emphasise and propagate missions. So it was that Kou Shih-yuan and I took two brothers each to Asian countries, including Japan, and to various places in the United States to begin enlightening the church about overseas missionary efforts.

Yet having heard little of the experience of Chinese in missions and having not experienced the life of a missionary myself, how could I understand the hardships they had to face and how could I communicate this to those to whom I spoke?

Coming back from our tour of Asia and the US, I discussed this lack with my wife, and she agreed with me that we would do well to experience missionary life first hand. As our church in Taipei was already quite stable, it seemed that setting up such an experience was quite possible. The church, in fact, not only gave us their approval, but they prayed for us, put their hands on us and sent us out as their representatives.

We planned to travel via Thailand to Singapore, where we would study the Indonesian language before going on to Indonesia. Because we were trying to save money, we took the train from Bangkok to Singapore – a fifty-six-hour journey that took us through Malaysia. As we approached Singapore, I prayed to the Lord for three things: a place to stay, a language teacher, and a church in which to be a co-worker. As Singapore is quite an advanced country, I knew renting a house would be costly. And while we learned Indonesian, I wanted a place of ministry: I could teach adult Sunday School, lead a youth fellowship, or lead a fellowship of the elderly, whether classes were big or small.

When we arrived in Singapore, Rev Hsu Sung-kuang came to pick us up at the train station. No sooner had we arrived than he said, 'I hear that you want to rent a place.' When I told him that we did, he responded: 'Let's go look at a house right now!'

Pastor Hsu took me to an apartment which was on the tenth floor. He asked me if I liked the place or not. I nodded. The place was quite roomy, with three bedrooms and two living rooms and was fully furnished.

'This is my house,' said this helpful brother. 'If you like it, you can stay here.'

'I like it very much,' I said, 'but for two people, the place is quite large.'

Sensing that I was afraid of paying high rent, he said, 'Don't worry. Stay here. I don't want any rent from you. In fact, I've already deposited some money in the bank for the electricity, water, and phone bills.'

What a servant of God! A pastor is never rich. If Rev Hsu had rented his home to others, he would have collected a large sum of money. But for the two years that we stayed in Singapore, this dear brother treated us as guests.

With my first prayer answered, someone then introduced me to a lady Indonesian instructor. Although she was an overseas Chinese, her Chinese was not nearly as good as her Indonesian. I told her that I hoped to have two-hour classes three times a week because I wanted to learn the Indonesian language fast. I also told her that because I was a missionary, I would not be able to pay as much as ambassadors did, but only so much an hour.

'Money is good,' she said seriously, 'but if I charge you a fee, I won't be able to say that I am your co-worker. I would very much like to be a part of your ministry for the Lord.' The second prayer was marvellously answered! What grace!

The third thing I asked for was an invitation to minister in a church. I was willing to teach any age except children. God's answer to my third request came when Pastor Hsu came to me to propose that I preach for him at Jubilee Chapel. 'If you are willing, I'll let you preach weekly so that I can accomplish other things in the church.' I agreed, grateful for the opportunity. And for two years I preached at Jubilee Chapel, with many other opportunities to share God's word with the brothers and sisters of that congregation.

Again we experienced God's working and his faithfulness in providing for our needs as we followed his will for our lives. In fact, our time in Singapore was extremely precious. For one thing, my Singapore family were all baptised in Jubilee Chapel and became active members of the congregation. So whenever I stood in the pulpit to preach, I could see my whole clan seated together. What a comfort to my heart! The promise of Acts 16:31: 'Believe in Jesus Christ, and you and your whole family will be saved', was indeed fulfilled in my family. Seeing my brothers, sisters, nephews and nieces worshipping the Lord together, I felt the Lord's faithfulness to me in a special way.

Also in our two year stay in Singapore Brother Teo Seng-hui took me out for breakfast daily, investing a lot of money, time, and effort in doing so. His love for us was very precious. I still think of him often. During one spring festival season, he bought me some sticky cake. Actually I don't usually eat it because it sticks to my false teeth. But because Brother Teo was warm and hospitable, I took some and was surprised that it didn't stick to my teeth at all. And was it good!

When I saw Brother Teo a few days later, he asked me how the sticky cake tasted. 'It tasted great,' I said and explained that I don't usually eat sticky cake because of the problem of my false teeth. 'But the cake you bought me was different. Not that sticky, it was easy to eat.'

When Brother Teo bought me some more the next day, I remembered what the Bible said about grace upon grace. Giving thanks to the Lord is important too, for if we thank him, grace is added to grace. Today few know how to give thanks to the Lord. We are often like the ten lepers whom Jesus healed. Though ten were healed, only one went back to thank Jesus. Today, then, if we receive God's blessing, let's go before him and thank him! Thankfulness will greatly increase our faith and our experience of the Lord's faithfulness.

Accused of being a wandering vagrant

When Brother Kou Shih-yuan and I went to Singapore to promote overseas missions, the churches in Singapore made arrangements for us to hold a series of rallies at the Victoria Opera House because it was easy to get to and could accommodate many people. Brother Kou and I planned to speak alternately.

When the Singaporean newspaper reported our rallies, two elderly ladies who had heard me preach in Penang saw the announcement and decided to attend. Sitting in the audience the first meeting, the elder sister said to the younger, 'Have you noticed how Mr Wu Yung's complexion has become fairer?'

'Yes,' the younger sister answered, 'it's because he lived in

Singapore before, and now he is residing in Taiwan. Singapore is on the equator, and Taiwan is not, and the people on the equator usually have darker skin than people living elsewhere.'

After a while the elder sister leaned over to her younger sibling and whispered, 'When Wu Yung preached in Penang, he had such a loud voice. Why isn't his voice loud anymore?'

'It's probably because of his advancing age,' guessed the younger. Satisfied with this explanation, the elder sister listened quietly for a while, then asked, 'Sister, did you hear him just relate his testimony . . . about his coming to Christ through his mother? Is that true? Don't you remember what he said when he preached in Penang? He told us that he came to trust Christ first and then later his father and mother came to know Christ. How could his testimony have changed after a few years?'

'Do you remember what he said before?' the younger sibling challenged.

'How could I forget it? He said he had had cancer and was healed by God. Then he came to Singapore and led his father and mother to Christ. Today he said his mother came to know Christ before he did. How could his coming to Christ be through his mother? How could this happen? This minister is like a wandering vagrant! He talks of one thing in one place and another in another place. This man is a liar!'

Furious, the two women rushed out of the meeting site during the final prayer. I happened to be standing right at the gate, waiting to greet the people as they were leaving. The sisters stared at me as they walked right past me. I was a little bit puzzled. As my heart was asking why, the younger sister came back and asked, 'Are you not Mr Wu?'

I said I was.

'We rushed out while you were praying. How did you manage to be standing by the gate so quickly?'

'I was not the speaker today,' I told her.

'Then who was?' she asked.

'Mr Kou Shih-yuan.'

'What? Mr Kou Shih-yuan?' she exclaimed, then turned and shouted to her elder sister, 'Sister, come back! The speaker today was not Mr Wu but Mr Kou Shih-yuan.'

I didn't understand what had happened between the two sisters, but later they related to me the whole event. Mistaking Mr Kou for me and misjudging the situation, they had come close to being instruments of Satan to cause trouble within Christian circles.

I have learned, on the other hand, if others misunderstand us, we don't need to be angry or rush to defend ourselves. Arguing in self-defence usually leads to greater misunderstanding. If we could only learn to deal with misunderstandings with gentleness, the misunderstandings would not as likely expand into greater conflicts. I shudder to think of the rumours that may well have spread had the misunderstanding between me and the two elderly sisters not been resolved. I might well have become known as a wandering, dishonest vagrant.

Preaching at Grace Gospel Church in Manila

While I was praying with my younger brother in Singapore one day, I sensed the Holy Spirit leading me to go to Manila in the Philippines. When we ended our prayer time, I told my brother about it. 'Do you know someone there?' he asked.

'No one I can think of,' I replied.

When he questioned how I could go to Manila, a place I had never been and where I knew no one, I dropped the subject.
But not long afterwards, when I was returning to Taipei and about to get out of the taxi from the airport, a Mrs Tan called out to me. 'Where have you been?' she asked.

'Singapore,' I told her.

'I've been looking for you,' she said. 'You came home at just the right time. Here is a letter for you from the Philippines that I was asked to hand-deliver.'

The letter was from Grace Gospel Church in Manila, inviting me to speak there. I decided to go, particularly in light of the earlier moving of the Holy Spirit in my heart.

Although the Grace Gospel Church was small at that time, meeting in the chapel of Grace Christian High School, God blessed the meetings. When the chapel proved to be too small, we changed the venue to a stadium. The stadium was also fully packed. God's wonderful and real leading in these meetings was evident.

But I also faced a test during my time in Manila. During one of my sermons I mentioned how Singaporeans eat hot spices with every meal, confessing how much I love to eat spicy food. As a result, my host ordered all spicy foods. But when I did not eat any, a little girl turned to me and asked, 'Mr Wu, didn't you say a while ago on stage that you like to eat hot and spicy things? Now that they are in front of you, why don't you eat any?'

At first I just smiled in response. But when she continued to probe, I replied, 'It's not that I don't want to eat it, but my boss won't allow me to.'

'Who is your boss?' she came back.

'My wife,' I confessed.

'Then are you afraid of your wife?' she asked.

'No,' I told her, 'I love my wife.'

Actually I really love to eat spicy things. But because highly seasoned foods might affect my health adversely, my wife doesn't want me to eat them. I normally don't eat any at home. But before this trip my wife asked me while I was at the airport not to eat spicy foods in the Philippines. Deciding that it was enough not to eat spicy foods at home and planning to eat as much of it as I could while in the Philippines, I ignored her as if I hadn't heard her. Unfortunately she knew that I was playing dumb, so she tapped my shoulder and looked me square in the eye and said, 'When you go to the Philippines, do not eat any spicy food. Okay?' With this eyeball-to-eyeball contact, I had to say yes! And having made a vow to her, I had to keep it. I ate no spicy food.

The Bible tells us that we have to keep our vows, or we will lose our trustworthiness. Because our Lord is faithful, we have to mirror that faithfulness, even in the matter of spicy food!

Tangle with ginseng

I went to the Philippines a second time to take part in evangelistic meetings sponsored by many churches. The series was held in a stadium which could accommodate thousands of people. As I hadn't had much experience with such big crowds then, I began to feel tense. Noticing in my first message that I spoke with an intense, loud voice and dripped with sweat, the wife of an ambassador to the Philippines stewed up for me two ginseng roots which were gifts to her husband from a Korean basketball team that had come for a game.

Only thirty years old then, I had no idea how powerful ginseng was. After I took the ginseng concoction, I felt very strong. But it so stirred me up that I could not sleep. The sleepless nights began to affect my perception, and I suffered panic attacks. When I was travelling in a car, for instance, it seemed as if the cars on the other side of the road were all coming right toward us. My memory also began to deteriorate. As I preached, I would forget what I had just said. I even forgot the names of people I knew. So when I returned to Taipei, my wife, knowing of my state of mind, came to pick me up at the airport and took me to Sun Moon Lake for a week of rest. Little by little my nerves relaxed until by the end of the week I was back to normal. I learned the hard way the dangers of ginseng.

The secret of a God-pleasing life

I often tell seminary students that there are no short cuts to spiritual growth and health. The spiritual vitality of a servant of God is the foundation of his pilgrimage and ministry. I consider consistent daily devotions to be the secret to that vitality and growth – in fact, primary and foundational to our Christian walk.

I was reminded of this conviction while I was in Manila, when a sister testified of the consistency of her mother-in-law's Christian testimony. In the ten years of her marriage this sister said that she had never seen her mother-in-law angry. One

Sunday, she said, her husband expressed concern about his mother. 'My mother is now more than eighty years old,' he noted, 'and she has never neglected her daily devotions from her youth until now. She gets up for her devotions before the sun rises. She could do it easily when she was young. But now that she is old and her bones are getting fragile, I am worried that she might slip and fall when she goes out to meet with other ladies at the church each morning. Do you think we could think of a way to ask her to stay home?'

'You should know that God has been her priority all her life,' responded the daughter-in-law. 'You and I are but second or third along the line.'

'Even so,' the husband insisted, 'I think we ought to think of a way to stop her from going out at dawn. What if she had an accident? We would all feel terrible.'

'How can we stop her?' the wife asked.

'Tonight we'll lock all the doors before we go to sleep so that Mom can't get out of the house,' the husband proposed.

The wife agreed because neither of them could think of any other way to achieve their purpose.

The next morning when they saw that all the locks were untouched, they thought that their mom wasn't able to get out that day. They continued locking the doors night after night for two weeks, smug with their success.

Then an old lady said to them, 'You have a great mother. Although she is already more than eighty years old, she leads our daily devotions every morning. If she didn't lead us in our daily Bible reading and prayer, our times would not be nearly as enjoyable.'

'Has my mother-in-law been meeting with you for daily devotions recently?' the wife asked.

'Oh yes,' said the old lady. 'She has never missed one.'

'Did she come yesterday?' the wife probed.

'Yes, she came yesterday,' the informant said.

'What about earlier this week?'

'Yes! Every day.'

The daughter-in-law was astonished. How had her mother-in-law led the daily communal devotions even when the doors were locked?

When the wife told her husband about the conversation, they agreed to get up early the next morning to see how his mother got out without touching the lock. At dawn the next day they watched from their hiding place as the elderly, not-so-steady mother-in-law put a small chair near the wall and climbed over the fence to make her escape to lead the group devotions at church.

This old lady thirsted for the Lord. She had read the Bible and prayed to be near God every day for many decades. The beauty of her life was a testimony to its efficacy. Neither her face nor her voice reflected anger. Once again I was impressed with the importance of a daily time with God and his word as a foundation for true Christian living.

Reading the Bible is a must. One should not only read through it, but also seek for important insights. God's servant must be able to meet the heavenly Father in such a way that they come to see earthly things from the viewpoint of the Bible. The reader must meditate on the word to absorb nourishment from it because only when food is digested does one get satisfaction, and only a satisfied life can produce power. Christians need power to fight the good fight for the Lord.

Prayer must also be a significant part of our communion with God. Only earnest prayer from the heart can cast out burdens, leaving our spirits free and relaxed, usable in God's work.

Without the foundation of daily exposure to God's word and communion with God himself, our spiritual life will be flimsy. We will not only be defenceless against the storms and challenges that come our way, but we will lack the power and usableness in God's hands that is his purpose for us.

Visit to India

Though I didn't know how God would use me there, I was moved by the Holy Spirit to accept an invitation to go to

Calcutta, India. It was a trip never to be forgotten.

When I arrived in Calcutta, the man at the immigration counter asked me, 'How did you come here?' Though surprised by the way he asked the question, I answered that I came by plane.

'No! No! I'm not asking about your means of transportation,' he came back. 'I'm asking about the type of visa you have.'

I explained that I had gone to the British embassy in Taipei to get the visa.

'How did they give you this visa?' he probed.

I confessed that I honestly didn't know. 'Why don't you ask the representative in the British embassy in Taipei?'

'Wait for me outside,' he ordered.

After waiting until almost sunset (I had arrived there about two in the afternoon), I went to inquire of the man at the desk again. 'Sir,' I said as patiently as I could, 'am I allowed to enter your country or not? If I am, can I enter now? If not, send me back to Taipei.'

The man told me to wait while he negotiated with his boss. When he came out, he informed me that I was to be allowed to stay only for five days. After subtracting my arrival and departure days, that actually gave me only three days. 'You may enter today, but come back to the immigration office at 9 a.m. tomorrow.' I nodded, and he pencilled into my passport a note stating the five-day limit.

The brother who had come to pick me up at the airport had been waiting since one o'clock in the afternoon. The sun was low in the sky then as he drove me over rough and potholed roads to the Baptist Seminary where I was to stay. When we arrived, nobody was around because a severe drought had forced a suspension of classes. As there was neither a guest room nor a dormitory room available at the school, I was sent into a storehouse to spend the night.

What a night! There was no water to take a bath or to drink. But as soon as I lay down, I began to snore. I don't know how long I had slept when I was awakened by someone knocking at the door. A bit frightened, I dared not answer the knock. But when the knock became a pounding, I had no choice but to open up. There in front of me stood a group of dark-skinned men.

'You made us lose a whole night's sleep,' charged one of them. 'When you arrived at immigration, we are the ones who had to sign in your passport,' they said when I protested that having arrived only that day, I could not have made them lose a whole night's sleep. 'Don't you remember us?' they asked.

Surely, I thought, *these men want to blackmail me, coming in the middle of the night like this*. But then, stepping inside, they said, 'Give us your passport. Though at first we wanted you to report to the immigration officer tomorrow, now you won't have to do that. As it is, he likely doesn't know that you have come. If you meet him tomorrow, then he'll for sure know that you came. Anyway, as there are already more than eight thousand Chinese in Calcutta, it won't make any difference if we add one more.'

Pleased that my not having to report the next day would save me a half day's time, I thanked the men. But that was not the end of the good news. Before they left they told me that the limitation for my stay in India was withdrawn, and apologising for awakening me in the middle of the night, erased the written limitation from my passport.

After my middle-of-the-night visitors left, I lay wondering what I should do in my suddenly extended stay. 'Lord,' I prayed, 'I didn't come to India for a tour.' Actually it didn't seem to me at the moment that there was anything worth looking at. The roads were in poor shape, the country was in the middle of a drought, and stores were closed because of a strike. Hordes of homeless people milled the streets. Even babies were learning to walk right in the middle of the street. Some picked through fallen coconuts for a sip of milk or a bit of the meat. Cows walked freely on the road, with nobody daring to shoo them away because cows are considered as gods. So both cows and vehicles were caught in traffic jams. However, as the cows couldn't understand the rules, car drivers were definitely better followers of traffic laws than the cows.

One day we were on our way by car to a village to visit a tannery, when I noticed many large birds flying around overhead. Their heads were featherless. One of the brothers with us told me that the birds were vultures and that the open ground over which they were circling was a graveyard. In India, he said, though many of the dead are buried or cremated, many are either thrown into the sea or abandoned above ground to be eaten by the birds. It was certainly not a pleasant sight.

Later in my stay in India, a brother with whom I was staying told me that a German lady who lived at the back of the apartment building cried day and night. She was married to a Hindu, whom she met while he was studying in Germany. They had settled in India after he completed his studies. Within two months she had had a nervous breakdown, unable to cope with the very different surroundings, language, and culture in India.

Missionaries also have to cope with different lifestyles, language, and culture. But because of their love for God, they are able to establish the roots they need to persevere. While the German lady broke down within a few weeks, missionaries usually stay for years, sometimes as long as ten years at a time in the adopted country. Some even die in the foreign land.

I met in Calcutta a white man whom I first saw sleeping outside the doorway of the Ling Liang Church. One seldom sees a white person do this. But this man was a believer who had come all the way from Scotland to pay his debt to the gospel. He laboured without the support of relatives, church, or mission group. As he was a farmer without much knowledge of the Bible, no church would send him as their missionary. But, strong in his determination, he came anyway and stayed on the street, subsisting mostly on noodles. To cook, he borrowed fire and a kettle from someone. Because he slept outdoors, in doorways or along the road, his body was full of mosquito bites.

When he heard that I had an invitation to preach the gospel in a place called Taba, this most unusual missionary asked for a supply of tracts. Explaining that he usually worked in the streets, he was at ease talking with people as they passed by. He would go to Taba, he said, pass out the tracts and invite Chinese to go to hear my preaching. I have rarely seen a more enthusiastic minister of the gospel than he, though he was all alone and living like a beggar.

At least partly because of this man's diligence, the meetings were well attended in Taba. In the three consecutive days of services, more than one hundred and fifty signed their names as having received Christ as their personal Saviour. As a result of the harvest of that series of meetings an overseas Chinese church was established in the town.

Touch with the Korean church

During one of my stopovers in Korea during the 1970s, Korean Pastor Li Man Yueh invited me to visit the Full Gospel Central Church. It was at that time the largest church in the world. When Pastor Li introduced me to the mother-in-law of Rev Yonge Cho, Rev Tsui Tzu Shih, she asked me how long I was staying in Korea and if I could preach at a meeting the next afternoon.

'Is there a regular meeting tomorrow afternoon?' I asked.

'No,' she answered, 'but the members here are easy to gather. If I told them to come, they'd come. If you are willing, I'll tell them at once. Please come and share with us tomorrow at 2 p.m.' So I agreed.

The next day I was surprised to see several thousand people fill the meeting place. Because it was daytime, most were ladies. When I finished preaching, I led in prayer and took my seat. But Rev Tsui asked me to return to the pulpit. Seeing that many in the audience had their hands on their heads, I asked her what they were doing. 'They want you to lay your hands on them,' she explained.

If there were tens or even hundreds of people waiting for me to lay my hands on them, I might be able to do so, I thought. But thousands? Not knowing what else to do, I held my hands up high as if to give a benediction as a symbol of the laying on of my hands. But Pastor Tsui pulled my arms down, saying, 'They are waiting for you to lay your hands on each person individually.' When I objected that to do so would take hours and that the ladies would have to go home to make dinner, she said, 'Don't worry. The members here are very patient. When they come to a meeting, they bring food supplies with them.'

So I did what they requested. I laid my hands on one head after another. Though at that time the central church had not grown to the one hundred thousand members it has today, I saw for myself how members thirsted for the Lord and how revival continued among them.

A miracle in Thailand

On my first trip home to Singapore I stopped over in Thailand to hold some special meetings. Because my plane was late, I asked the believers who came to pick me up not to take me to dinner but to go directly to the meeting site.

When we arrived, though it was time to start the meeting, only a few people sat scattered in the large auditorium. I felt cold as I made my way to the platform. But a servant of God should never let the number of listeners affect his delivery of the word of God. The meeting went on as planned.

In the overseas Chinese churches in Thailand, one does not just go to preach, but has to help with the visiting and the inviting as well. In the process we went to visit a stroke victim who had been bedridden for five years. A native of Chaozhou, the lady said to me, 'Mr Wu, I don't think I'll ever be well again.'

Answering her in her native language, I said, 'Sister, that's not true. We usually experience God in a special way when we are in trouble. You can't experience God's abundance without experiencing your own poverty first. You cannot experience his salvation before going through disaster or healing without being sick. The way to spiritual blessing is usually along such a pathway of trial.'

Understanding my point, the bedridden woman said, 'Okay, then pray for me!'

After I prayed, the lady called her daughter to her and ordered, 'Support me. I'd like to stand up.'

The daughter did as she was told, and the patient, whose body was paralysed on one side, moved her legs out of the bed and pulled herself to a standing position with her hands on a table in front of her. 'Leave the room,' she told us; 'I want to accompany you out.'

Panicking, the daughter said, 'Mom, you don't have to do that! They don't want you to escort them out of the door.'

But the older woman insisted on seeing us out of the door herself. With both hands on the table, she straightened her body. And as she moved, I saw drops of perspiration on her forehead. She was exerting much effort. But she was moving the paralysed side as she eased away from the table! 'Mr Wu,' she repeated, 'leave the room now. I'll see you to the door slowly as I move along the wall.'

Refusing her daughter's help, the older woman ordered the younger to go ahead and open the door. And by faith the stroke victim walked – slowly, mind you, but all by herself. How could one ever strike down faith as big as hers?

The news of the miracle spread rapidly among the overseas Chinese community. When the evening service started, the large auditorium was fully packed.

Jesus is the same yesterday, today and forever. He performed a miracle then, and he can also do so now.

Satanic attack in Thailand

On one of my trips from India to Singapore, our plane had a layover in Thailand. Because the plane from Calcutta was late, I missed the connecting flight back to Singapore and had no choice but to stay overnight at a guest house. Catching me while I was registering, an elder called out to me, 'Elder Wu! When did you arrive in Thailand? Why didn't you let us know in advance of your trip here?'

I told him that my trip to Thailand was unplanned, that I was on my way to see my relatives in Singapore. I explained that delay in getting in from Calcutta had forced me to stay overnight.

'What are your plans for tomorrow,' he asked.

'I'll go to a nearby church to worship,' I told him, 'then take the afternoon flight back to Singapore.'

'Don't do that,' he said. 'It would be a shame if you didn't preach.'

When he offered his church, I objected. 'Your speaker for the worship service is already scheduled. How can I butt in like that?'

'No problem! Our own pastor is the speaker tomorrow. I'll call him up and tell him to let you take his place.'

I protested. I was sure that the pastor had already prepared his sermon, and I didn't feel right taking his place after he had expended so much effort. But I said I would be willing to preach if the pastor himself called me.

So the elder called up his pastor, and a while later the pastor called me. 'Elder Wu, it is a rare opportunity for you to come to preach in our church. I would like you to preach tomorrow. I preach regularly in our church.'

After I had agreed to preach, the elder asked me if I could give a message concerning elders. 'Whenever we have an election for elders,' he explained, 'not only are there arguments, but some people also physically fight.' The problem, he said, was that leadership in any organisation among the overseas Chinese in Thailand, including church leadership, was highly coveted. 'If you preach a sermon concerning the choice of elders,' he said, 'they would come to know what being an elder is all about.'

'I don't know if I can do that,' I said, 'but I will pray about it.' Before he left, the elder promised to pick me up in the morning for breakfast before going to church.

That night I was awakened from my sleep. Immediately a wave of fear washed over me. As I got out of bed, I heard something move. I thought I was feeling an earthquake. Yet I wasn't quite sure whether it was the room moving or whether it was I who couldn't balance myself. But then I fell to the floor and, feeling nauseated, began to throw up, soiling my clothes with my vomit. Needing to steady myself, I rolled to one of the legs of the bed and grabbed hold of it. Then I started to pray to God. I asked the Lord to let me know what was happening. A thought came to my mind that perhaps what was happening was connected to my preaching tomorrow. *Could the sermon be so important that I would be attacked by demons? If so, I thought, then I can thank the Lord for his grace, claiming his promise that greater is he that is in me than he that is in the world.* I did just that.

Once my focus was on the Lord, I ordered the bad spirits to leave the room at once in the name of our Lord Jesus. The shaking came to a stop, and I stood up. I then took a bath, changed my clothes, and washed the soiled clothes so that they would be dry for my trip to Singapore.

After I preached my sermon that morning about serving God and being an elder, the election of elders that followed was the most peaceful one in the church's history. Thankful for the impact of the sermon, many elders and deacons came to send me off at the airport that afternoon. I thanked God for the overnight delay, putting me in the right place at the right time, and for his gracious working.

34

Travels in the West

Six pews, four missionaries

While in Finland, I was preaching in a small village. As I waited for the service to begin, I glanced at the church's bulletin board and noticed pictures of two couples. 'Who are these people?' I asked.

A missionary who once went to Taiwan explained that they were the church's missionaries.

I looked around the church with its six pews. If every pew were fully occupied, I figured, the congregation would number thirty-six. In Taiwan a church with only thirty-six members might well have difficulty just paying their pastor's salary. *How could they afford to send out missionaries?* I wondered.

'In Finland,' the missionary told me, 'every church sends out its own overseas missionaries. If a church cannot afford to send one itself, other churches will assist them.'

I was impressed. Finland is indeed a missionary country. Although the country may be poor, they are rich. Although they may be weak, yet they are strong.

Visiting the China Inland Mission in London

The very first thing I did when I landed in England was to visit the China Inland Mission. Early in my ministry in Taiwan, many of my co-workers were from CIM. CIMers started the annual Bible study summer and winter camps for Taiwan youth.

When I walked through the main entrance of the CIM building in London, I immediately saw two hangings of Chinese calligraphy. One said 'Jehovah Jireh', and the other one said 'Ebenezer'. The phrase 'Jehovah Jireh' means 'the Lord will provide' and is truly illustrated by the CIM in their many missionary efforts. Founder Hudson Taylor was once travelling by train, for example, when a member of the upper class transferred from first class to the ordinary class section in order to talk with him. As the two men talked, the missionary leader shared something of his deep concern for the people of China. Upon the rich man's departure, he handed Hudson Taylor a cheque for fifty pounds, saying, 'As I was listening to you, I became burdened for your ministry. Take this money and use it for your work in China.'

Not finding anyone around when he reached the office, Taylor went down to the prayer room and found the staff together in prayer. Because that day they had come up forty-nine pounds and eleven shillings short to cover the workers' living allowance, they were now asking God for that amount. When Mr Taylor showed them the fellow traveller's cheque, they rejoiced that God had not only answered for the forty-nine pounds and eleven shillings, but more!

'Ebenezer', which means 'until today Jehovah is our help', also is still descriptive of the CIM today, although they have changed their name to Overseas Missionary Fellowship. From the founding of the mission in 1865 to the present, the organisation has steadily grown stronger, with currently over nine hundred missionaries serving in many corners of East Asia. Even today Jehovah is helping them.

When I went to the CIM office, representing the Taiwan church, I expressed our sincere gratitude for the work CIM has done in Taiwan.

Visiting the founder of the Chinese church in London

The second thing I did while in London was to visit Pastor Stephen Wang. In his youth he was a student of Leighton

Stewart, the former president of the Yenching University (now Beijing University). When Leighton Stewart was the American ambassador to China, Wang was one of the go-betweens between the two countries, contributing much to China's welfare at the time.

Later, when the communists had taken over mainland China, Wang and his family were the target for persecution. Eventually Wang's oldest daughter was exiled to Tibet, and Wang fled to England. Devastated by the separation from his family, he was contemplating suicide one night on a train when, just in time, someone shared the gospel with him. He became a faithful Christian, trained by the Lord himself.

Getting a good job in England, Stephen Wang eventually searched out the Chinese in London and founded a Chinese church among them. Once an English mission leader suggested that Chinese migrating to England ought to join the English church rather than organising a church of their own and separating themselves from Western people.

'The Chinese people here in London are like lost sheep,' said Wang. 'We have come, not only to search for them, but to shepherd them. No English church has done anything about these Chinese immigrants.'

Now that the Pastor Stephen Wang is with the Lord, the Chinese Overseas Christian Mission, under the leadership of Miss Mary Wang, has carried on his vision and expanded his ministry. Among the missionaries they have sent to other parts of Europe to search out the Chinese is Brother Chia from our church in Taiwan. He has gone to Sweden to plant a Chinese church.

Although I was in London only for one day, Pastor Wang arranged for me to speak at one of their summer camps. Impressed with the size of the camp property, I was told that a young pastor had donated it. He inherited the land at his aunt's death. Suddenly a millionaire, he asked the Lord how to deal with such a fortune and dedicated his wealth fully to the Lord. How much people are used of God, I believe, is determined by the amount they are willing to give up for him.

First visit with the 'Queen of the Dark Chamber'

'Have you heard of the "Queen of the Dark Chamber", Christiana Tsai?' asked Rev Moses Chow at the New York City airport.

'Yes,' I said enthusiastically. 'She was the president of the Shanghai Jiang Wan Theological Seminary. She was greatly used by God.'

Rev Chou told me that Miss Tsai wanted to see me as soon as possible and had asked him to drive me to her place directly from the airport.

When we arrived at Miss Tsai's residence in Paradise, Pennsylvania, it was almost midnight. The drive seemed very long to me, as I was already exhausted from the long flight over the Atlantic. Waiting for us was a note of apology from Miss Tsai. She had gone to bed on doctor's orders, the note said, but would see us in the morning. I was just as glad to go to bed.

In the morning I went to see Miss Tsai in her room. She was quite frail, and her voice was gentle and refined. As a peculiar disease had made her eyes intolerant to light, the slightly built sister wore dark glasses in the shade-darkened room. After we greeted each other, she asked me to share my testimony of how the Lord had healed me and also how I was called into his service.

I, in turn, asked 'the queen' about her ministry in 'the dark chamber'. She said that she served the Lord through prayer, then showed me her prayer notebook. Glancing through the booklet, I saw my own name among perhaps two hundred others. I learned too that Miss Tsai also regularly invited Taiwanese military officers at the Naval Academy in Pennsylvania to her home for a meal to tell them the good news. Browsing through the booklet, she pointed out a name to me and asked me to help her to follow up a military officer who had recently returned to Taiwan. Having received Christ, he was in need of discipling. I copied down the man's name and address.

'How many people have you led to the Lord?' I asked.

'Most of the people in this book,' she answered, joy lighting up her face.

Thinking again of the two hundred names on those pages, I praised the Lord for his grace in this small woman. Though confined indoors in what amounted to a personal cell, she was remarkably fruitful in witness.

I had a wonderful time talking with the 'Queen of the dark Chamber' that entire morning and was sorry I had to continue my journey to Miami and could not spend longer with her. The insights this elderly servant shared were invaluable to me. Later Miss Tsai was to donate her farmland to Rev Moses Chow for his ministry to the Chinese (Ambassadors for Christ).

Preaching in Cantonese – a miracle in Trinidad

When we organised a meeting for Chinese in Trinidad, both Cantonese-speaking Chinese and the local-born Spanish-speaking Chinese attended. So if I would have spoken in Mandarin, then had my message translated first into Cantonese and then into Spanish, both the speaker and the listeners might have forgotten what was last said. So would I speak in Cantonese, local people wanted to know. Then what I said could be interpreted into Spanish.

But I knew how to preach only in Mandarin! How could I preach in Cantonese? My Cantonese to this day is not very fluent, good enough only for buying things and asking directions. I understand only about a fifth of the Cantonese I hear. When I expressed my objections, the Western missionary suggested that I speak half Mandarin and half Cantonese. As long as she understood me, she said, she could translate what I would say into Spanish.

I prayed to the Lord, urging him to repeat for me the miracle of Pentecost for the sake of evangelism in Trinidad. I prayed that through the Holy Spirit's intervention the locals would hear the sermon in the language they understood.

Bravely I took the stage to try out my grotesque Cantonese, with the OMF missionary poised to translate my sermon into Spanish the best she could. Marvellously the Lord answered my prayer. Both groups understood the message. Just as in Acts, chapter 2, I was able to preach in an unknown (or nearly so) tongue as clear as can be. People even accepted Christ in response to the Cantonese I spoke!

Mistaken for an ambassador in Argentina

When I was going through customs in Argentina, the immigration officials couldn't decipher the handwriting on my visa because of the bad penmanship of the official who was drunk when I had applied for it. After some time someone declared that I was an ambassador. *Yes,* I thought, *an ambassador for Christ!*

Not only was my luggage not inspected, but the Republic of China ambassador to Argentina met me and, though he didn't know me, held a banquet in my honour! This made my contact with the local people as well as the overseas Chinese very easy. Among both Chinese and Argentineans I was able to gather in an ample harvest. I even had opportunity to preach to Koreans.

The Argentineans wake up early to open their businesses, then close down at two in the afternoon and reopen at six for the evening. As they eat supper at eleven at night, meetings begin at twelve. Preaching at midnight was a new experience for me.

After a Korean who knew Chinese interpreted a message for me to the Korean group, they gave me an expensive, locally manufactured leather coat. I still wear it today whenever I am in a cold place; and when I do, it brings back fond memories of Argentina.

Surprises on revisiting Brazil

Returning to Brazil after my ministry in Argentina, I was surprised to find the Brazil Overseas Chinese Church already built. In the year between my visits, the living standard of the overseas Chinese had greatly improved. Instead of the one jeep during the church's planting stage, many cars were parked outside the meeting place the night of our revival meeting. Brazilians had responded positively to the travelling markets the Chinese had established.

While in Brazil I heard of a Christian couple who had bought land in the village of Chia Yi and who had constructed a meeting place for the church while they lived in a tent nearby. They had put God first in their lives. God blesses those who do. The Bible tells of many such people. Noah, for instance, when he left the ark, did not first build his own house, but rather built an altar to the Lord. The New Testament Christians also demonstrated this principle in worshipping the Lord on the first day of the week. Evidence of the Lord's blessing, the vegetable gardens of this couple in Chia Yi produced an abundant crop, and their chickens laid many eggs for their egg business.

I was amazed at the size of the Japanese church in which I was invited to speak, with Mrs Wang Kuo-liang interpreting. While the largest church in Tokyo has but two hundred members, and most churches in Japan have fewer than twenty or thirty, this church had seven or eight hundred members. In the Japanese homeland among hindrances to the faith are culture, pressure from jobs, relatives, and friends, and demonic power. In Brazil many of these limitations and restraints have been removed, and Japanese hearts are wide open to the gospel. We thanked the Lord for the remarkable church growth there.

Noticing how tired I was, local Christians took me to the tourist Mecca of Rio de Janeiro. There I was able to walk the beaches, with their fine, white-as-snow sand and scenic beach houses. After a few days' rest, I was able to return to Sao Paulo.

Meeting an Auca on the way to Berlin

A telegram awaited me in Sao Paulo from United Airlines. Earlier the Billy Graham Evangelistic Association had arranged a flight for me to fly from Taipei to attend their first Congress on Evangelism in Berlin. Thousands of ministers of God would be assembling there from all over the world. But, committed to this ministry in Brazil, I called BGA while I was in the United States to say that I was sorry to be unable to join the conference in Berlin, though I was delighted to be invited, explaining my situation. No problem, they told me. If I would give them an address in Brazil where I could be reached, they could authorise airline tickets for me by telegram, and I could fly from New York instead of Taipei.

While I was in New York, Pastor Torrey Shih took me to a department store and bought a hat and coat for me, knowing how cold Berlin would be. I still have the hat, and whenever I have a chance to wear it, I remember Pastor Shih's warm friendship.

When I boarded the plane for Berlin, I was assigned a seat beside a man who looked familiar, but who looked like an aborigine. Because the man made me feel a little nervous, in a little while I got up and moved to another seat. When I did, an American woman came to me and asked, 'Sir, are you going to the conference in Berlin?'

'Yes,' I said.

'A while ago you were seated over there,' she continued. 'Then suddenly you changed seat. Did you feel uncomfortable sitting there?'

I smiled. The man was indeed a little bit frightening.

The woman asked me if I had seen the strange man somewhere.

'No,' I said, but then, with her continued probing, I remembered that I had seen his face in a magazine. Then this fellow passenger told me that the man was of the Auca tribe of Ecuador. Then I remembered how Auca Indians had killed five American missionaries in Ecuador's jungles.

'My husband was one of those men martyred back then,' the lady told me, then went on to relate how she had gone back to plant a church among the Auca. 'At first,' she said, 'they resisted and fled, probably because they felt guilty about what they had done. Later their fears and doubts were wiped out by the love and care I showered on them. Then we became friends, and I used their language to tell them of the Gospel.' Among those who had come to Christ, she told me, was this man. He had become a minister for the Lord. 'I have brought this man to the

Berlin conference so that he can testify for God,' she said. 'He is fruit from a gospel seed watered with blood. At last it is bearing fruit.'

I was deeply touched. Later at the conference the Auca man sang a hymn with a tune using a three-note scale.

While I was in Berlin, I spoke in a large Baptist church. An exchange student, Hsu Chih-wei, who later returned to Taiwan and became one of the directors in the Department of Education, interpreted for me. Germans seem quite different from Americans. Concealing their feelings, they are serious and quiet. When you go to a restaurant, it is as though no one is around. Yet because many cried and were moved when I preached, the pastor asked me to preach again at their Tuesday prayer meeting.

Later when I was marching in a parade organised by the conference to mark Martin Luther's birthday, some people in the crowd chanted, 'Wu! Wu! Wu!' They were from the Baptist church and recognised me. Government officials commented that I had brought some recognition to our country, the Republic of China, though actually the incident was just friendliness from people I knew.

After the conference our host wanted to give us a tour around both East and West Berlin. As the bus approached East Berlin, we passed by the Berlin Wall, now gone. At customs, though customs officials granted other participants entry into East Berlin without hassle, when I showed my passport, they did not allow me to cross into the communist side of the city because they did not recognise the Republic of China as a country. Though being denied entry into a country is not uncommon for citizens of an unrecognised country, being treated coldly is not a nice experience, to say the least.

Fall from a tree threatens ministry in the US

Before a planned trip to the US a young black brother looked strangely at me during one of my speaking engagements in Zion Church, Mucha. He said that he had seen me in a dream. He told someone at the church that during this trip to America I would suffer. Because the man was young and a foreigner, I didn't take him seriously at the time.

But I had reason to remember his prediction a few weeks later in the US as I lay on my back struggling to breathe. Trimming a tree, I had fallen off the ladder from a height of more than ten feet. Unable to utter a sound at first, I could not even give voice to my cry to the Lord. Only after I was able to draw air into my lungs was I able to call out to my wife. When she heard my call, she ran out into the backyard. Seeing me on the ground with such a pale face, she knew I was hurt badly. So she called out for all of our seven children as though their dad was soon to leave this world. They all came to my side. My oldest son quickly called an ambulance from a mobile phone.

X-rays at the hospital showed that six of my ribs were fractured. Admitted to the hospital, I lay on the bed unable to move my neck or straighten my legs. Indescribable pain permeated my whole body.

Worst of all, I was supposed to preach in a series of meetings arranged by the Chinese Congress on World Evangelism to promote the congress. Dr Timothy Lin was to be responsible for four locations, and I was to be responsible for six.

When Dr Lin heard of my fall, he offered to take all the locations. At first this seemed ideal, for Dr Lin is a well-respected speaker and theologian in the US. Everyone would be happy about his coming. I thanked him.

But then when I considered Dr Lin's age, I wondered if taking all ten locations would be too much for him. If his health suffered, it would be my fault. So I decided I would take the challenge of attempting to do my share myself.

But normally recovery from a fracture takes more than three months. Yet the first of my meetings was to start in only two weeks. How could I possibly handle it? Discussing the challenge with my wife, I said that if God made it possible for me to get out of bed within a few days, I would know that the Lord's grace was upon my body and that he was making it possible for me to accomplish the original plan.

After four or five days, my neck began to move a little. Slowly my feet began to respond as well, and soon I could get out of bed and make my way with a lot of effort to the bathroom. I was thus encouraged to believe God would enable me to proceed with my speaking assignments.

I was still hurting and struggling to get around when a friend introduced me to a well-known orthopaedic surgeon, Dr Walter of the Long Beach Memorial Hospital. I went to see him. After examining me, he agreed that my fall and fractures were serious. I asked him to help me bandage my body so that I could handle my speaking commitments. 'You are not out of the critical stage yet,' he objected, 'with six of your ribs fractured, pneumonia may set in, endangering your life. Do you take your life so lightly?'

'Please bandage me,' I instructed. 'Whether I preach or not is my own business.'

So he used an elastic bandage to wrap my chest.

Admitting that I was a tourist who didn't have any health insurance, I told him that he should bill me direct, and I would pay him.

'You don't need to pay me,' he said. 'I never bill a missionary. You may go now.' So I walked out of his office all bandaged up, amazed that this very prominent California doctor did not charge me for either consultation or the medication he prescribed. I know that getting medical help in the US usually costs a considerable amount of money if you don't have medical insurance. I thanked God for his mercy and his grace through one of his servants.

As the time neared for me to go to San Francisco for the first of my meetings, I still hurt, though the pain had decreased a lot. My daughter had planned to drive me to the airport, but when it was time to go, I couldn't get into the car because I couldn't bend my head or my spine. So she rented a minibus to pick me up. I was carried onto the plane, also onto the platform that night. I spoke while sitting, with a microphone aiding my weak voice.

Every word I spoke caused pain, and I was aware of a rising fever. Finally I became dizzy and could no longer see the congregation. Seeing how ill I was, someone shouted, 'Don't let him continue talking . . . he may die!' As volunteers hurriedly carried me off stage, they noticed my high fever. Alarm filled the hall, and people, many of them from Taiwan, scrambled to help and give advice.

Eventually someone contacted Dr Walter. 'Sorry,' he said, 'I am helpless because the patient is in San Francisco, and I am in Los Angeles. He might have pneumonia, and his life may be in danger. If you are his friends, take him to a hospital right away. You may still save his life.' So my friends contacted a hospital in San Francisco and prepared to take me in.

'Wait until 2 a.m.,' I begged, sure that God's grace was sufficient for me. Had I not been able to move my neck and get out of bed in a short time, and had the doctor not charged me? Were not all these evidences that God would guard me until I finished his work? 'If my fever isn't down by then,' I bargained, 'then I'll be willing to go to the hospital.' I felt that if the fever did go down, I could be sure that the Lord's glory would be revealed in my recovery. Though worried, my care-givers could do nothing but what I had requested.

About 1 a.m. I began to perspire heavily. Before 2 a.m. the fever and pain were gone. I was completely healed.

On the second day I walked under my own strength to the pulpit. I was like a healthy person, a living testimony of God's working. Though what the young black brother prophesied came true, God promised peace in the midst of tribulation; this too proved true in my life. And I was able to finish the task the Lord had given me in all six locations.

Impromptu conference at Yellowstone

During one of my trips to a wonderful summer conference held in the city of Denver, Colorado, Sister Chen Ke-min came to see me. 'Mr Wu,' she asked, 'would you dare hold a summer conference at Yellowstone National Park?'

I asked, 'Why did you say "dare"?'

She said, 'Because this conference would be different from all the other conferences you know of. When others invite you to speak at a conference, it is usually sponsored by a church or a para-church organisation with financial support. But this time the conference would be sponsored by neither.'

'If no one is supporting it, why then should we hold one?' I asked, curious.

She explained: 'I asked you whether you dared hold one because I will write letters to all the people I know to see whether or not they would be willing to join Mr Wu Yung's summer conference at Yellowstone National Park.'

'It would be quite impossible to hold this conference,' I objected, 'because driving from New York would take three or four days. From San Francisco, it would take two or three days to drive. The whole occasion would use up almost ten days of the participants' time. Who would be willing to take such a long leave from work in this busy American society?'

Sister Chen was not put off by my objections. 'If they want to come, they will be willing to pay the price. If they are not willing, the conference would not benefit them anyway. If they come, they will bring their hearts with them because they will have invested that much time and money in this conference. They will concentrate at every session. So if you dare to hold this conference, we'll do it. If you don't, we'll give up the whole idea.'

Thinking to myself, *What strong determination this lady has for the Lord! Why can't I be like her?* I agreed to the conference. We set a date in August.

When my wife and I arrived in Yellowstone, we discovered that there weren't any dormitories for rent. Everyone would have to stay at the hotel, and we would hold our meetings in the hotel's conference hall – expensive, but really quite convenient.

We came to Yellowstone a day before he camp began. I walked around to see if anyone was around. We seemed to be the only ones there. As in America people's time is very precious, we figured that participants might come just when the camp was about to start. We checked accommodations to be sure that when the people came, they would have a place to stay, for everyone was responsible for their own accommodation and meals.

The next day I stood by the doorway to wait for the participants. But nobody came all day, none even by 2 p.m. When a
car arrived with a lady and her children in it, I went to talk with
them. They were not Chinese. They were Japanese and were
there on vacation, not for the conference. At 4 p.m. a family
came. And about ten minutes before the first session, surprisingly, just about everybody came. Like a sudden downpour of
rain, more than sixty showed up!

Sister Chen showed herself a lady of faith. Without telling the
hotel staff how many would come, she just told them that we
would hold a conference there, asking if we might use the conference hall free. For a week she prayed without receiving any
response from the hotel. But a few days before we were to begin,
the hotel people welcomed us, agreeing to let us use the conference
hall for free. When we began our first session, there were already
seventy to eighty people.

Sister Chen was right. Having invested so much in being
there, the participants came with eager hearts, ready to study
God's word. The atmosphere of the whole conference was unlike
any that I had ever known. God made his presence felt, and
people simply savoured the Holy Spirit's working among us.
Insights gained were incredible. It was a wonderful conference.
People had such a precious time that during the sharing time at
the close, many said that they would be willing to come next
year.

But Mr Chen would have none of it. 'You don't know how
much my wife put into this conference. I am her husband. I
know how much time, phone calls, and thought she put into it.
Although she coped with the load, I wasn't quite able to.'
Because of this, Mrs Chen couldn't guarantee that there would
be such a conference every year.

Yet Mrs Chen had the inspiration, faith, and courage to hold
this conference that blessed many of her friends. In the end more
than ninety attended from all over. Faith made everything
possible, and everybody drew from the abundance of our Lord.

'Martha' service spoils a conference

When a lady from Houston who attended the Yellowstone conference saw the blessing achieved, she came to talk to me. 'Mr Wu, are you willing to hold a conference in Houston?' she asked. 'My husband and I have lived in Houston for many years now, and we have many friends. We can handle the invitations, the other chores, and the meals.'

I told her I would be willing.

Thirty to fifty people attended the conference in Houston. The lady who organised the meetings took charge of the business matters as well as the cooking. It was a lot to handle. Things seemed to be going well until during one of the sessions I was leading our hostess came rushing in from the kitchen, shouting, 'You're all sitting here listening to the sermon while I am left all alone in the kitchen. How come nobody cares to help me?'

Like Martha, the lady found herself overwhelmed by too much to do. Though she took on the tasks out of a simple love for the Lord, she let the flesh take over and let irritation spawn impatience with the others. All of us who serve the Lord easily make the same mistake. Too much of our service is done without the Lord's presence. It is done in our own fleshly strength and by our own planning. It is not beautiful; it does not glorify the Lord; it is not fruitful.

In this case, in fact, the lady's irritated outburst put a damper on the whole spiritual atmosphere. The openness of hearts disappeared. I was unable to preach further.

A son's wounding brings me to his side

One day in 1980, when I was home in Taiwan, my children called from the States to tell me that my youngest son had had an accident and was in the hospital, but assured me that his condition was not too serious. But children are treasures. Because the older children didn't explain clearly what happened to our hospitalised son, my wife and I became worried and restless. I felt I could do nothing but secure an airline ticket and rush to his side.

When I arrived at the airport in the United States, my children told me the whole story: my youngest son had been parking his car at night when a man accosted him to rob him. The robber got my son's keys and asked him to take off all his clothes except his undergarments. When the boy started to leave as directed by the robber, the robber shot him in the back. My son could easily have been killed. Praise the Lord, the bullet hit him in the shoulder, away from vital organs.

With two surgeries, the shoulder was almost as good as new. Although he has a little problem with his fingers, he can use them quite adequately. We are grateful. God's grace has been sufficient.

Visiting Rev Beard in New Zealand

Rev A.E. Beard was an OMF missionary in the Pescadores. I recall him returning to New Zealand to retire, and he was staying a few days in our home while he waited for his flight. Arriving home one day, I heard sounds of laughter coming from upstairs. I followed the sound and came upon a scene that touched me. The elderly pastor/missionary was playing with my youngest son. They were happily chasing each other. Rev. Beard even crawled on the floor while my son chased after him.

The apostle Paul said he 'became all things to all men so that by all possible means he might win some'. Having spent decades working among Chinese on the mainland and in Taiwan, Rev Beard had learned to adapt to the people to whom he ministered. And now he was acting like a child because he was with a child.

When Rev Beard saw me standing by the stairway, he stood up to talk to me. He said, 'Brother Wu, I'll be leaving tomorrow,' and his eyes teared up. Leaving the land and people he loved was obviously coupled with feelings of reluctance; so I comforted him, saying, 'Rev Beard, I will find a chance to visit you when you are back at home.'

'Visit me? It is a long way to travel from Taiwan to New

Zealand. You would have to fly eight or nine hours,' he said.

'That doesn't matter,' I said. 'I often go abroad. If God gives the opportunity, I'll visit you in New Zealand.'

He thanked me for my warmth and not long afterwards left to return to Auckland.

A year later I went to visit him as I promised. I stayed in Auckland a few days, and Rev. Beard was very happy about it. He hadn't really expected me to fulfil my promise, at least that soon.

When I went on to Wellington after my visit in Auckland, I discovered to my dismay that all the hotels, even the second-class ones, were fully booked. How could a country like New Zealand, so removed from the rest of the world and with such under-developed transportation, have fully booked hotels? 'Is it because I am Chinese?' I asked one hotel receptionist.

'No,' he said. 'Don't misunderstand us. There is a rose contest going on right now. Rose growers from all over the country are bringing their roses to Wellington for the exhibition and judging. There won't be any hotel rooms available in Wellington for the next couple of days.'

I was beginning to feel a bit anxious, wondering if I would have to sleep out in the cold, when I remembered Rev. Beard's mentioning a Mr Meyer, who lived above a bookstore and who would help me if I needed assistance.

When I found the bookstore, Mr Meyer was doing bookwork on the upper level. Eager to finish his accounts before getting involved with this stranger at his door, he asked me to wait. He was a man about fifty years old.

Assuring me that he could make arrangements for me after I told him of my problem, he said, 'Let's have dinner first. Then we can go up the mountain for a good view of Wellington.'

Mr Meyer took me to a Chinese restaurant. When we were almost finished eating, I went to the counter to pay the bill. But my host grabbed me from behind and remonstrated with me: 'I understand the customs of the Chinese,' he said. 'But paying the bill is the business of the locals; so take your seat and don't cause me any trouble.'

After a pleasant view of Wellington from the mountain top, we were on our way home when he asked me a startling question: 'Mr Wu, do you look down on others?'

I thought before answering. Why would he ask such a question? Why would I look down on him? 'What do you mean?' I asked him.

'Nothing really,' he said. 'It's just that many who come to Wellington look down on the locals.'

'Why?' I asked. 'The people here are warm and hospitable. Why would others have any bias against locals?'

'The people you see walking down the streets have ancestors who were pirates or robbers,' he explained. 'The English government used to exile their pirates and robbers to New Zealand, so most locals have the blood of pirates and robbers in them. I am an exception.'

'Why are you an exception?' I wanted to know.

'Actually, my great grandfather on my mother's side was also a pirate, but he was not willing for his daughter to marry a pirate. To find someone who was not a descendant of a pirate, he went all the way to England to find himself a non-pirate son-in-law. But no decent man would come to such a remote and unpleasant place. One day he saw a young man walking along the road and followed him. When it was dusk, he put a bag over the man's head and kidnapped him, smuggling him to Wellington to become his son-in-law. So, though my grandmother has pirate blood, my grandfather doesn't. I, therefore, have only a small amount of pirate blood in me. If you want to look down on me, you must look down only a bit.'

I laughed quite loudly at his last comment, wondering why my host would tell me all this. Perhaps, I decided, he wanted to lessen my inhibitions while at his home, so that I could relax and enjoy his hospitality without bias. Actually I did feel happy and relaxed, quite at home during my two-day stay.

35

A Helpmeet from God

When I finished the recording of these memoirs, I gave them to my eldest son-in-law, Henry Huang Xi Zhen, to put in order. After listening to the tapes, he felt that I had mentioned too seldom the relationship between my wife and me and and her place in my ministry. Though I would rather the praise come from others, the more I think about it the more I agree, that the work she has done and continues to do to support me is by no means inferior to God's work through me. And who else knows her better than a person who has lived with her for fifty years? Furthermore, the purpose of this life testimony is to give aid to younger ministers through examples. Thus if I, by what I add in the following pages, can encourage the wives of ministers today to be helpers rather than obstructors, I will have fulfilled my purpose to a greater degree.

For many of the years we were raising our seven children, we lived by faith. During those challenging years my wife had to care for both her home and her church. If it were not for the Lord's adding strength and bestowing grace, we would not have dared to continue in the ministry.

The Chinese traditional designation of a wife as 'the inner person' is consistent with the teaching of the Bible. When God led Eve to Adam as his helpmeet, Adam said, 'This is bone of my bone, flesh of my flesh', meaning the inner person. We Fujian people call man 'the hunter', meaning someone who goes outside to hunt and fish, and woman 'the house sitter', meaning someone who keeps house and looks after the children.

A wife should live up to her role as the internal helper of her husband. Say the husband has character deficiencies. Other people can't easily or clearly see them because they see only the bright outside, not the dark side. A wife knows her husband inside and out. A good internal helper not only can comfort her husband when he is sad and encourage him when he is in despair, she can wisely help him change character defects such as untruthfulness, boastfulness, envy, pride, indecent behaviour, irate speech, irresponsibility, and arrogance. However successfully a man hides such weaknesses from other people, they are always exposed to his wife. She should not blindly encourage him to do what he wants or nurture a haughty spirit. Though Chinese ancients taught that a woman should be obedient to three people (to her father before marriage, to her husband during married life, and to her sons in widowhood), this obedience has a limit; it does not mean she should blindly obey in both the right and the wrong. A true and wise internal helper is one who corrects her husband's errors.

My wife is such a person. Of course, she stands with me most of the time. But there have been many occasions in which she would not do so. President Lincoln once said: 'I don't stand on your side, nor do I stand on my side. I stand on God's side.' My wife uses this principle to deal with me. If I don't stand on God's side, then she will not stand on my side. She does this to stop me from offending God. When I feel sad, she comforts me; when I fall into despair, she encourages me; but when I am wrong, she resolutely refuses to align with me. Although my 'flesh' at times does not appreciate this, afterward I realise the way she acts is truly best.

'Since your wife is so virtuous,' a British reporter challenged a Member of Parliament, 'does she obey you in everything?'

The Member of Parliament answered, 'If she listened to me in everything, then she would not have any substance in my eyes.' I have come to appreciate the wisdom of his answer. A good internal helper not only aids her husband in his work; she also helps him with his personal character. My wife is really my good helpmeet in both these realms, I believe, in the way God meant when he created a helpmeet for Adam (Genesis 2).

An internal helper should never become an internal obstructor. I have discovered over the years that when a husband fails in the ministry of the church, the wife is often to blame. When a husband becomes the object of another person's anger at church, for example, the wife becomes an obstructor when she goes to the church seeking revenge for him. When a husband comes home and shares some unhappy affairs between church members, hoping that his wife will join him in prayer for them, she becomes an obstructor when instead of praying for them, she spreads the news to other families. An idle wife also becomes an obstructor by leaving the household chores for the husband to do. This makes her husband like a candle which burns on both ends. Very soon he is spent both spiritually and physically.

A husband who works hard in the church often finishes a day exhausted. He wants to go home at night for peace and to clear his mind. He needs family warmth to dissipate his worries; he doesn't need family problems to increase his anxieties. I pity a man whose wife chatters incessantly about how a sister in the women's group said something impolite to her that day or grumbles about all the housework she has to do while he cares only about the church and its members. A husband whose wife has little to share with him but complaint is a victim of both internal worries and external attack. In ministry a man who lacks an internal helper is as worthy of pity as a man who has but one leg.

I am a man with two legs. My wife has never been an up-front person; she has just served in support ministries in the church, quietly dedicating her heart and effort. At home she has done her best to do all the household chores, seeking my help only when she has had absolutely no other alternative.

My wife is always concerned for the needy. When brothers and sisters showed their love for us by sending us gifts at New Year and other festivity times, she always passed them along to brothers and sisters in need. In spite of the fact that we had times of affluence, so generous was she, in fact, that when I was already fifty-five years old, our family still had absolutely no savings.

As I recall almost half a century of sharing life with my wife, I am profoundly grateful to her. She has cared for me and put up with me in all my ailments – para-sinusitis, heart trouble, tuberculosis of the right lung, colon cancer, and blood pressure problems.

Though by no means a person without emotions, when I am sick, my wife does not express her sorrow outwardly for the duration of the illness. She has always seemed as though she was as stable as the giant Tai Mountain. She has made the Lord her rock and her help, knowing that if she becomes panicky or weepy, wailing to heaven and earth, it would make me worse. Over the years she has truly acquired the gentleness and self-control which are among the fruits of the Holy Spirit.

My wife never stops looking to buy things that might be beneficial to my health. Though now I am over seventy, and she is not young, in this she has never changed. If she has money with her while shopping, she always buys food supplements for me. She never thinks of buying anything for herself.

In fact, my wife carries out her selflessness to such a point that sometimes it irritates me. She always chooses the worst for herself. I do not eat leftovers; she eats them all. She is so thrifty for my sake that she is inclined to eat even food that has spoiled. Occasionally I have had no way to deal with her except to remove the bad food from her mouth. Thus I always have to keep an eye on the refrigerator to remove soured or rotten food and throw it away. I have to do it discreetly, though, because if she catches me, she scolds me.

In the last few decades my wife has been a biblical watchman, watching her family and her church. From childhood to adulthood both the children and her church have been the subject of her prayers. The content of her prayer is very rich, and the time of praying is very long.

Of course, I am also a recipient of my wife's prayers. As I serve in the Lord's ministry she is afraid that I might become proud upon success or disheartened upon failure. Just like Joshua when he led the Israelites to war against the Amalekites, he won because Moses supported him with prayer. I can still stand today because of my wife's long-term and constant prayer and the prayers of the churches for me.

My wife and I have worked together, going from one house to another, visiting people. Whenever someone is in want, she assists. Whenever someone is sick, she goes to help. Whenever someone is sad, she comforts them. She has assisted women in labour though she was neither midwife nor doctor – she goes to give spiritual support. For twenty-eight years she took charge of the ministry at the female prison. When we started the Hsuchang Street Church, she joined in building up the youth fellowship. When we established a branch church on Nanking East Road, she joined in to build it. Nominated many times for the position of deaconess, she has consistently refused it. Although her work was in no way inferior to a full-time minister's work, she has wanted only to give and not to get, not even recognition.

When the time came for the church to write its history, many people paid attention only to Brother Wu Yung, not to Mrs Wu Yung's work. Even so, I have never heard her expressing indignation or complaining about this. In establishing the church, she has sometimes carried heavier responsibilities than I. She has been like Ruth, who collected grains quietly, unnoticed. My wife has wanted only to spread the name of the Lord so that it would be glorified; she has asked for nothing more.

She has been the same with our children. If they give her a small present, she is greatly moved. If her children are busy with their own business and forget to send her a present, she never complains. She treats them equally, never liberal to one and stingy to another. She can keep on giving without complaint not expecting anything in return because she has a feeling deep inside her heart that to have the Lord is enough.

I thank the Lord for his grace in giving me such an internal helper. The Book of Proverbs says that a virtuous woman is her husband's crown. My wife makes me gain and never lose; she totally fulfils the office which God has given her. She is an example of what a minister's wife should be.

Here at the end of this book I have said a great many words from the bottom of my heart, hoping not only to reaffirm my gratefulness to my wife, but to help young people learn something about choosing a spouse. I hope also to help women who are already wives of ministers to renew their determination to be strong internal helpers and gentle companions to their husbands. What a beautiful thing it is for husband and wife to be of one heart in the ministry and to walk in step to please the Lord!

English-speaking OMF centres

AUSTRALIA: PO Box 849, Epping, NSW 2121
Tel (02) 9868 4777. Freecall (outside Sydney)1800 227 154
email: omf-Australia@omf.net   *www.omf.org*

CANADA: 5759 Coopers Avenue, Mississauga ON, L4Z 1R9
Toll free 1-888-657-8010. Fax (905) 568-9974
email: omfcanada@omf.ca   *www.omf.ca*

HONG KONG: P O Box 70505, Kowloon Central Post Office, Hong
Kong email: hk@omf.net   *www.omf.org*

MALAYSIA: 3A Jalan Nipah, off Jalan Ampang, 55000, Kuala
Lumpur email: my@omf.net   *www.omf.org*

NEW ZEALAND: P O Box 10-159, Auckland
Tel 09-630 5778 email: omfnz@omf.net   *www.omf.org*

PHILIPPINES: 900 Commonwealth Avenue, Diliman, 1101 Quezon
City email: ph-hc@omf.net   *www.omf.org*

SINGAPORE: 2 Cluny Road, Singapore 259570
email: sno@omf.net   **www.omf.org**

SOUTHERN AFRICA: P O Box 3080, Pinegowrie, 2123
email: a@omf.net   *www.omf.org*

UK: Station Approach, Borough Green, Sevenoaks, Kent, TN15 8BG
email: omf@omf.org.uk   *www.omf.org.uk*

USA: 10 West Dry Creek Circle, Littleton, CO 80120-4413
Toll Free 1-800-422-5330 *www.us.omf.org*

OMF International Headquarters:
2 Cluny Road, Singapore 259570.